Contents

CANCELLED 10p.

D0258255

Preface to the fourth edition

Apart from metrication changes it is eleven years since this book was over-hauled and it is perhaps apt that this should occur again at its coming of age at twenty-one years.

A number of changes have been made but the major alterations are to be found in the tools section, including the extraction of references to wooden planes. I was loath to part with these old friends and for this reason, and because of the part they played in establishing the great traditions of wood-craft, a representative selection has been put together in a full-page illustration purely for historical interest. No excuse is offered for having done this.

Many new drawings are included; some provided by manufacturers, whose interest and help is always readily forthcoming in the provision of sound technical information via their education services.

Readers may be surprised that the bone glues are given a brief mention, but these are still in demand and supply, although much reduced — the modern adhesives offering so many advantages in handling, application and effectiveness.

Veneering by 'hand' methods also came up for review and although this kind of work is perhaps not so commonly practised today, it is nevertheless a branch of the craft offering satisfaction for the creative urge and is therefore retained with some changes and one half-tone added to illustrate the kind of things which can be made, using cauls and exotic woods.

A few references in imperial sizes will be found in respect of some twist bits, all of which are not yet fully metricated and also in reference to saw teeth, the universal 'P.P.I.' (points per inch) still being in common use at present.

Throughout the book, the word 'medullary' is not used in connection with 'rays', these groups of cells being correctly known now as 'rays'.

G. H. L. 1979

1

Drawing

General notes
The ability to make clear and accurate drawings is essential to the complete craftsman. It is necessary to be able to put ideas on paper in such a way that other people can read and understand them, and this is particularly important in the drawing test which always forms part of an examination in any practical subject. For the purpose of this book, it is assumed that the student has had some elementary training in technical drawing at the draughtsman's board with tee-square and instruments.

Particular attention should be paid to the method of projection, over which so many candidates make fundamental errors in the examination room. The student must also study the types of line to be used for the various parts of his drawings and should pay due regard to the finish and general neatness of his work.

Cleanliness Drawings handed in at examinations should be spotless and to ensure this, meticulous attention must be paid to cleanliness of the hands before starting work. Fingers must be kept off the paper as much as possible, and when lettering, a slip of paper can be placed under the hand. Erasing must be kept to the very minimum, in the first place by avoiding mistakes and secondly by making the preliminary laying out of the drawing very faint indeed, so that errors can be removed by the merest flick of the rubber over the paper. Heavy erasing roughens the hard surface which then collects and holds dust. Celluloid set-squares and protractors can be washed occasionally in lukewarm soapy water, whilst a few slips of gummed paper or stamp edging stuck under the blade of the tee-square raise it sufficiently to prevent dust being rubbed into the surface of the paper. These slips are quickly cleaned or replaced at intervals.

Lettering A poor lettering style can seriously mar an otherwise good drawing, and so often does, especially in examinations when the time limit imposes restrictions on the finishing touches which can be applied. The student is advised to adopt and practise a uniform style throughout all work at the board and should remember that perfectly plain block letters, neatly formed, look far more appropriate than any fancy shapes, with, perhaps, incorrectly formed serifs and other superfluous embellishments. Over-large lettering should also be avoided as it takes much more time to form the shapes, and the proportions between the parts of each letter become of paramount importance. All lettering should be formed between two very faint guide lines, and for this purpose an F pencil will be found suitable whilst for the drawings themselves an H or 2H pencil will be quite hard enough.

Common SI units of length

Unit	Symbol		
millimetre	mm		
centimetre	cm	= 10 mm	
decimetre	dm	= 10 cm	(100 mm)
metre	m	= 10 dm	(100 cm 1000 mm)
kilometre	km	= 1000 m	

Decimal notation To obviate errors in reading dimensions in decimals, the following conventions should be observed: (1) the decimal point is placed level with the middle of the figure, but in typewritten work the full stop is acceptable, (2) with numbers of less than one, the decimal point is preceded by a zero (e.g. 0.3), and (3) where five or more digits appear, the thousand marker is best indicated by a space, the use of a comma being liable to misreading as a decimal point.

Dimensions   The figured dimensions on drawings are best made using one unit throughout and for most purposes the millimetre is convenient. When this is done, the symbol mm can be omitted from each dimension and a reference to the unit included in the title box, e.g. ALL DIMENSIONS IN MM.

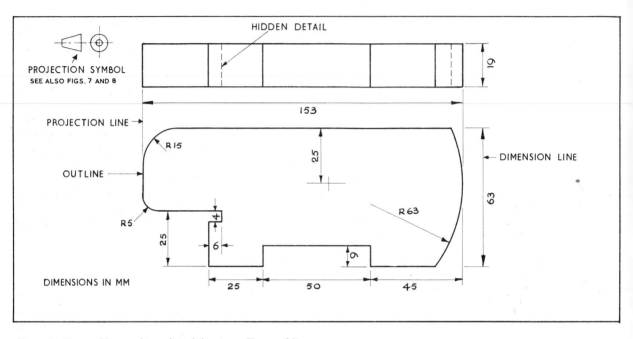

Figure 1   Types of line used in technical drawing

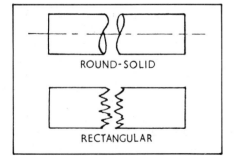

Figure 2   Conventional breaks

Types of line

The various types of line used in technical drawing have been standardised, together with the methods of dimensioning, and attention is directed to the following points:

Thick continuous lines   The most important part of a drawing is the object itself and for this reason, main outlines are drawn in thick, continuous lines which stand out boldly. Care should be taken to maintain an even thickness of line throughout the drawing.

Thin continuous lines   This kind of line is used for dimension lines (arrows) and for lines projected from the outlines to facilitate the insertion of dimensions. The projection lines do not normally connect with the outlines (see Fig. 1) but can do so when used to indicate points on surfaces.

Other uses include: (1) the outlines of parts adjacent to the object which may be needed to indicate a location or for other reasons, (2) for hatching (diagonal lines) used in sectional drawings, and (3) for leaders which are used to show where notes or dimensions are meant to apply. A leader should finish with an arrow head if to touch a line or with a dot if finishing within an outline.

In examination work, geometrical construction lines should not be erased as they may be required for the purpose of marking. They should be fine and quite unobtrusive.

Hidden details   Hidden details are indicated by thin, short dashes.

Centre and section lines   A long chain line is used to locate centre lines of round parts as in Fig. 2 and is also used to show section planes as in Figs.

Ref	Size in mm
A0	841 × 1189
A1	594 × 841
A2	420 × 594
A3	297 × 420
A4	210 × 297

Figure 3   Standard sizes of trimmed drawing sheets

17 and 18. It is also used to show path lines indicating movement as in Figs. 12 and 23.

Dimensioning   The dimensioning of a drawing must be done with care to avoid confusion and, as far as possible, dimension lines should be placed outside the main outlines of the object with the actual figures standing normal to them (at right angles) so that they are read from the bottom or the right-hand side.

Radii and diameters should be indicated as shown in Fig. 1 and wherever possible should be placed outside the outlines.

Scales

Technical drawings are always made to a selected scale which indicates the ratio between the size of the object and the drawing. Many objects can be drawn to full size and this ratio is shown on the drawing as: SCALE 1:1. With larger objects, a smaller scale is employed to reduce the drawings to more convenient proportions and recommended divisors are 2, 5 and 10 which give ratios of 1:2, 1:5, 1:10, 1:20, 1:50 and 1:100, e.g. SCALE 1:2 (i.e. half full size).

With small objects, drawings can be made larger than full size so that details can be shown and dimensioned clearly, the ratios already mentioned being reversed as 2:1, 5:1, 10:1 and so on. Such a ratio would be shown as, e.g. SCALE 2:1 (i.e. twice full size).

All parts of the drawing are reduced or enlarged proportionately and this is done by means of a suitable scale rule. The particular scale chosen will depend on the size of the object, the amount of small detail to be shown and of course, on limitations imposed by drawing facilities available. The scale should be indicated clearly in the title box.

Orthographic projection

This is the method adopted for the preparation of working drawings and involves the making of elevations, plans and sections of any object by projecting views on to flat surfaces known as 'planes of projection'.

Generally, two elevations (side views) and a plan (bird's-eye view) are sufficient to convey a complete picture of the object, but extra elevations are drawn when the article is of a complex nature.

For the purposes of orthographic projection two planes are assumed to intersect, the line of intersection being known as the 'xy' line or 'ground' line and the four angles thus made as dihedral angles, which in this case are all right angles. Note the abbreviations for vertical and horizontal planes, viz. V.P. and H.P. as in Fig. 4.

First angle projection

The four dihedral angles are numbered for reference and of these the first and third angles are used in standard practice for all projections.

An extra vertical plane at the end (V.P.²) is usually employed as shown in Fig. 5, and on to this is projected an end elevation. End vertical planes can be at either or both ends, depending on the amount and location of the detail to be shown, but where one only is required, it is normally placed as shown in the illustration.

The object is arranged with its front or face side parallel to and facing away from the V.P.¹ and with its base parallel to the H.P. for projecting the views. One of the most important points to remember is that the lines of projection are always perpendicular to the planes of projection.

Fig. 6 a shows, in pictorial form, the projections of an object on to the three

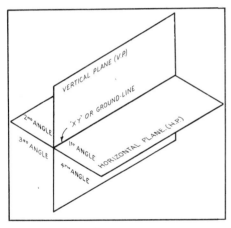

Figure 4   Planes of projection

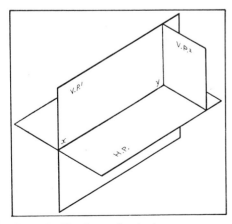

Figure 5   The planes of projection

planes which in Fig. 6b are shown opened out to form a set of working drawings.

It should be noted that the object is placed between the viewer and the plane of projection so that the view obtained from the left appears on the right of the elevation and vice versa. This is first angle (or European) projection.

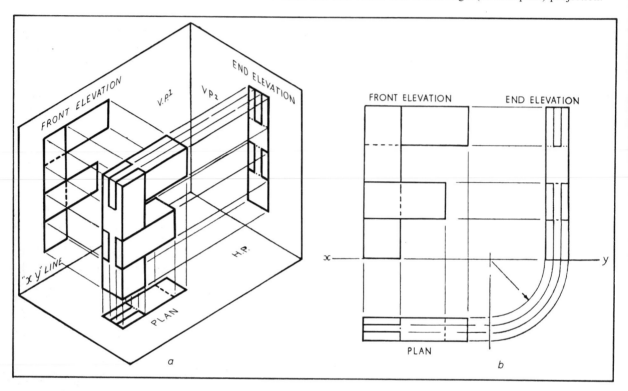

Figure 6 a and b   First angle projection

Third angle projection

This method of projection, used in America, employs the third angle which brings the plan above the elevation. End vertical planes are employed for the projection of other elevations but in each case the projection shows that side of the object *adjacent* to the plane concerned. This is the reverse of the first angle method.

In Figs. 7 and 8, first and third angle projections are demonstrated more fully with the viewing directions shown but with no planes of projection indicated. In both cases six views are shown and these could be needed with a very complex subject, but with this letter 'F' two elevations could convey all the necessary information. Note the symbols used to denote first or third angle projection.

Examples in orthographic projection

Figs. 9, 10 and 11 give examples in pictorial form for conversion to orthographic projection as exercises. Fig. 11 a gives an example which compels us to complete the end elevation first in order that we may project back to the front elevation and thence to the plan. This reverses the usual procedure whereby the front elevation is completed first.

In Fig. 11 b is shown an octagonal box which, when drawn in orthographic projection, requires completion of the plan first in order to complete the elevation.

A small hopper is shown in Fig. 12 and it is required to find the true shape of the side marked A, for in none of the views do we see this. Note how the

Figure 7   First angle projection

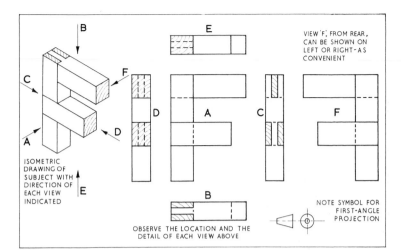

Figure 8   Third angle projection

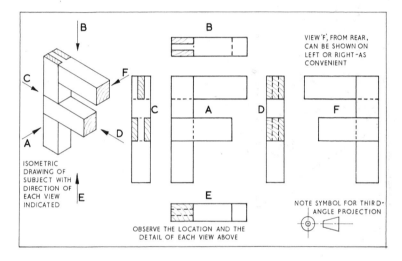

Figure 9   Examples for conversion to orthographic projection

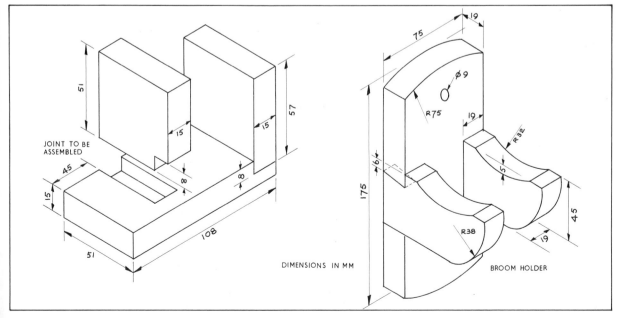

Figure 10   Example for conversion to orthographic projection

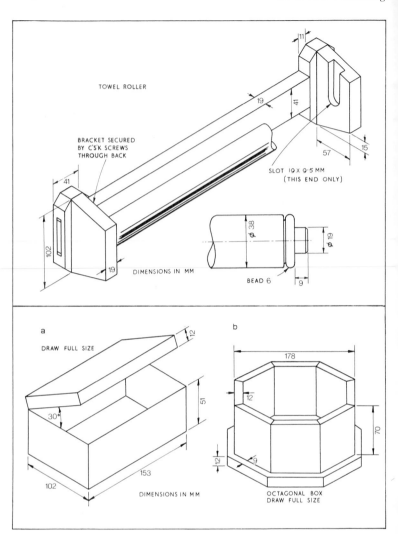

Figure 11 a and b   Examples for conversion to orthographic projection

side is swung down to the horizontal in the side elevation, enabling its true width to be projected to the plan. By combining the true width with the lengths at the top and bottom edges, the true shape of the side is found. This is known as a 'development'.

Auxiliary projections

New plans and elevations   So far we have considered projection only where the object is viewed from the front, end or top. Sometimes, because of a peculiar shape and in order to convey a complete impression, we are required to project views at various angles to the vertical or horizontal planes.

Fig. 13 gives an example in which the need for an auxiliary view is amply illustrated. In this case an auxiliary or 'new' elevation is required, for in neither of the normal elevations are the true shape or sizes of the corner face of the building shown. The direction in which the new elevation is projected is indicated by the arrow on the plan. The new ground line, $x^1 y^1$, is drawn at right angles to the arrow at a convenient distance from the plan from which all the salient points are projected at right angles to, and well past, the ground line. The various heights of the building are transferred from the original to the new elevation by means of dividers, after which the elevation may be lined in.

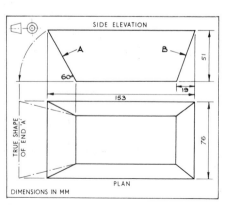

Figure 12   Development of true shape

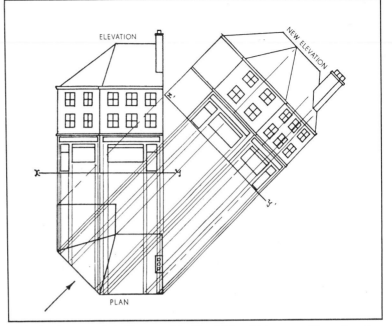

Figure 13   Projecting a new elevation

A simple example is illustrated in Fig. 14 in which an auxiliary elevation is required, projected from the original plan in the direction of arrow, A. Remembering that the lines of projection are always perpendicular to the plane, we erect an auxiliary vertical plane (V.P.³) whose line of intersection with the horizontal plane is along $x^1 y^1$, and at right angles to the arrow. On lowering V.P.³ away from the object, the projection will appear as shown. It is actually prepared on the drawing board by projecting from all points on the plan, at right angles to $x^1 y^1$, and passing by this ground line far enough for us to transfer the vertical heights from the original elevation. In making this new elevation, only the length and breadth of the model are affected, heights remain unchanged.

In Fig. 15 we see an auxiliary plan projected from the original elevation, in the direction of the arrow, B. In this case, an inclined auxiliary plane intersects the V.P.¹ along $x^1 y^1$ at right angles to arrow, B, and the new plan is projected as shown. This time the width of the object is unaffected whilst the

Figure 14 (left)   Projecting a new elevation. First angle projection

Figure 15 (right)   Projecting a new plan. First angle projection

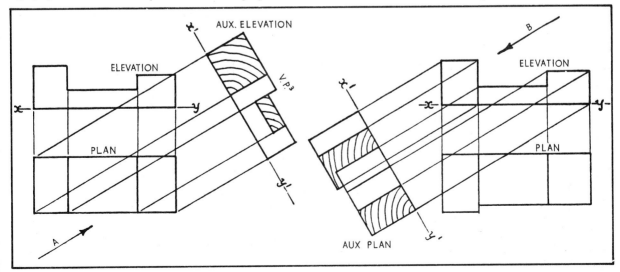

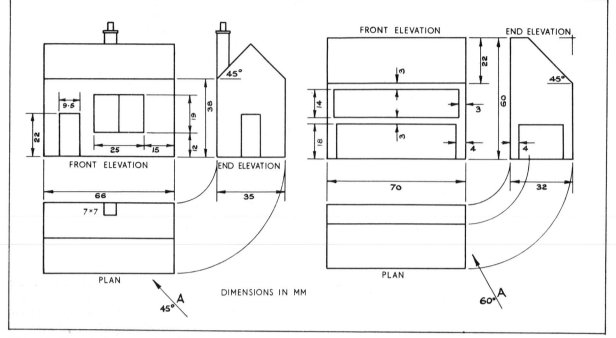

Figure 16   Examples for practice in making auxiliary elevations. First angle projection

length is changed by foreshortening.

These two examples should be worked by the student, and he must remember at all times that new elevations come from original plans and that new plans come from original elevations.

Fig. 16 gives examples for practice in making auxiliary elevations.

Sections

It very frequently happens that the normal projections do not convey complete details for use in the workshop because of some peculiarity in the shape or construction of the object. The draughtsman then resorts to 'sectioning' in various ways to give a more complete and accurate picture.

The object is cut by a 'section plane' which is represented by a chain dotted line as in Fig. 17. From this plane, which can be set at any angle to the planes of projection, extra elevations or plans are projected in the normal manner. A sectional drawing is always labelled clearly as such, with a reference to the section plane concerned, e.g. 'Section on A A or B B' and when representing

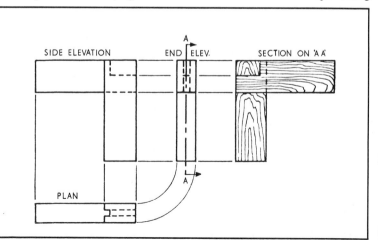

Figure 17   Projecting a section

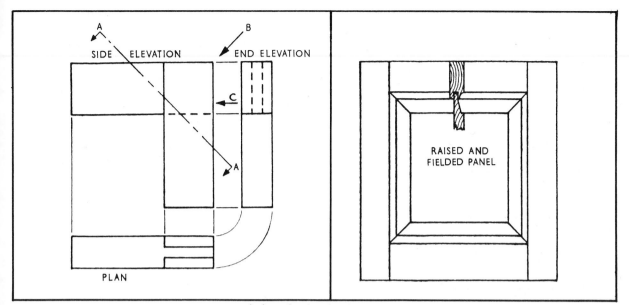

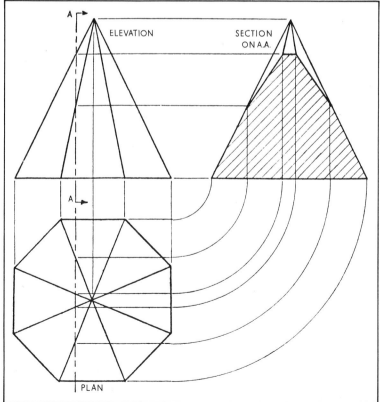

Figure 18 (above)   Example for sectioning. First angle projection

Figure 19 (above right)   'Scrap' section

timber, the drawing is 'grained' to represent long or cross grain.

Fig. 17 shows a haunched mortise and tenon with a sectional elevation added, and Fig. 18 gives an example for practice. Sections are required on A A from the directions of both arrows, B and C. It must be remembered that all parts of the object *beyond* the section plane should be included in the drawing, but these will not, of course, be grained.

In Fig. 19 we see a method of 'scrap' sectioning which is often used as a space and time saver.

Figure 20 (above)   Truncated pyramid

Figure 21   Vertical section of a pyramid

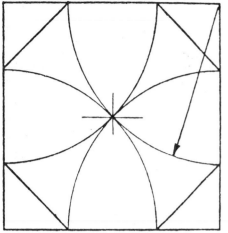

Figure 22   Constructing an octagon in a given square

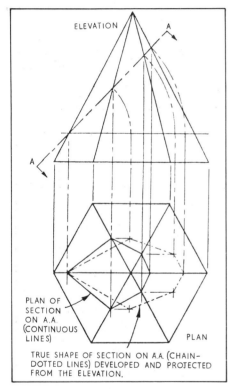

Figure 23   Oblique section of a pyramid

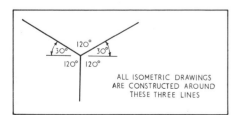

Figure 24   The isometric axes (making 3 angles of 120°)

In Fig. 20 we see a hexagonal pyramid cut by a horizontal plane, the section being projected on to the plan. The lower part of the pyramid is known as a frustum. Before drawing this example, the pyramid should be rotated through 30° to make AB horizontal on plan so that the true length of AB can be obtained from the elevation. As shown, it is a false length in both drawings. Take a vertical height of 8 cm and the sides of the base as 4 cm.

Fig. 21 shows an octagonal pyramid which is cut by a vertical section plane, with a sectional elevation projected to the right. Note the method for constructing an octagon, Fig. 22, and work this example with a pyramid whose height is 10 cm with a base of 9 cm across the flats.

In Fig. 23 is shown a hexagonal pyramid cut by an inclined section plane. The section is shown on the plan together with the development of the true section. This example should be worked using a pyramid with a base of 5 cm side and a vertical height of 10 cm.

Isometric projection

This is one of the forms of pictorial representation which is used for conveying compact and clear impressions. It is not used in the drawing offices of industry, but is nevertheless of great educational value and is used to clarify constructions and mechanical details in textbooks. The student, in making such projections, gets practice in thinking and visualising solids in three dimensions. A further point worthy of note is that many examination questions are set in isometric projection for reproduction in orthographic projection.

This rather rigid geometrical method of picture making always produces some apparent distortion because it does not follow the laws of perspective, but this does not detract from its value to the craftsman, for the drawing is mechanically correct and can be used for taking off sizes.

Fig. 24 shows the three isometric axes around which all drawings are constructed. Two examples are given which can be used for practice – they should be turned through 90° and viewed from the opposite corner. In Fig. 25 a the construction lines for erecting the roof have been left in for guidance and it should be noted that in Fig. 25 b the complete box enclosing the bureau was drawn before putting in any detail.

When dealing with multi-faced objects, the rectilinear solid (or box) which will contain the object is first drawn in isometric projection and then, by measurements along or parallel to the axes, the object is constructed inside. In Fig. 26 is shown the frustum of an octagonal pyramid converted from orthographic to isometric projection by this method.

Curves are dealt with in a similar manner, by drawing first the rectilinear figure which contains the curve, in isometric projection, and then transferring points on the curve by means of measured ordinates. The method is demonstrated in Fig. 27.

Isometric scale   It will be observed that all faces of the object recede from the viewer at the same inclination, and the foreshortening of these faces is sometimes accounted for by using the isometric scale. This produces a drawing proportionately smaller than full size and the scale is constructed as shown in Fig. 28. Conventional isometric projection, i.e. to full size or to any of the common scales, is much more generally used, and the student should employ these unless specifically asked to work to *isometric* scale.

Oblique projection

This is another commonly used form of pictorial drawing. One face of the object is always parallel to the viewer whilst the top and sides recede at any desired angle – usually 45°. It will be noticed that a front or side elevation in orthographic projection can readily be converted to oblique projection.

Figure 25 a and b   Examples in isometric projection

Figure 26   Isometric projection

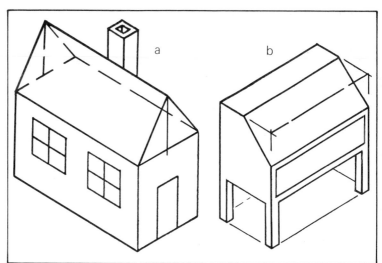

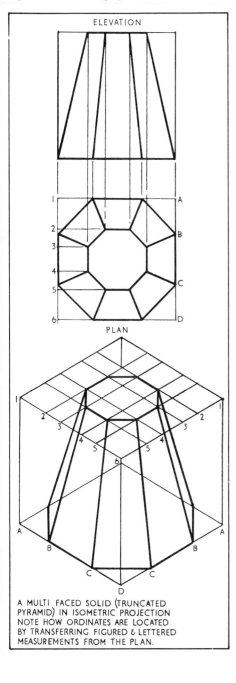

A MULTI FACED SOLID (TRUNCATED PYRAMID) IN ISOMETRIC PROJECTION NOTE HOW ORDINATES ARE LOCATED BY TRANSFERRING FIGURED & LETTERED MEASUREMENTS FROM THE PLAN.

Two examples are given in Fig. 29, whilst Fig. 30 b shows how curves are dealt with.

Fig. 30 a shows another form of oblique projection in which the plan is parallel to the viewer. This is known as planometric projection which is sometimes inaccurately known as axonometric projection. The method is quite simple and is readily adapted to a plan of the subject.

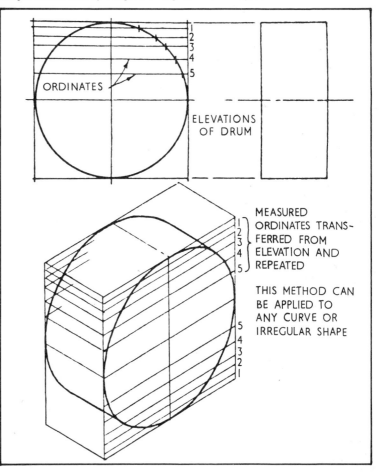

Figure 27   Curves in isometric projection

Figure 28 (*right*)   *Constructing an isometric scale*

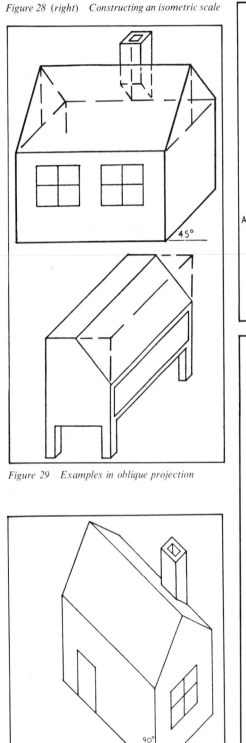

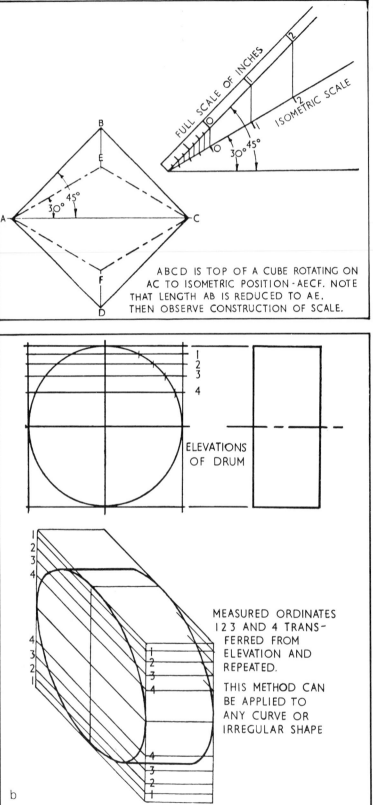

ABCD IS TOP OF A CUBE ROTATING ON
AC TO ISOMETRIC POSITION - AECF. NOTE
THAT LENGTH AB IS REDUCED TO AE.
THEN OBSERVE CONSTRUCTION OF SCALE.

Figure 29   Examples in oblique projection

ELEVATIONS
OF DRUM

MEASURED ORDINATES
1 2 3 AND 4 TRANS-
FERRED FROM
ELEVATION AND
REPEATED.

THIS METHOD CAN
BE APPLIED TO
ANY CURVE OR
IRREGULAR SHAPE

Figure 30 a   Example in planometric projection
Figure 30 b (*right*)   *Curves in oblique projection*

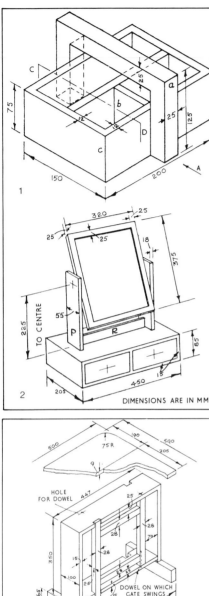

DIMENSIONS ARE IN MM

DIMENSIONS ARE IN MM

Questions

(1) The figure shows a sketch of a box. Draw a plan, an elevation looking from A, and a sectional elevation on the line C D. Also show the joints you would use at a, b and c. Scale: 1:2. Assume any dimensions not given.

(2) *Fix your drawing paper with a long edge at the top.*

The drawing shows the main proportions of a stand with a swinging mirror.

(a) Near the top of your paper, make a scale of 1:2 so that lengths up to 450 mm may be scaled from it.

(b) Draw the front and end elevations of the complete stand, using the scale you have made, with the mirror in the vertical position. Hidden details of the carcase and back are *not* required.

(c) On the back of your paper, draw a full-size front and side elevation of the pillar, P only, which you are asked to design. Your drawings, which should be dimensioned, should show a suitable shape for the pillar within the limits given on the drawing provided, and the method of joining it to the base and to the connecting rail, R.

(CL)

(3) *Note*—Use your discretion to supply dimensions or other details which are not given.

The construction of the table is *not* to be shown.

Gate-leg table

(a) Make a free-hand sketch, showing piece, B, suitably shaped to form the foot of the table, keeping to the general overall sizes.

(b) To a scale of half full size, draw a plan and an end elevation of the table with one of the gates opened to an angle of 60°. On this elevation show the design of the foot and draw two adjacent pieces of the top; show also the same two pieces in broken lines, on the plan.

(c) Insert *six* of the main dimensions.

(d) In a suitable panel add the title 'GATE-LEG TABLE – HALF FULL SIZE'. Use capital letters.

(O and C)

(4) The lower drawing gives the general form and main dimensions of a magazine rack.

The ends, bottom and partition are 12 mm thick and the sides are 10 mm thick. Joints at D, E and F are common dovetail, mortise and tenon, tongue and groove respectively.

All other sizes and details not shown are left to your discretion. Arrange your paper on the drawing board with one short edge at the top.

Draw to a scale of 1:2:

(a) a front elevation viewed in the direction of arrow, A,

(b) an end elevation viewed in the direction of arrow, B,

(c) a plan projected from the front elevation.

You are to show on your drawings details of the joint and shaping for the ends, partition and feet.

Draw, also, a suitable shape for a handle that could be cut in the partition. Add the title 'A magazine rack' and dimension the end elevation.

(L)

2

Tools

Steel and tool steel

A number of impurities are always associated with the ferrous metals and all have marked influences on the physical properties. Carbon is the most important of these impurities, about 3% being present in pig (crude) iron. In the refining processes which follow in steel making, the levels of the impurities are adjusted, carbon being controlled at from 0·1 to 1·2%.

'Pure' iron is soft and ductile, but when alloyed with carbon, a range of steels is produced whose properties are governed mainly by the carbon content which is varied to give the precise qualities of hardness and toughness as required. Certain heat treatments are employed which produce increasingly marked and important physical changes through the range of steels from low to high carbon contents. In general, a low carbon content (0·1 to 0·3%) is associated with mild steels which lend themselves to forming, bending and machining, a medium carbon content is related to toughness with considerable hardness which becomes more pronounced as the carbon content progresses from 0·4 to 0·6%, whilst high and very high carbon contents from 0·6 to 0·9% and thence up to 1·2% produce tool steels which, when heat treated, are extremely hard and still tough enough to withstand stresses imposed when they are used in making cutting tools.

The chemistry of steel is very complicated, but in simple terms it may be taken that carbon goes into solution in iron, forming a chemical compound and at about 1·2% C, the solution is in effect, saturated. Carbon in excess of this percentage would remain 'free' in the metal which would exhibit the properties of cast iron whose composition resembles the metal from which steel is made.

Wood-cutting tools are made from steels of 0·9 to 1·2% C, and in the final stages of their manufacture they are given heat treatments known as 'hardening and tempering', the effect of which is to leave the steel hard enough to hold a cutting edge for an appreciable time and yet tough enough to withstand reasonable stress without fracture. These treatments are connected with the finely balanced relationship between carbon and iron, hardening being brought about by quenching in water from red heat, making the steel 'dead hard'. In tempering, the steel is again heated, but to a lower temperature after which it is quenched or allowed to cool slowly. This removes some of the extreme hardness and provides a compromise between the desirable qualities of hardness and toughness.

With careless grinding, cutting edges readily heat up above the tempering heat; if this happens, that part of the cutter will be spoiled. With the temper 'drawn', it becomes soft, will not hold a cutting edge and will probably fracture. For this reason alone, the greatest care must be taken when grinding tools to avoid overheating which is indicated by blue-purple discoloration on the bright surface of the steel.

Saws

Hand saws

All saws cut through the action of a number of teeth on the blade passing in rapid succession across the wood, each tooth removing a portion of wood fibre which is then carried forward in the gullets between the teeth and dis-

Figure 31   Hand saw

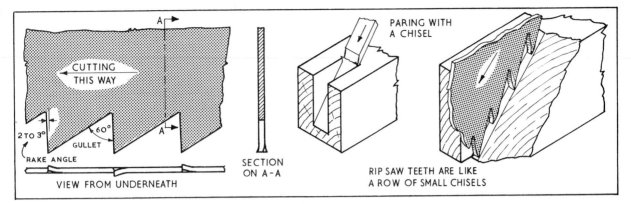

Figure 32   Rip-saw teeth and their cutting action

charged on the opposite side. Clearance for the free passage of the blade in the kerf (saw cut) results from the setting of the teeth points alternately to right and left and this makes a kerf a little wider than the blade thickness.

Different kinds of saws are made for various purposes, but for the moment let us consider only the hand saws, generally made in lengths from 500 to 650 mm. Among these we find two basic tooth forms, viz.: one for cutting along the grain in the *rip saw* and one for cutting mainly across grain in the *cross-cut saw*. Comparing Figs. 32 and 33, we see that although the gullet angle is 60° in both cases, there are differences in the rake- and sharpening-angles which give the two types their distinctive cutting actions. See Fig. 38.

A point to remember when selecting a hand saw is that while a cross-cut saw will also cut along the grain, it is almost impossible to cut across grain with a rip saw. With small power tools so readily available nowadays it is perhaps hardly necessary for the amateur to own a hand rip saw, nevertheless many jobs will turn up where the rip saw is needed, and these tools are still in good supply.

One will naturally be anxious about identifying a good saw when buying, but there is no certain way of judging the quality of a blade simply by handling or examining it. Inferior steel in a blade will be discovered only after some use, the real assurance of quality being found in a reputable maker's name on the blade.

In choosing a saw, one must consider the kind of work expected of it, remembering that a long saw with large teeth will not cut small sections or thin wood cleanly, and that a short saw with small teeth will make hard work of cutting large timbers. Teeth are usually referred to as 'points' and vary in

Figure 33   Cross-cut saw teeth and their action

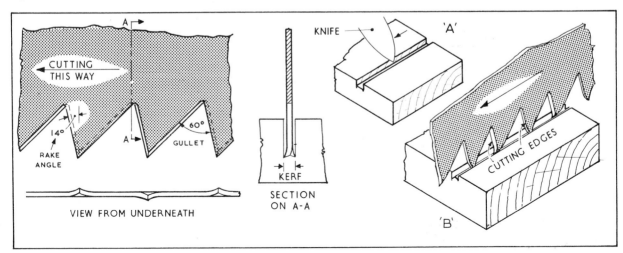

size from 10 per inch on short, thinner blades to 6 per inch on the longer
saws among which we find the rip saws with only 5 points per inch.

Saw blades   In the better-quality saw blades alloy steels are used and these
contain, in addition to carbon, the elements chromium and vanadium or nickel
chromium and molybdenum in small and accurately portioned quantities.
These additives give the steel excellent wear-resisting and edge-holding qualities and blades can be spring-tempered and tensioned to give fast and accurate
cutting.

Tempering   The tempering process is of great importance in achieving a
balance between hardness and toughness. If left too hard, a blade may fracture
in use and although the teeth might hold cutting edges for a long time, they
could fracture when being set. If left too soft, the blade might distort in use
and teeth will dull very quickly. A properly tempered blade will bend in a
uniform curve and spring back quite straight on release.

Setting   The slight angling of teeth alternately to right and left enables the
saw to work properly and provides clearance for the blade in the kerf. Most
saws are machine set nowadays but hand setting is still employed on fine
quality saws. This is a highly skilled operation carried out with the simplest
of tools, viz.: a setting hammer and an anvil with a slightly bevelled edge over
which the teeth are set by striking them lightly.

Taper grinding   In addition to being hand set, good hand saw blades are taper-
ground, giving a slight reduction in thickness from teeth to the back. This
helps in obtaining sufficient clearance in the cut with a reduced amount of
set. Such saws produce quite fine kerfs.

Handles   These are either of close-grained hardwood fitted tightly to the blade
and secured with special screws or of a virtually unbreakable plastic material
moulded on to the blade. The 'balance' of a saw is achieved by the handle
being fitted at an angle which will take a thrust line to about halfway along
the saw.

How a saw works

Reference has been made to the two basic tooth forms and we can now look
at these in more detail.

Rip saws   The action of the rip-saw tooth can be demonstrated with a narrow
chisel as in Fig. 32. Paring away a little wood at a time, the piece of wood
can easily be cut in two along its whole length. The rip-saw teeth are readily
seen as a row of narrow chisels with leading edges at an almost vertical rake
angle and sharpened square across the blade. A properly sharpened rip saw
will cut very cleanly and because of this, will work well with slightly less set
than on a cross-cut saw.

  The rip-saw teeth are usually reduced a little towards the saw tip since full-
size teeth here would tend to bite deeply and cause the saw to whip.

Cross-cut saws   The way in which a cross-cut tooth works is demonstrated
in Fig. 33 at A in which a sharp knife is being drawn across the wood, cutting
two deep lines close together. As the cuts deepen the short wood fibres between
them crumble and fall away, and if the piece of wood were thin it would be
possible to cut right through in this way. The teeth seen at B resemble knife
points, each being sharpened at an angle across the blade to produce knife
edges. With the points set over a little at alternate sides of the blade they
produce a cut wide enough for the blade to pass freely.

Saw maintenance

The best of saws will of course need re-sharpening from time to time and if
previous maintenance has not been done carefully, then all four of the following processes will be needed: (1) *topping*, (2) *shaping*, (3) *setting*, and (4)
sharpening.

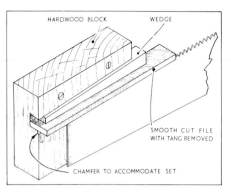

Figure 34   Topping clamp for aligning saw teeth

Topping   The teeth points are re-aligned by levelling off along the saw with a smooth-cut file (or mill file) held in a hardwood block as in Fig. 34. Even if the saw only needs sharpening it is usually topped, the small flats or 'shiners' which appear on the tooth points being of great help in shaping and sharpening. Topping is an essential feature in the 'doctoring' of a saw which has suffered from unskilled sharpening leaving misshapen and undersized teeth. See Fig. 35. If the teeth are in very poor alignment or if any are very small, the topping should be done in two or more stages, being followed by shaping each time. One very heavy topping could make the shaping process quite difficult.

Shaping   This is only necessary when teeth are incorrectly angled, of different sizes or misshapen. After topping – and with the saw in a vice – alternate gullets are filed square across the blade to bring each tooth to its correct shape and rake angle. See Fig. 38. The shiners on each side of a gullet serve as guides in shaping and exactly one half of each should disappear as the gullet is filed. The other two halves will go when the alternate gullets are filed from the other side of the saw. Any teeth untouched in the topping should not be filed until a later topping produces shiners.

Very careful filing will be needed when the shiners on either side of a gullet are of different sizes, a small shiner (or perhaps none at all) indicates a small tooth which will quickly become smaller with unskilled filing.

Setting   This is the slight bending of tooth tips alternately to right and left, never more than one half of the tooth being set. The plier-type saw set seen in Fig. 36 gives quite satisfactory results if adjusted carefully for the right depth of set. One must be very careful to set *alternate* teeth in the correct direction, for if a tooth tip has to be reset in the opposite direction it may fracture.

After setting it is usual to side dress the teeth to remove any irregularities. This is done with the blade laying flat on the bench, an oilstone slip being drawn lightly along the entire line of teeth on both sides.

Sharpening cross-cut saws   The bevel on cross-cut teeth – which produces the knife edges – must not be too 'flat', for although this will give thin, keen edges to the teeth, they will wear rapidly and need sharpening more often. Before sharpening begins, the teeth should be lightly topped and the saw then set up in the vice with about 10 mm protruding and the handle to the right.

Sharpening is perhaps best commenced at the saw tip, placing the file in the first gullet seen to have the right-hand tooth set forwards, the left-hand tooth being set to the rear. The file is kept horizontal and is then slanted across

Figure 35 (left)   *Topping of saw teeth*

Figure 36 (right)   *The plier-type saw set*

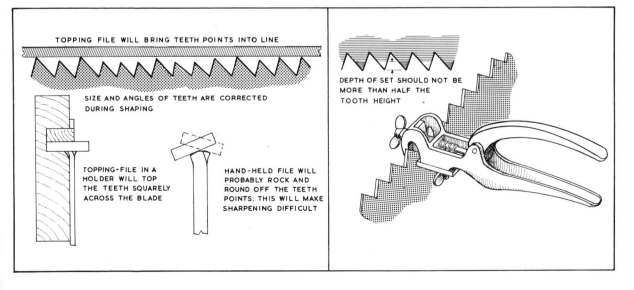

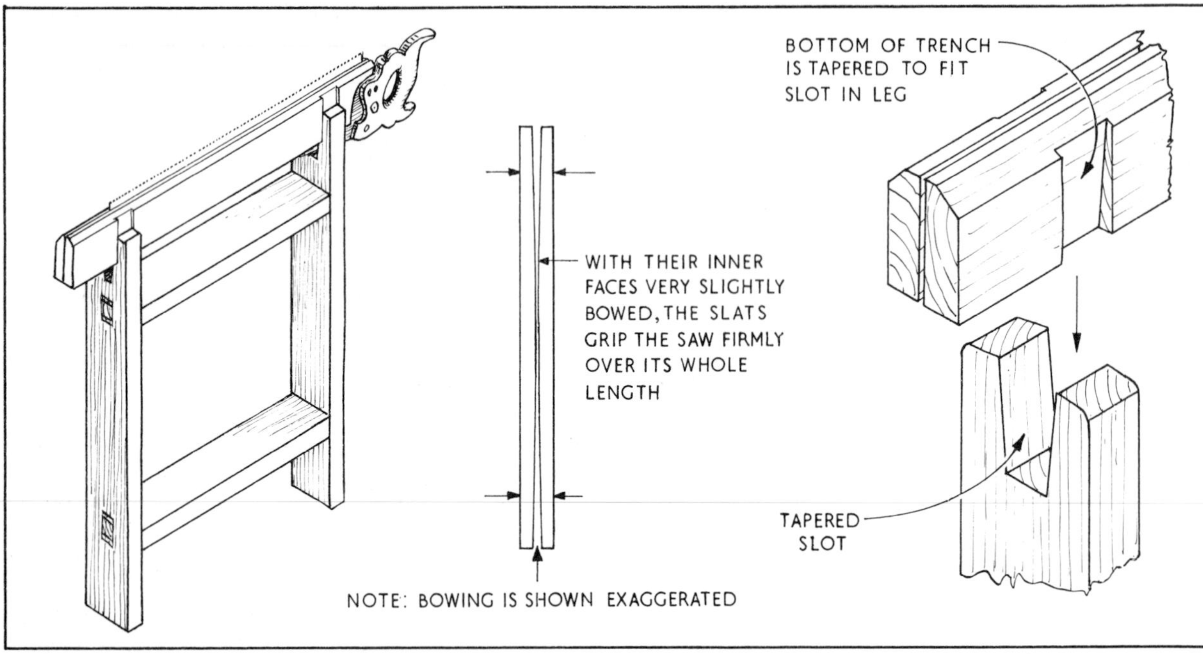

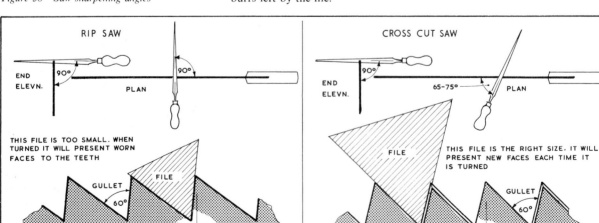

Figure 37   Saw sharpening vice

Figure 38   Saw sharpening angles

at between 65 and 75° pointing to the right and is then rotated a little to produce the desired rake angle, up to 14°.

It is in maintaining the angles for bevel and rake that the greatest difficulty will be experienced by the beginner: this is one of those tasks in which only 'practice makes perfect'. Two or three steady strokes are made until one half of the shiner on each side of the gullet has disappeared. The file is then transferred to the next gullet but one for like treatment, and so on along the blade. As the front of each tooth is sharpened, so is the rear of its neighbour.

It is a good thing for the beginner to work quite slowly and deliberately, and having started sharpening one should traverse the whole length of the saw without taking the file away which might result in coming back at a different angle.

Saw and vice are now reversed and sharpening can begin again, dealing with those teeth which were omitted on the first pass. Each shiner should disappear after two or three strokes. The saw is then lightly side dressed to remove any burrs left by the file.

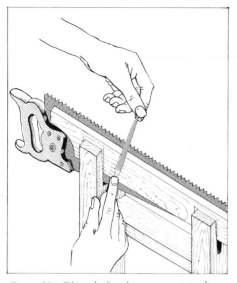

Figure 39   Filing the bevel on cross-cut teeth

Sharpening rip saws   After topping, the saw is set up in the vice as already described. Sharpening proceeds in the same manner as for the cross-cut saw except that the file is held quite square across the blade and is rotated so that the leading edges of the teeth are pitched at only 2 or 3°. Alternate teeth are sharpened, one half of each shiner disappearing at each pass along the saw and sharpening is followed by a light side dressing.

Other hand saws

A few innovations worthy of mention have appeared in recent times and amongst these are the Teflon-coated blades noted for their reduced friction levels and their rust resistance. Notable also is the 'universal' tooth form which is a compromise between the rip and cross-cut tooth. Saws with these teeth will cut across and along the grain but at the cost of slower cross-grain cutting.

Some saws are made with hardened teeth which cannot be file-sharpened and these find acceptance with the occasional user. These saws keep their edges four or five times longer than usual and to the person who uses one only occasionally, this probably represents a lifetime of service.

In building work saws are often at risk from severe working conditions, accidental damage or loss, and the craftsmen often prefer to use the inexpensive 'fleam'-toothed saws with hardened teeth and simply buy another when necessary. The fleam tooth is a fast-cutting form with deep gullets of less than the normal 60° angle. Unhardened fleam teeth can be sharpened with a 'cant' saw file which has a flattened triangular section.

Tenon saws

The tenon saw, also known as a 'back' saw, is made for fine work and with a thinner blade and smaller teeth it is stiffened with 'U'-sectioned back of brass or steel which grips the blade firmly. Because this saw is used in general work at the bench, it must cut across and with the grain and so its tooth form is that of the cross-cut saw, with tooth rake angle about 16°. Tenon saws are commonly available in lengths from about 205 to 350 mm, the smallest having 15 points per inch and the larger, 13 points.

The dovetail saw is a small version of the tenon saw with a thinner blade and usually 25 points per inch. It is used for fine and accurate work including, of course, dovetailing.

Maintenance of tenon saws   These saws are sharpened exactly as for cross-cut saws, using short 'slim taper' files of 100 to 125 mm length. Much greater care is needed to keep the small teeth of an even size and shape.

Tenon and dovetail saws should always be kept quite sharp so that no forcing – which could lead to distortion of the blade – is needed. Very slight distortion of the blade can sometimes be rectified by tapping the back lightly with a hammer, but if this fails the saw should be returned to the manufacturer for repair.

Care of saws   Apart from the normal maintenance in sharpening, a few common-sense precautions will prolong the useful life of all saws. Rust is an enemy common to most tools and if allowed to form on saw blades it will spoil cutting edges and make sawing difficult because of the extra friction. It also gives the saw a neglected appearance. Saws should not be left laying about on the bench when not in use but should be hung on racks kept specially for them. Dull saws will need forcing at work and might be distorted; this applies particularly to back saws. When using hand saws, the trestle should be high enough to ensure that the saw tip does not strike the floor and to avoid injury small pieces for hand sawing should be gripped in the bench vice.

Figure 40 a   Back saw

Figure 40 b   Circular saw for use with power drill

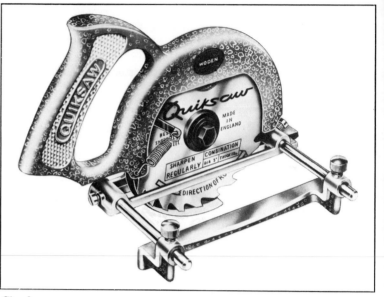

Circular saws

Small power saws are in general use nowadays either as drill attachments or as portable or bench-mounted units and each will only give good service if good-quality blades are fitted and properly set and sharpened. Blades coated with friction-reducing Teflon give increased cutting speeds and are rust-resistant. A choice of tooth forms is available and for general purposes, the gullet (or 'combination') tooth is a good choice as it will cut across or along the grain. Its deep gullets give fast cutting and good dust clearance and less power is needed in driving it. With fewer teeth to set and sharpen, maintenance is that much easier. It is seen in Fig. 40 b.

The cross-cut tooth is not very satisfactory in long ripping operations but it does leave a good surface and is very effective in cutting plywood and hardboard.

Using circular saws   It is unlikely that pupils will be allowed to use circular saws in schools but they may well have access to them at other places and a few words of warning will not come amiss.

One must never forget that power-operated tools can inflict serious injury if handled carelessly. The importance of keeping saw blades properly set and sharpened cannot be over-emphasised, a dull blade will cut slowly and probably overheat whilst a real element of danger will exist because work will have to be forced against the machine to make it cut.

Manufacturer's guards should always be used as recommended and bench saws, wherever possible, should be operated with saw guard and riving knife in position. The guard is there to stop things falling on to the saw and to stop work being thrown upwards whilst the riving knife will hold the newly made kerf open to prevent the wood from binding on the back of the saw. A 'push stick' with a V notch at the end should be used to feed slender work past the saw – for obvious reasons.

In using bench saws, the work should be held firmly down on the table whilst cutting to prevent the saw from snatching.

In using portable saws, a wise practice is to hold the machine with both hands with the work clamped to bench or trestle so that there is less chance of one's free hand being at risk whilst steadying the work.

When fitting saw blades care must be taken to get the correct rotation, and before changing blades the power should be switched off at the wall plug. The starting switch does not really give adequate protection against accidental starting, especially with hand-held units where a press-button switch might easily be operated inadvertently.

Maintenance of circular saws This work involves processes identical with those for hand saws but until one has become experienced on these, it is recommended that circular-saw sharpening is entrusted to a professional saw doctor.

It is the topping process which presents a problem since this can only be done with the blade set up in a bench saw (not a hand-held unit) and running under power. Topping is done by resting a piece of abrasive stone flat on the saw table and then presenting it very lightly and quite square to the blade as it turns. This job is *not* for the beginner. The remaining operations – shaping, setting and sharpening – are carried out as for hand saws but special setting pliers will be required. Combination tooth gullets are reshaped with a round-edged mill file and for these operations the blade can be gripped between two stout wooden discs held in a vice.

Figure 41 a   Bow saw   b   Coping saw

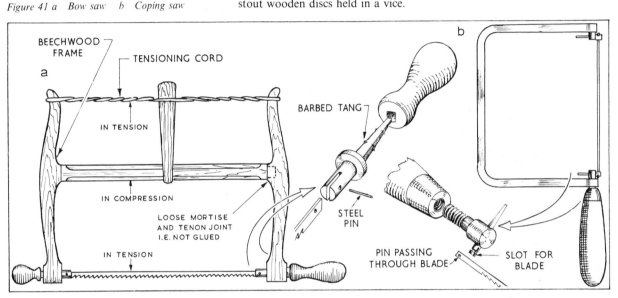

The bow saw

The bow saw

With a wide gap in the frame and a narrow blade, the bow saw is designed for cutting contours. The blade can be turned to cut in any direction by rotating the handles, taking care not to twist the blade. Also illustrated is the coping saw, used for small work. Its blade can be turned in any direction and is tensioned by turning the handle clockwise, drawing in the threaded end of the blade holder.

The pad saw

The pad saw is used for cutting curves where the bow-saw frame would be an obstruction as in piercing. The compass saw is used for heavier work.

Planes

First let us consider the types of plane in general use.

The jack plane

This is so called because of the variety of tasks to which the craftsman applies this plane. Its main jobs are: (1) to clean surfaces by removing saw marks, (2) to prepare surfaces to a reasonable degree of truth, and (3) to bring timber to size. Because this plane is used with a fairly coarse cut, the cutting iron is usually sharpened with a slightly rounded edge as in Fig. 44. If sharpened

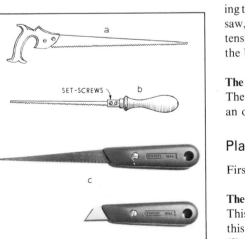

Figure 42 a   Compass saw   b   Pad saw
c   The Stanley saw knife

Figure 43   Choosing the right plane

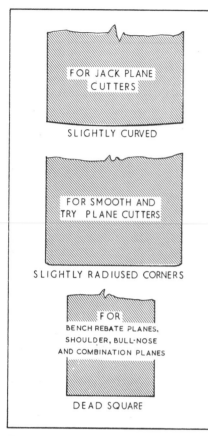

FOR JACK PLANE CUTTERS

SLIGHTLY CURVED

FOR SMOOTH AND TRY PLANE CUTTERS

SLIGHTLY RADIUSED CORNERS

FOR
BENCH REBATE PLANES,
SHOULDER, BULL-NOSE
AND COMBINATION PLANES

DEAD SQUARE

Figure 44   Plane iron (cutter) shapes

Figure 45   The common planes compared
a   Smoothing
b   Jack
c   Trying

A short plane will not plane a long edge straight.
A long plane will bridge the hollows

as for other planes, surfaces would be left with ridges and taking a wide, thick shaving, it would be tiring in use. Surfaces left by the jack plane are not regarded as finished, further treatment with other planes follows later.

The trying plane (try plane)
If the timber is of considerable length and requires accurate preparation, e.g. for edge-to-edge joints, then the trying plane is used. It is seen compared to other planes in Fig. 45. The cutting iron is sharpened quite straight with the corners rounded a little – this plane is only used with quite fine settings. The extra length causes the plane to span depressions without cutting whilst high spots are removed. The trying plane can be used on the shooting board for short edge-to-edge jointing work. Metal trying planes (or 'try' planes) are available in several lengths from about 450 to 600 mm, the shorter ones being known as fore planes and the largest as jointers.

The smoothing plane
The plane seen in Fig. 46 is representative of the modern bench planes. Although the smoothing plane has many varied uses, its main work is in finishing – its fine setting and straight cutting edge removing small irregularities and defects leaving clean surfaces in readiness for scraping or glass-papering.

Plane irons (cutters)
The double irons with which the common planes are fitted merit attention in some detail. Modern cutting irons are made from alloy steels which hold a cutting edge for long periods whilst cap irons are usually made from low-carbon steels since they are not actually involved in cutting.

The cap iron (also known as the 'back' iron) is secured to the cutting iron by a cheese-headed screw passing through a keyhole slot and because of its shape it makes close contact with the cutting iron, close to the edge.

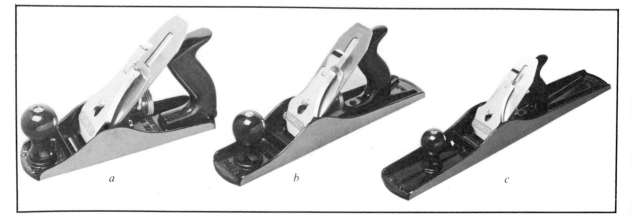

a   *b*   *c*

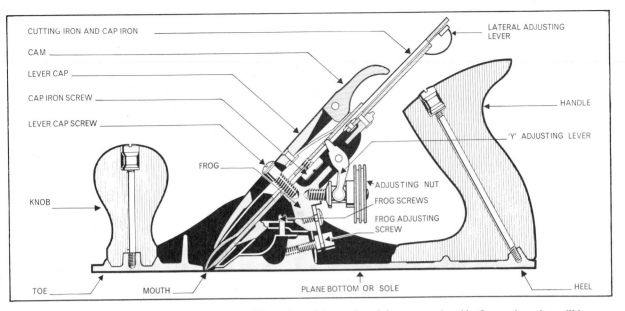

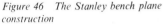

Figure 46 The Stanley bench plane construction

The action of the cap iron is best appreciated by first seeing what will happen in a plane having no cap iron as in Fig. 47. The plane will work well enough whilst *with* the grain (usually producing a straight shaving), but if the grain should change direction, the shaving will become thicker and stronger and will lift further and further in advance of the cutting edge until either the sliver will be torn from the wood or the plane mouth will become choked and stop working. A wide mouth will aggravate this fault.

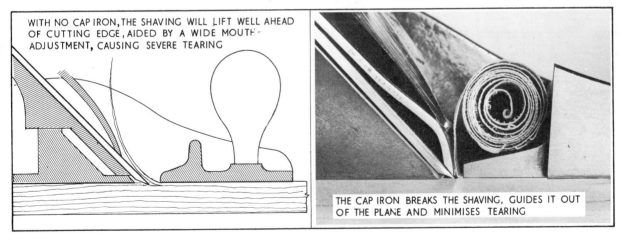

Figure 47 Showing the need for a cap iron and how it works

Fitted with a properly adjusted cap iron and with the mouth suitably adjusted, the effect is as seen in Fig. 47. The cap iron breaks the shaving, guides it out of the plane and minimises tearing. Because it is broken, the shaving has no strength and is unable to lift itself by bearing against the cutting iron. So instead of finding a few deep tears in the surface, produced by a single iron working over short grain, we shall find a large number of very small ones which will not necessarily ruin the surface finish. The size of these tears can be reduced to a minimum by: (1) setting the cap iron very close to the cutting edge, (2) setting the cutting iron to take only very thin shavings, and (3) by keeping the mouth as small as possible.

In working on timbers with wild and wandering grain, these fine adjustments are important and help considerably in getting a good finish. Timbers with

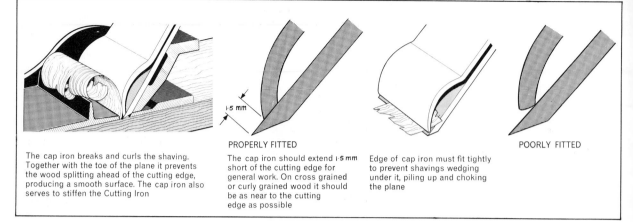

The cap iron breaks and curls the shaving. Together with the toe of the plane it prevents the wood splitting ahead of the cutting edge, producing a smooth surface. The cap iron also serves to stiffen the Cutting Iron

PROPERLY FITTED

The cap iron should extend 1·5 mm short of the cutting edge for general work. On cross grained or curly grained wood it should be as near to the cutting edge as possible

Edge of cap iron must fit tightly to prevent shavings wedging under it, piling up and choking the plane

POORLY FITTED

Figure 48   Plane irons

'double' grain are difficult to finish well, whilst with figured wood like flamed maple and some of the exotic woods such as Rio rosewood, it is often well nigh impossible to plane along the grain effectively without bad tearing. In such cases, the expert will plane across the grain with good results, finishing with the hand scraper.

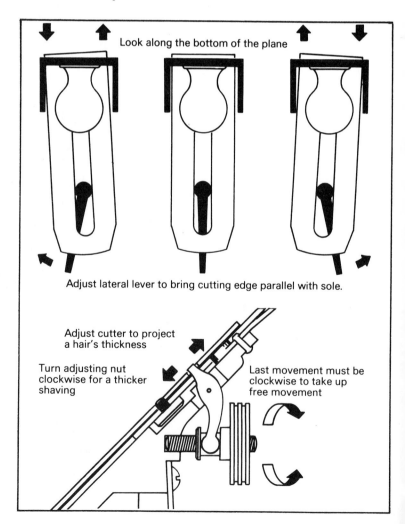

Look along the bottom of the plane

Adjust lateral lever to bring cutting edge parallel with sole.

Adjust cutter to project a hair's thickness

Turn adjusting nut clockwise for a thicker shaving

Last movement must be clockwise to take up free movement

Figure 49   Setting a plane

The maintenance of planes

(1) *General*   Attention to a few points will ensure good service from planes: (1) most metal plane bodies are castings and will break if dropped heavily, (2) plane soles should be kept clean and bright, (3) bedding surfaces on frog and cutting irons should be kept quite clean, (4) all assembly screws should be checked at intervals for tightness, and (5) most modern cutting irons are made from alloy steels and it is just as important to take care against burning at the grindstone as with ordinary carbon steels.

(2) *Bedding of the cap iron*   It is very important that the edge of the cap iron should fit accurately against the cutting iron. See Fig. 48. A hollow-worn oilstone will produce a rounded surface when backing off, thus spoiling the bedding of the two irons. The only cure for this is to reface the cutting iron on a flat oilstone – not an easy task by any means. If the edge of the cap iron is at fault, the cure is more easily made since the surfaces can be trued with a fine-cut file.

(3) *Cleanliness of the cap iron*   When working on soft, resinous woods the cap iron will quickly collect a deposit of resinous matter as the shavings pass over it. This sticky mass will retard the action of the plane and may finally cause a blockage in the mouth when a shaving finally sticks to it. The cap iron must be kept clean and bright, attending to this whilst sharpening.

Grinding and sharpening

One will learn that without good maintenance, the finest tools are of no more use than the most inferior. Apart from cleanliness and rust prevention, the most important aspect is in the preparation and preservation of cutting edges

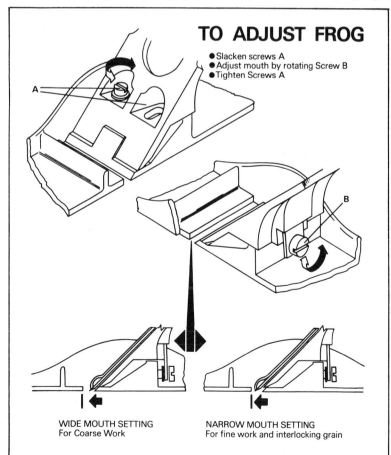

TO ADJUST FROG
- Slacken screws A
- Adjust mouth by rotating Screw B
- Tighten Screws A

WIDE MOUTH SETTING
For Coarse Work

NARROW MOUTH SETTING
For fine work and interlocking grain

Figure 50   Adjusting the frog

and it must never be forgotten that from the moment a cutting edge is formed, it becomes the most delicate and vulnerable part of any tool.

Damage can be avoided in common-sense ways, e.g.: (1) by cleaning dirt, grit, paint, etc. from wood surfaces before planing them, (2) by resting planes on their sides so that the cutting edges do not get rubbed on the bench top, (3) by keeping the bench cleared of nails, screws, etc., (4) by replacing saws and chisels in their racks after use, and (5) by laying tools down on wood surfaces only. Shavings and chippings should not accumulate on the bench, they should be swept off with a brush (not the hands) to avoid injury.

A cutting edge is formed at the intersection of the faces of a wedge form. In general the harder the material to be cut, the larger is the wedge angle – known as a cutting angle or bevel. For example, tools for cutting steel in a lathe require a cutting angle of around 70° so that the tool point is well supported against the load imposed in cutting. On the other hand a thin blade with a cutting angle of only a few degrees will be quite efficient in cutting a material life soft balsa wood. In both cases the cutting edges are cleanly formed at the intersection of two smooth, flat surfaces. In other words, both tools must be sharp.

Figure 51 a (above)   Honing. Inset: grinding and sharpening angles   b (below)   Removing the wire edge (backing off)

Figure 52 Honing with the Stanley honing gauge

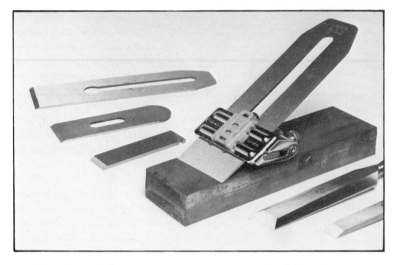

Although the timbers in common use vary considerably in hardness and texture, it is found that one standard angle of 25 to 30° is more or less suitable for all. In Fig. 51 it will be seen that there are in fact two angles or 'bevels', viz.: a *grinding* bevel at 20 to 25° and a *sharpening* bevel at 25 to 30°. The grinding bevel is formed on a grindstone which cuts rapidly and leaves a coarse finish and the sharpening bevel is formed by honing on an oilstone of fine texture which leaves a very smooth finish.

The two bevels are used only for convenience as it is not easy to maintain a constant angle when honing the full width of the bevelled surface. The surface readily becomes rounded, necessitating early regrinding of the tool. With the grinding angle being smaller, only a part of the bevelled surface needs to be honed and this simplifies the process. An aid to maintaining a constant angle is found in the honing gauge seen in Fig. 52.

It is not at all essential to form two bevels, and in fact many craftsmen maintain one bevel only, at about 25°, on their tools just by honing. This calls for a steady hand and long practice and once such a skill is acquired, it will never be necessary to wear away tools at the grindstone. For most of us it will be necessary to regrind tools from time to time and with careful honing, regrinds will be few and far between and our tools will have longer lives.

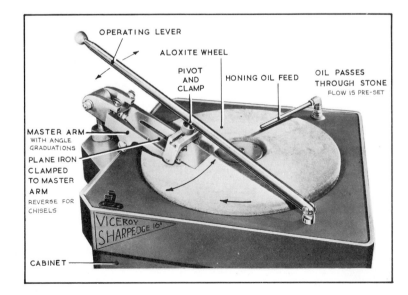

Figure 53 The 'Viceroy Sharpedge' tool sharpening machine for plane irons, chisels, gouges, etc.

Grinding wheels

The old-fashioned sandstone grinding wheels, at one time the only means of grinding tools, have now been superseded by man-made grinding wheels produced by the bonding together of grains of very hard materials such as aluminium oxide, carborundum, etc.

These grinding media can be moulded into any desired section in addition to the plain disc wheels. At the same time the grain size can be chosen to give a range of cutting properties, from those needed in heavy grinding operations to requirements for the finest precision grinding. These wheels are usually run at high speeds and can be used in wet or dry grinding conditions. In wet grinding, a thin oil or oil emulsion is flooded over the work for cooling and to flush away grit and metal particles. Using a coolant always requires the use of splash guards and some means of collecting, filtering and circulating the fluid.

The well-known bench grinders, with wheels of up to about 200 mm, can be used only in dry grinding and are not really suitable for the woodwork shop. The wheel size produces a marked hollow-grinding of cutting bevels, and with the consequent thinning and weakening at cutting edges, the risk of burning (overheating) is increased considerably.

A modern development in grinding technique is seen in the horizontal grinding wheel as shown in Fig. 53. These machines are commonly used nowadays in woodwork shops. They are very efficient since they exploit the rapid cutting properties of artificial abrasives without the risk of burning, a coolant in the form of a special honing oil being flooded over tool and grinding wheel. With chisel or plane iron gripped in the holder, it is a simple task to produce correctly angled and flat bevels very quickly.

Oilstones

After grinding, the keen edges for clean cutting are made by honing on oilstones of natural or artificial materials, the trend today being towards the artificial stone for general use. The best known of the natural stones are the Arkansas and the Washita stones from North America, with Turkey and Charnwood Forest stones also coming to mind. These natural stones all produce very fine edges because of their fine, close textures but they vary a little in quality and are costly.

Artificial stones are made from hard abrasive materials which, in the form of a grit, are bonded together in any desired shape to form bench oilstones and slipstones. The uniformity of the grit in size, hardness and cutting power ensures consistent results. Norton's 'India' oilstones are well known, they are made from an aluminium oxide abrasive known as 'alundum'. Bench stones, which come in three grades (coarse, medium and fine grits) are also made with one side of coarse and the other of a finer grit and this latter kind are known as 'combination' stones. Slipstones, for sharpening gouges and other shaped tools are available in a wide range of shapes and sizes. See Fig. 72.

Bench oilstones should be housed in wooden boxes with lids, best made from solid wood blocks – the making of which provides a useful exercise for the beginner. A good anchorage on the bench is obtained by driving in a small panel pin underneath each corner, leaving about 3 mm protruding and pointing each with a file.

Light machine oils are generally used in honing to float off grit and metal particles which would clog the stone. Heavy oils are not suitable and linseed oil must be avoided at all costs as it will harden and clog the stone. After use, dirty oil should be wiped away and the lid replaced.

To avoid uneven wear of the stone, the entire surface should be used, avoiding the rubbing of narrow chisels along the middle only. A figure of eight movement can be used to help in even wearing of the stone and a further aid

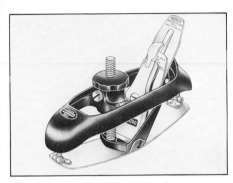

Figure 54   The 'Record' circular plane

Figure 55   The 'Record' 010 bench rebate plane in use

Figure 56 a   Stanley bench rebate plane
b   Stanley 'duplex' rebate plane

is the provision of two small hardwood blocks recessed into the box, one at each end and laying flush with the stone. These allow cutters to pass right over the far end of the stone which is turned end for end (with its box) after each honing. Passing cutters over the block at the near end is not always satisfactory. Every effort should be made to ensure even wear since refacing can be a lengthy task involving rubbing against another abrasive stone using silver sand or other grit as a grinding medium.

Sharpening (honing)   With some light oil on the stone and with the tool held at the correct angle the bevel is rubbed along the length of the stone, working over the whole surface. Quite soon, a small lip or 'wire edge' will be pushed up at the cutting edge and the tool is then ready for 'backing off' and this is done by holding it down firmly on its flat face, whilst rubbing it back and forth a few times. It is most important that the cutter is held quite flat on the stone as a slight bevel on the face of a plane iron may prevent the cap iron from bedding properly whilst a bevel on the face of a chisel will prevent it from paring flat surfaces.

The slight rounding of a jack-plane iron (see Fig. 44) will present no problem in honing – it is the easiest thing in the world to produce a rounded edge. Keeping the edges straight on smoothing-plane irons calls for careful control at the oilstone, likewise for shoulder- and rebate-plane irons.

Other planes

The circular (compass) plane   This metal plane has a sole of thin, spring steel which can be adjusted for working on large-radius concave or convex curves. Such curves are often referred to as 'sweeps'.

The rebate plane   A rebate (or rabbet) is a stepped surface formed along the edge of a piece of timber. The Stanley 'duplex' plane seen in Fig. 56 is designed for making rebates, the fence guiding the plane from the edge of the wood whilst the depth gauge stops the plane at any predetermined depth. A spur makes a cut line in front of the cutter, ensuring a clean edge to the rebate and is particularly effective when working across grain. The cutter can be moved forward for working into a stopped end.

The cutter must be sharpened quite square and straight and must be set up accurately in the plane, otherwise ragged or tapering rebates will be formed. Rebates too large for the plane's capacity can often be made by ploughing two or more grooves and sometimes going in from both face side and face edge.

The plough plane   A typical modern plough plane, used in making grooves along the grain, is seen in Fig. 57. This one is supplied with a range of cutter sizes from 3 to 16 mm. Care must be taken to hold the plough level and without wobbling, otherwise ragged edges will be left, especially if the groove is deep.

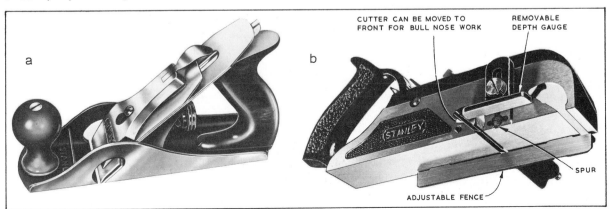

CUTTER CAN BE MOVED TO
FRONT FOR BULL NOSE WORK

REMOVABLE
DEPTH GAUGE

a

b

STANLEY

SPUR

ADJUSTABLE FENCE

Figure 57   The 'Record' 044C plough plane

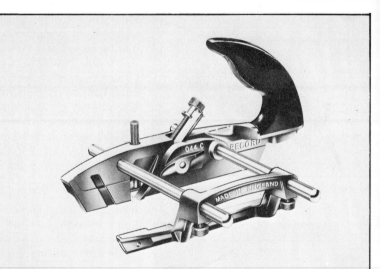

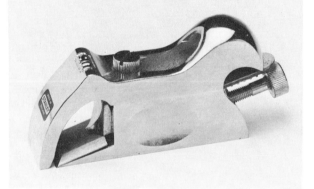

Figure 58   The Stanley No. 92 shoulder plane

Figure 59 (right)   The Stanley No. 90 bull-nose shoulder plane

Figure 60   The Stanley No. 9½ block plane

The shoulder plane   A metal rebate plane intended for use on work demanding a fine finish. It is especially suitable for trimming the shoulders on hardwood tenons required to fit accurately. Note the low-angle cutting iron which is reversed (with the bevel on top). This has much the same effect as the cap iron in other planes. See Fig. 58.

Figure 61   The 'Record' multi-plane

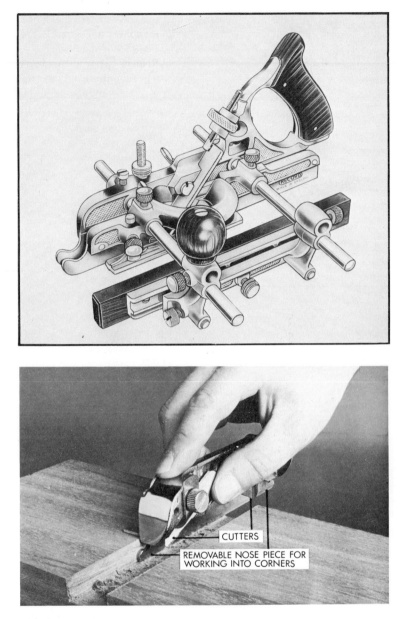

Figure 62   The Stanley side rebate plane. Used in widening plough grooves and housings.

The bull-nose plane   A small metal plane resembling the shoulder plane but only about 100 mm long and with the cutting iron set close to the nose. Especially useful for cleaning up stopped rebates and chamfers. See Figs. 59 and 119.

The block plane   A small metal 'smoothing' plane suitable for all kinds of small and fine work as in trimming of mitres and for planing across end grain. It has a low-angle cutting iron as in the shoulder and bull-nose planes. See Fig. 60.

Combination planes   These planes as in Figs. 61 and 63 will produce plough grooves, dados (wide shallow recesses), rebates, edge and centre beads, tongues and grooves. Other planes of this kind are provided with cutters for a variety of mouldings, replacing the moulding planes of former times.

Spokeshaves   The spokeshave is, in effect, a very short plane provided with handles for its manipulation and it is used in truing and smoothing curved surfaces. Modern spokeshaves are made in cast metal with flat or round faces for convex or concave curves. Cutters can be held in a wooden holder, as in Fig. 65, for sharpening.

Routers   The router is used in levelling and cleaning up the bottoms of trenchings (housings) and other recessed surfaces. Two modern routers are shown in Fig. 66 and the old-fashioned wooden router is seen in Fig. 67.

Figure 63 (right)   The Stanley 18-blade combination plane

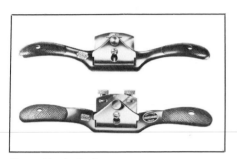

Figure 64   Spokeshaves

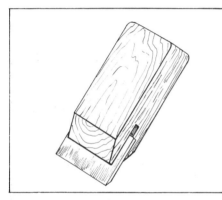

Figure 65   A wooden holder for spokeshave cutter sharpening

Figure 66a (above right)   The Stanley No. 71 Router

Figure 66b (below right)   The Stanley No. 27 Router

Figure 67 (opposite page)   A selection of wooden planes, not now in common use. It will be of interest to compare these with their modern counterparts previously illustrated

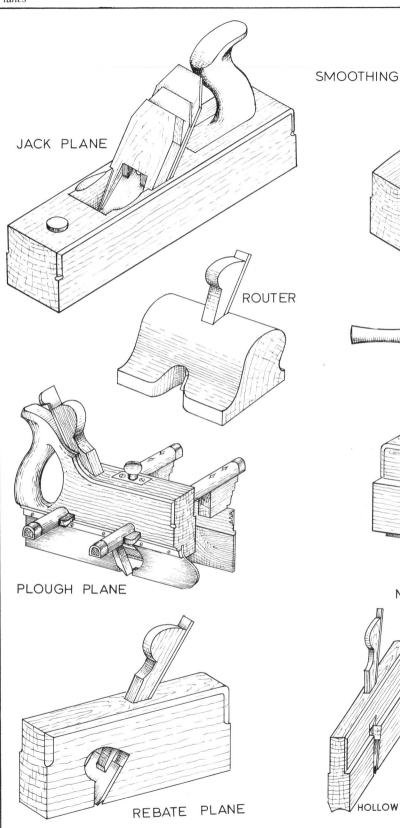
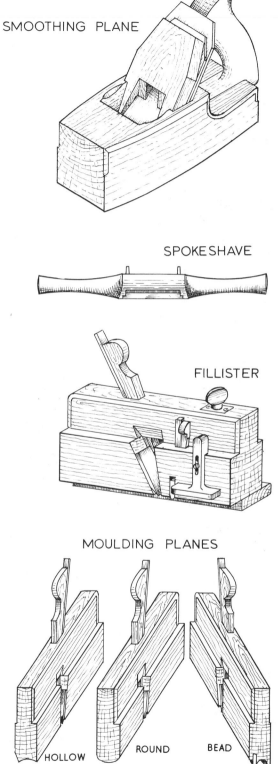

JACK PLANE

SMOOTHING PLANE

ROUTER

SPOKESHAVE

FILLISTER

PLOUGH PLANE

MOULDING PLANES

REBATE PLANE

HOLLOW   ROUND   BEAD

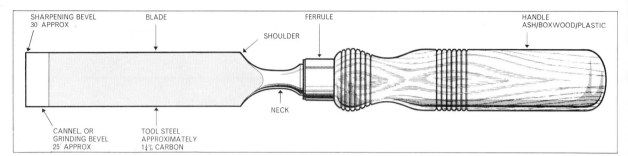

Figure 68   The parts of the chisel

Chisels and gouges

A selection of wood chisels is shown below with notes as to their various uses. Bevel-edged chisels are specially useful in paring dovetails where a square-edged chisel would damage the sloping surfaces. Handles are commonly made of ash, beech, box or plastics. Ash and beech will not withstand constant, heavy use of the mallet and in the registered pattern chisel, used in mortising and other heavy work, the beech handle has an extra steel hoop (or ferrule) to prevent splitting. Box takes a smooth finish, is hard wearing and is used for handling mortise chisels and higher-priced bench chisels. Note the stout leather washer fitted at the ferrule on mortise chisels to absorb some of the shock and to stop damage to the handle. Plastic handles are much in favour nowadays and are reckoned to be virtually unbreakable.

Figure 69   Types of chisel

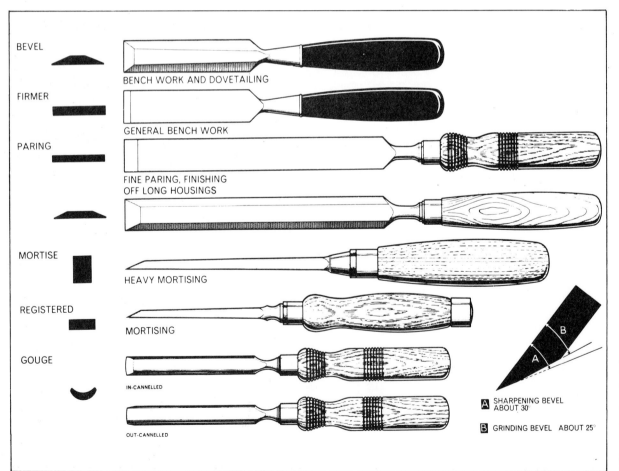

Figure 70   Methods of fixing blades to handles

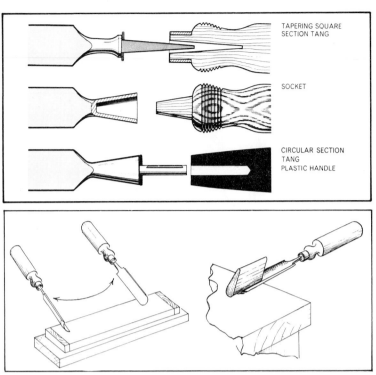

TAPERING SQUARE
SECTION TANG

SOCKET

CIRCULAR SECTION
TANG
PLASTIC HANDLE

*Figure 71   Sharpening a firmer gouge and
removing wire edge with a slipstone*

Firmer gouge   Ground on the outside, this gouge is suitable for any kind of scooping-out operation and is sometimes referred to as a carving gouge. Gouges are measured across the sweep (curve), from edge to edge and are made in a range of sizes up to 25 mm. They are ground with a rocking movement on a flat-faced grindstone. Sharpening is done on the oilstone as shown in Fig. 71, and the wire edge is removed by means of a slipstone.

Scribing gouge   This is the opposite of the firmer gouge – being ground on the inside – and is used for contour work where hollow or concave curves are required. The grinding of a scribing gouge necessitates the use of a special stone with a rounded edge. The sharpening is illustrated in Figs. 72a and b, the bevel being sharpened with a slipstone whilst backing off is done on the oilstone.

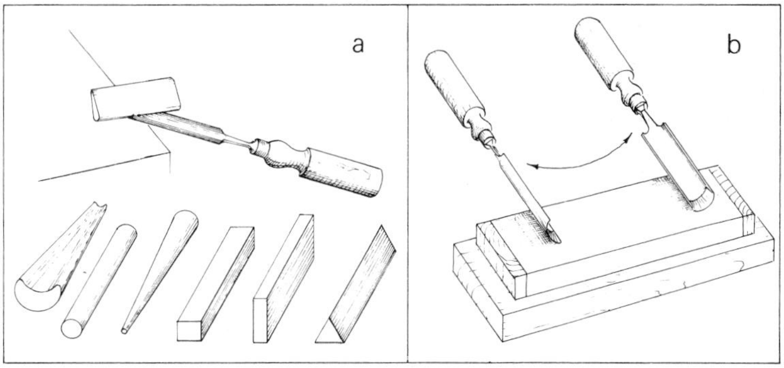

*Figure 72 a   Sharpening a scribing gouge.
Slipstones*

*Figure 72 b   Removing the wire edge from a
scribing gouge*

a

b

Figure 73   Chisels used in fitting locks

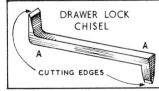

DRAWER LOCK
CHISEL

A   A

CUTTING EDGES

FOR WORKING IN RESTRICTED
SPACE IN MORTISING TO RE-
CEIVE DRAWER-LOCK BOLTS.
THE CHISEL IS STRUCK WITH
THE HAMMER AT POINTS "A"

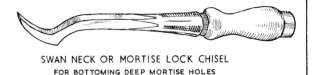

SWAN NECK OR MORTISE LOCK CHISEL
FOR BOTTOMING DEEP MORTISE HOLES

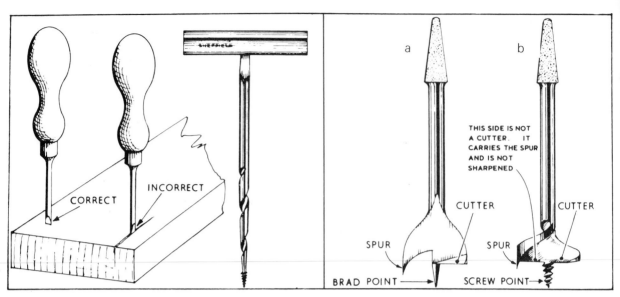

Figure 74 (*left*)   *The bradawl and gimlet*

Figure 75 (*right*)   *a   Centre bit*
b   Screw-point centre bit

Boring tools

The bradawl   Fig. 74 shows a bradawl in use. Note that the blade is entering the wood *across* grain to avoid splitting. Bradawls are used to make holes for nails or small screws and the largest size makes a hole of about 4 mm.

The centre bit   The three main features of this bit are: (1) the *centre* (*or point*) which locates the bit, (2) the *spur* (*or scriber*) which cuts the circumference of the hole, and (3) the *cutter* (*or router*) which removes the waste wood. The spur cuts the wood in advance of the cutter, which with a smaller radius ensures clean cutting. The plain (brad-point) centre bit is not in such general use today, the screw-point bit finding more favour since it is self-feeding and much faster cutting. Still available in imperial sizes, $\frac{1}{4}''$ to $2\frac{1}{4}''$, i.e. from approximately 6 to 55 mm. If used in deep boring, these bits will be found to wander off course.

The auger (twist) bit   For use in the carpenters' brace, the Jennings pattern ranges from $\frac{3}{16}''$ to $1\frac{1}{2}''$ (approx. 4·5 to 38 mm), whilst the solid centre bits are now available in metric sizes from 5 to 40 mm. These bits are used in boring

Figure 76   Sharpening of centre and auger bit. Smooth-cut files are used

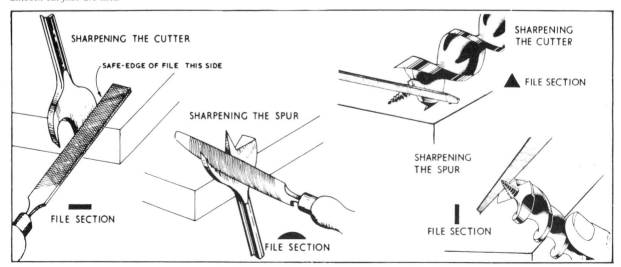

Figure 77   Auger (twist) bits

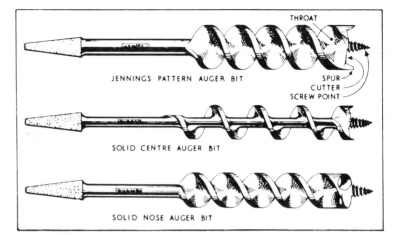

deep holes, the long spirals helping to maintain alignment as the bit penetrates. The screw point pulls the bit into the wood, the two spurs scribe the diameter of the hole in advance of the cutters which then lift the chips, passing them up the spiral. Auger bits can be sharpened as in Fig. 76, but too frequent application of the file can be avoided by taking great care of these tools, keeping them in a strong canvas roll or in a special rack. The solid nose auger is used in tough jobs and is specially suitable for boring at angles, the cutter form allowing the screw to get well started before boring begins. This bit cuts well in end grain. In the absence of spurs, the solid nose bit does not make as clean an entry across grain as the Jennings or solid centre bits.

Other bits   *Expansive bit* This bit, made in two sizes, is fitted with an adjustable cutter which slides in a dovetailed keyway. With extra cutters available, the full range of both bits is from a $\frac{1}{2}''$ to 6″. Holes of any size can be bored

Figure 78   Other bits used in woodworking

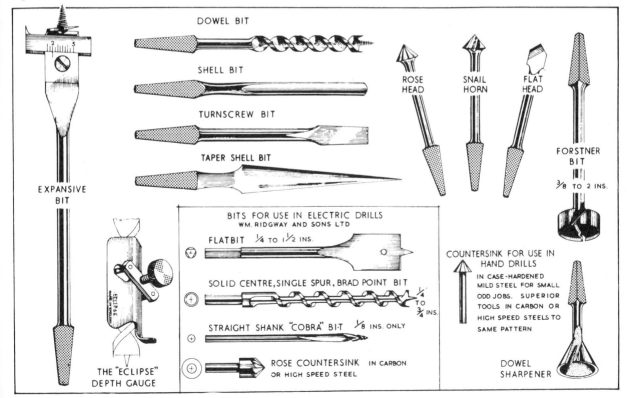

within these limits. These bits are difficult to use on hard wood. *Dowel bit* A short, precision-ground bit intended solely for boring accurate holes for dowels. *Bit stock* A square-shanked twist drill for general use in the brace. Does not always make a clean entry but bores quickly and accurately. *Shell bit* A simple, inexpensive and robust bit for boring clean, short, small-diameter holes. *Turnscrew bit* Used in the carpenters' brace, this tool provides a powerful screwdriver. *Taper shell bit* Used for riming (enlarging) or making tapered holes. *Countersinks* These form conical recesses to receive countersunk screwheads. *Forstner bit* Guided solely by its circular rim, this bit bores true, clean, flat-bottomed holes which can be overlapped without difficulty. Often used in decorative work and in pattern making. *Dowel sharpener* For pointing dowels to facilitate their entry into accurate holes. *Electric-drill bits* These are specially designed for use in small-capacity power drills which are so widely used nowadays.

Figure 79 a   Hand drill (wheel brace)
b   Twist drill with straight shank
c   Breast drill

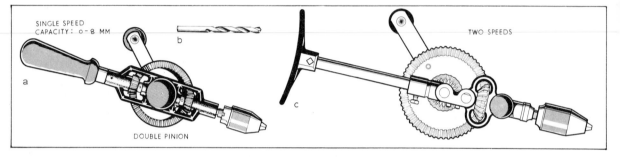

The carpenters' brace

The ratchet brace shown in Fig. 80 is fitted with universal jaws which are shown and explained alongside. The older type (and still commonly used) alligator jaws are also shown. In both cases the jaws are closed on to the bit as the chuck shell is screwed home, an internal taper pressing against the sloping point of each jaw. Plain braces (without the ratchet mechanism) are available, but the ratchet is very useful when working in confined spaces and when driving screws. The size of a brace is measured by its 'sweep', i.e. the diameter of the circle described by the handle, usually 200, 250 and 300 mm and of these, the 250 mm sweep is commonly used.

Screwdrivers

Many different kinds and sizes of screwdrivers are available and in addition to the well-known cabinet and London patterns, screwdrivers for special purposes together with many types of ratchet and spiral ratchet screwdrivers are made. The latter kind, especially, are great time savers where many screws are to be driven. They are supplied with interchangeable bits for slotted or recessed screwheads, with drill points and countersinks. In Fig. 81 is seen a Phillips recessed screw-head together with a screwdriver tip. This type of head is commonly seen today and is found on self-tapping screws, a more recent type of recessed head being the Pozidriv, also shown. Screwdriver blades for general use are often of carbon steels whilst those of high quality are of alloy steels, all being suitably hardened and tempered to withstand torque loads (twisting) in the blade and damage to the point. Blades for Phillips or Pozidriv screws are made from very high-quality alloy steels. Plastic handles are moulded over the blade shank on which are formed two or more small 'wings' to prevent rotation and separation.

To work efficiently and without damaging slotted screw-heads, the screwdriver tip must be properly formed and with cleanly ground faces and the edge square to the blade. A badly formed tip will cause the screwdriver to

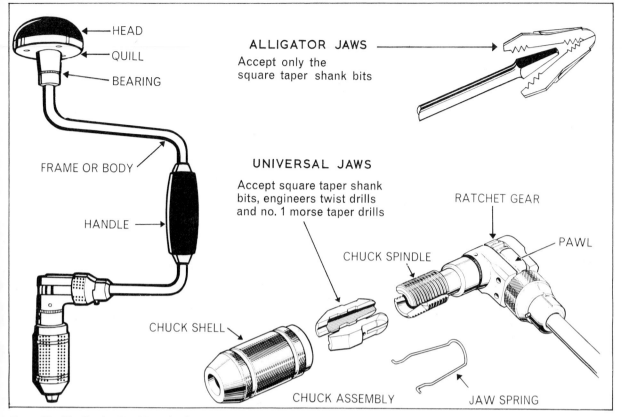

HEAD
QUILL
BEARING

ALLIGATOR JAWS
Accept only the
square taper shank bits

FRAME OR BODY

UNIVERSAL JAWS
Accept square taper shank
bits, engineers twist drills
and no. 1 morse taper drills

RATCHET GEAR

HANDLE

PAWL

CHUCK SPINDLE

CHUCK SHELL

CHUCK ASSEMBLY

JAW SPRING

*Figure 80   The Stanley No. 73 ratchet brace
with universal jaws. Alligator jaws and chuck
assembly with universal jaws*

ride out of the slot and damage it, preventing the screw from being driven
right home or, at least making it look very untidy and amateurish. In Fig.
82 are shown good and faulty screwdriver tips. The screwdriver must of course
be held in line with the screw to avoid damaging the slot and to drive it home
straight.

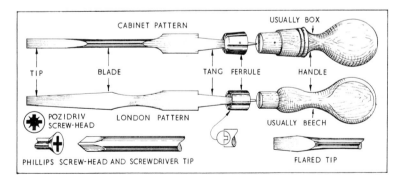

USUALLY BOX

CABINET PATTERN

TIP   BLADE   TANG   FERRULE   HANDLE

POZIDRIV
SCREW-HEAD

LONDON PATTERN

USUALLY BEECH

PHILLIPS SCREW-HEAD AND SCREWDRIVER TIP

FLARED TIP

Figure 81   Screwdrivers

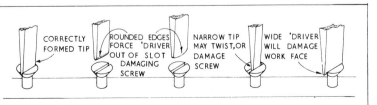

CORRECTLY
FORMED TIP

ROUNDED EDGES
FORCE 'DRIVER
OUT OF SLOT
DAMAGING
SCREW

NARROW TIP
MAY TWIST, OR
DAMAGE
SCREW

WIDE 'DRIVER
WILL DAMAGE
WORK FACE

Figure 82   Screwdriver points

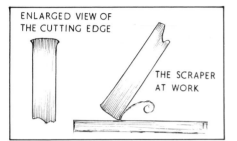

Figure 83   The scraper

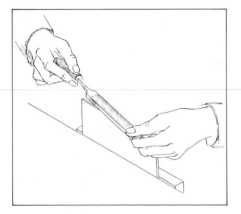

Figure 84   Truing a scraper edge with a smooth-cut file

Figure 85   Forming a cutting edge on the scraper

The scraper

This is a very simple tool, being merely a rectangular piece of thin steel plate of about the same grade as saw steel. It is used in the finishing of hardwoods, being particularly useful on short grain where there is a danger of tearing the surface with even a very finely adjusted smoothing plane. With the scraper inclined in the direction of working, very fine shavings are removed by the keen, hooked edge and this scraping action is very different from that of a plane cutter which lifts the shavings off. The scraper follows the smoothing plane on solid woods, removing plane marks and leaving very good surfaces, on veneers it is usually the only cutting tool used in finishing. Fig. 83 shows, first, an enlarged section of a correctly sharpened scraper, and second, an enlarged view of the cutting edge at work. Incidentally, it is most important that the scraper should be kept quite free of rust for the oxidation forms minute pits in the surface of the metal which prevent the forming of the very keen edge required.

Assuming that we have a scraper which is completely dull, let us study the sharpening process in detail.

It is necessary first to make the edges of the scraper quite square and smooth. This is done in the vice with a fine-cut file as in Fig. 84. Only a few strokes with the file will be needed and great care should be taken to keep it level. The ends of the scraper edge can be rounded off slightly as sharp corners here are undesirable. The next step is the removal of any burrs left on the cutting edges from the filing and this is done by laying the scraper flat on the oilstone, rubbing it along two or three times using a fair pressure. The absence of any burring can be checked by drawing the thumb across the scraper edge.

The edges of the scraper are next finished off on the oilstone to ensure that corners are clean and sharp. A little oil is needed and only *very* light pressure.

It remains only to form the corners into the shape shown in Fig. 83. This is done with a burnisher which is simply a piece of round tool-steel about four inches long and fitted into a handle. In Fig. 85 the method of forming the cutting edges is demonstrated. Three firm strokes are needed, the angle increasing with each, up to a maximum of from 10 to 12 degrees, which should not be exceeded or the edge of the scraper will become 'dubbed over' instead of assuming a good cutting edge.

Each stroke with the burnisher is made upwards, starting with the handle close to the scraper and finishing near the tip, the burnisher moving across and along the cutting edge which is being formed. It is the pressure and movement of the hard, smooth steel burnisher across the smooth and not-so-hard

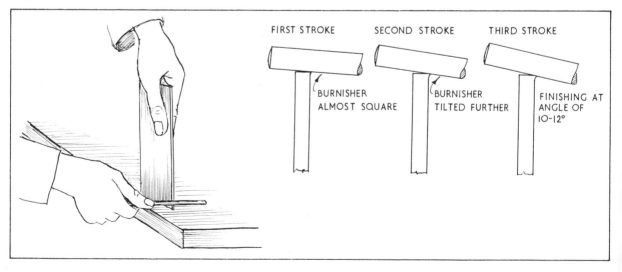

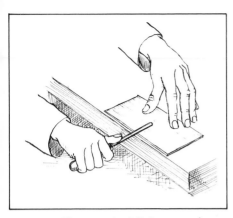

Figure 86   Flattening the dulled scraper edge

Figure 87   The Stanley No. 80 cabinet scraper

steel of the scraper which forms the keen-edged lip from end to end.

When the scraper becomes dull, it is not necessary to file the edges again so soon. A modified process is adopted, as follows. The scraper is laid flat on the bench, near the edge, and the lip is flattened with several strokes of the burnisher as shown in Fig. 86. The scraper is then sharpened as before, and when, after repeated treatment, we find we can no longer obtain a cutting edge with the burnisher, the scraper edges are retrued with the file and oilstone. Generally, the scraper needs retruing after four or five sharpenings.

Hammers and mallets

The hammer most commonly used by joiners and cabinet makers is the Warrington pattern, shown in Fig. 88. The claw hammer, much favoured in America, is the tool commonly used by carpenters in this country. It can be used for extracting nails and so saves the workman carrying pincers with him. The sectional sketch shows how the head is fitted to the shaft and secured with a steel wedge.

Hammers may be obtained in various weights, the very smallest being known as pin or tack hammers. The striking face of a hammer is rounded slightly to prevent it from marking the work badly if it should come into contact by accident. Nails should be left standing slightly proud of the face of the work and then driven home with a suitable-sized punch. If it becomes necessary to drive or hit the work, then a small piece of waste wood should protect the surface – or, better still – we should use a mallet. Hammer handles are usually made from ash, an elastic wood. Hickory is generally used for the handles of heavier tools such as sledges and axes.

The mallet is always used for driving chisels and for knocking together pieces of woodwork where the hammer would cause damage. Both head and handle are commonly made from beech, though ash is also satisfactory. The handle passes through a tapered mortise in the head, which holds the two together. Note that the striking faces radiate from a point at the operator's elbow, allowing the blow to fall squarely on the work (see Fig. 89).

Pincers

The most commonly used pincers are the Tower pattern shown withdrawing a nail in Fig. 90, the work being protected with a small piece of wood.

Figure 88   Hammers

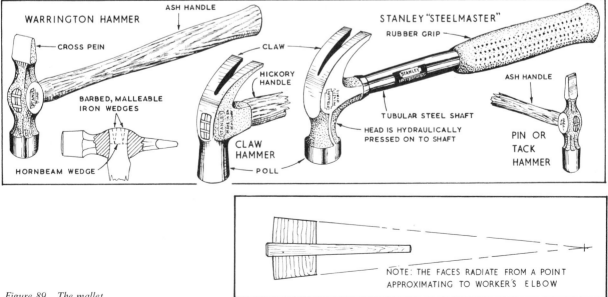

Figure 89   The mallet

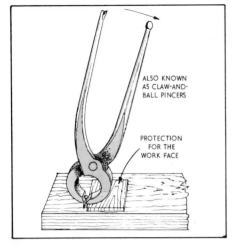

Figure 90   Tower pincers

Gauges

Two marking gauges are shown, on the left a traditional pattern with brass inserts in the stock to reduce wear, and on the right, a modern tool by Stanley, the shaped stock giving a natural holding position with the spur trailing correctly over the surface. These gauges are used in scribing lines parallel to a finished surface, in gauging wood to width or thickness and in marking out for joints. The cutting gauge, fitted with a small knife blade is useful in marking across grain and in cutting thin wood and plywood. It can also be used for cutting lines into solid or veneered surfaces for inlaying and for this, the blade must have one flat face to produce square-cut edges. A mortise gauge is shown (see also Fig. 126), the adjustable spur being set, after slackening off the set screw, by turning the thumb-screw. The panel gauge, usually home made, is used in marking wide boards to width and the thumb gauge, made from a small block of wood, is used with a pencil in marking chamfers.

The carpenters' square (try square)

The blade is of hardened and tempered steel and the stock of ebony, rosewood or plastic and faced with brass. Sizes in common use are 152, 228 and 300 mm. Squares should be tested for accuracy as in Fig. 92 using a straight-edged board. A cut line is struck with the knife and on reversing the square, a second line should coincide with the first. Any error in the square will be doubled and clearly seen.

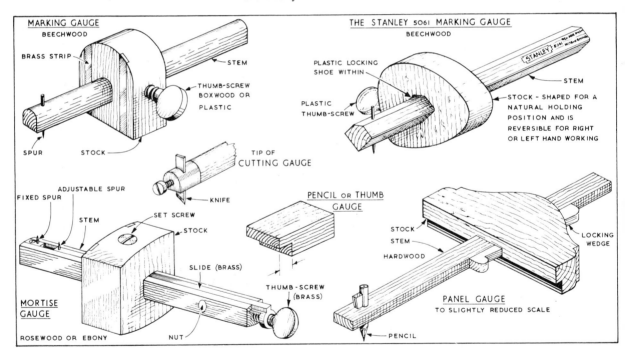

Figure 91   Gauges in common use

The sliding bevel

For marking out and testing angles other than right angles. The blade, as shown in Fig. 93, is slotted and is partly concealed in the stock when not in use.

The scratch-stock

A simple tool for working small mouldings by scratching away the waste. A piece of scraper blade, filed to the required contour is gripped in a hardwood block with the cutter inclined in the direction of working. It will work along or on end grain but not across grain.

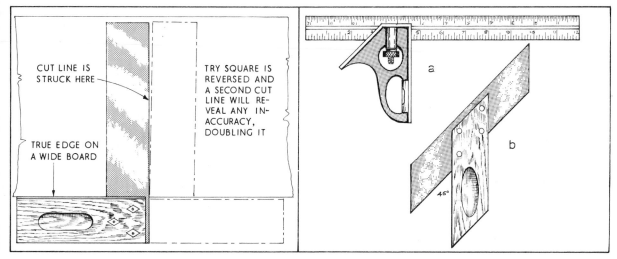

Figure 92 Testing a try square
a Combination square
b Bevel (mitre) square

Surform tools These modern tools employ multi-tooth blades in coarse or fine cuts and can be used effectively on wood (coarse blade) and other materials, including plastic laminates. They can also be used on metals and masonry but at a more rapid expenditure of blades. These are inexpensive and quickly fitted.

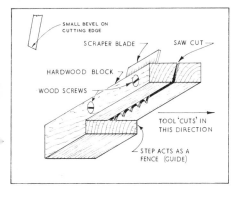

Figure 93 Sliding bevel

Figure 94 (below) Scratch-stock

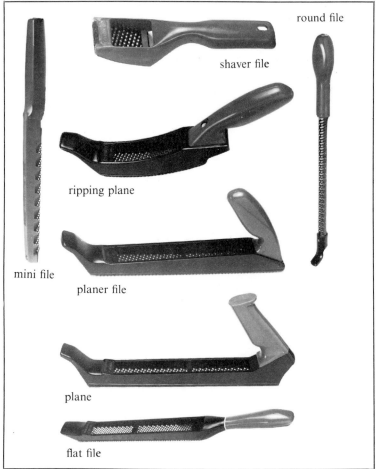

Figure 95 (right) Surform tools

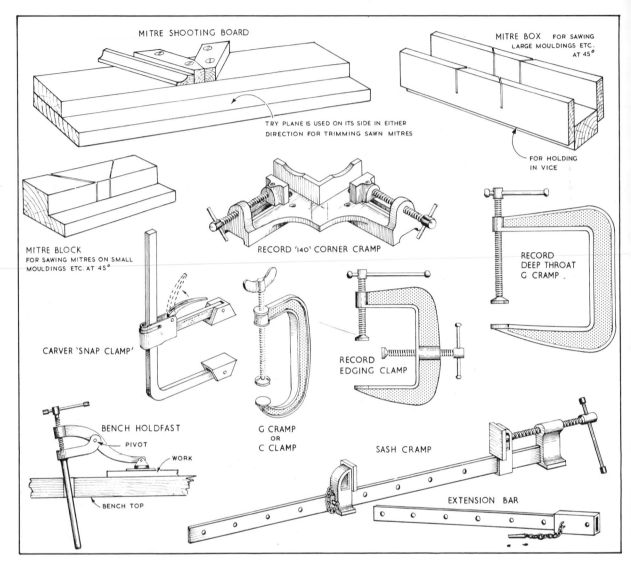

MITRE SHOOTING BOARD

TRY PLANE IS USED ON ITS SIDE IN EITHER
DIRECTION FOR TRIMMING SAWN MITRES

MITRE BOX   FOR SAWING
LARGE MOULDINGS ETC.
AT 45°

FOR HOLDING
IN VICE

MITRE BLOCK
FOR SAWING MITRES ON SMALL
MOULDINGS ETC. AT 45°

RECORD '140' CORNER CRAMP

RECORD
DEEP THROAT
G CRAMP

CARVER 'SNAP CLAMP'

RECORD
EDGING CLAMP

BENCH HOLDFAST

PIVOT

WORK

BENCH TOP

G CRAMP
OR
C CLAMP

SASH CRAMP

EXTENSION BAR

*Figure 96   Tools for cutting mitres and
a selection of cramps*

Questions

(1) Make sketches with explanatory notes on any four of the following: toothing plane, veneering hammer, coping saw, winding strips, mitre block, sash cramp. State the uses of the four tools which you have chosen.

(L)

(2) The cutting iron of a plane tends to split ahead of the cutting edge when a shaving is being made. How is this tendency overcome, and to a large extent prevented? Use sketches in your explanation.

(SU)

(3) Sketch and name three kinds of cramping device often found in a woodwork shop, and name one example of the most characteristic use of each kind.

(CL)

(4) Describe the uses of the following planes: jack, try, smooth, shoulder, bullnose. Explain the features which make each plane suitable for its special purpose.

(N Counties Tech)

3

Timber

The classification of the timber trees

All plants are grouped into five great divisions, each of which is made up of several classes which are themselves divided up still further for identification.

Two of these divisions are of interest to the woodworker: (1) the Gymnosperms, and (2) the Angiosperms, the first of which contains the class known as the Coniferae, the second containing the class known as the Dicotyledoneae. These two classes include the trees which provide the timbers in common use – the 'timbers of commerce'.

Each class is divided into families or 'kinds' of trees, each of these families is divided into 'genera' and each 'genus' into 'species'. In order to name any tree properly it is necessary to quote its genus and its species.

Thus, for example, in the class Dicotyledoneae is a family known as the Fagaceae – the family of noble trees which includes the oaks, the beeches and sweet chestnuts. Of these three let us consider further the oaks whose genus (or generic name) is *Quercus*. This genus includes different species, for example, *Quercus robur* and *Q. petraea* from Britain, *Q. cerris* from Turkey, *Q. alba* from America and so on. These botanical names are rarely, if ever, used in the timber trade. The first two examples given above would be simply English oak, the next Turkey oak and the last, American white oak.

The Conifereae (*conifers*) With a few exceptions these are the cone-bearing trees with needle leaves, whose seeds are produced 'naked'. Included are the pines, firs, larch and spruce which provide the 'softwoods' of industry. Most conifers are evergreen.

The Dicotyledoneae (*dicotyledons*) These include our deciduous trees whose broad leaves are shed in winter, and whose seeds are borne enclosed in cases. Included are the oak, ash, elm, sycamore, walnut, birch, beech, etc., which provide the 'hardwoods' of industry. Many tropical kinds are evergreen.

The terms 'softwood' and 'hardwood' are not entirely accurate as some of the softwoods are quite hard, whilst some of the hardwoods are soft and easy to work. The division is purely a botanical classification and concerns not only the foliage and seeds, but more important, the structure of the wood itself. However, the terms hard and soft, as used, are generally satisfactory and might be referred to as a trade convention.

Both the coniferous and the deciduous trees are known as *exogens*, or outward growers, because they add to their girth by forming new wood outside the old, as opposed to the *endogens* which form new wood on the insides of their hollow stems, as in the bamboo.

The growth and structure of wood

Like all living organisms, trees, which are the most highly developed plants known to man, are composed of immense numbers of minute cells or sacs of differing shapes, structures and purposes, all of which are combined to make up the tissues of the various parts of the plant. The cells are box-like structures whose walls are of cellulose when first formed, and they are then quite thin and soft, each cell containing a quantity of a thin, slimy liquid known as protoplasm, together with a nucleus. This is the living substance of the plant.

Certain changes take place in the cells as they age, most types lose their protoplasm but some retain it, according to the work they are doing, but in general the protoplasm disappears from the older cells, whose walls become

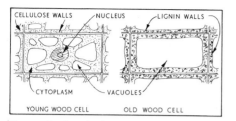

Figure 97   Wood cells

thickened and hardened, and this is known as lignification. They are dead in the sense that they cease to grow or change and serve only to give the tree the strength to hold itself erect. Fig. 97 shows typical woods cells, both young and old. Growth in the tree is promoted by the elongation and division of cells in the trunk, in the crown and the root system.

The cell type and the formation of the wood tissue differ considerably between the conifers and the dicotyledons, but there are certain superficial similarities in growth and overall structure which permits of a combined study in the first stage. In Fig. 98 is shown a typical cross-section of a trunk with all the parts named.

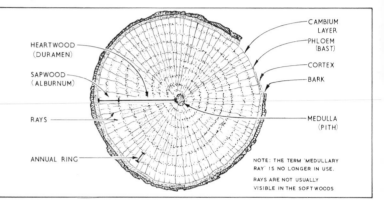

Figure 98   General structure of a tree

Pith   This is a cylinder of soft, dead tissue which is surrounded by the layers of wood cells. It represents the earliest growth of the sapling and extends throughout the length of the trunk, being formed in the crown or leading shoot as it extends upwards.

Annual rings   Sometimes referred to as growth rings. They each represent one season's growth in the tree, from spring to autumn, and are all quite clearly divided into two distinct layers, the innermost being the spring wood and the outer layer the summer or autumn wood. Spring wood is softer than that formed in summer, mainly because of its larger and thinner-walled cells. In most tropical timbers these rings are not very clear or may be absent as growth is even all the year round.

Heartwood (*duramen*)   This is the wood which has ceased to play any active part in the growth of the tree beyond giving it strength and in some cases serving for the storage of waste products such as resin, gum and tannin. It is made up of lignified (hardened) cells and provides durable timber, being the part most resistant to decay and attack by insects and fungi. It is often much darker than the sapwood and in most cases is readily distinguished.

Sapwood (*alburnum*)   This is the newly formed wood, the cells of which are not yet fully lignified. It is through the cells of the sapwood that water and dissolved mineral salts are conducted to the branches and thence to the leaves where food is manufactured. The sapwood is usually lighter in colour and in most cases is discarded by the woodworker because it is softer than the heartwood, offering less resistance to decay and attack by insects and fungi.

In the very young tree almost the entire section of the stem is required for conveying sap, but as the girth increases, the proportion of sapwood needed becomes progressively smaller by comparison with the trunk diameter.

Cambium layer   This is composed of a layer of cells completely encircling the sapwood, and it is here that growth takes place through the active enlarging and division of the cells, both radially and tangentially.

Wood cells are formed on the inside of the cambium whilst on the outside, and to a lesser extent, bast or phloem cells are formed. Both wood and bast cells become very much elongated in the direction of growth.

Bast or phloem   This is a layer of green tissue surrounding the cambium, and through its tube-like cells the manufactured food from the leaves is passed for distribution throughout the entire tree – twigs, branches, trunk and roots. The amount of bast is small by comparison with the wood tissue.

Cortex and bark   The cortex consists of a layer of cells with numerous air spaces and encloses the bast. The cells of the outer layer of the cortex become active and are known as the cork cambium whose duty it is to replace the layer of cork when it is ruptured by the expansion of the trunk. It is then cut off from further food supplies and it withers and dies but does not fall off at once.

The new cork layer is somewhat elastic and can accommodate an increase in the girth of the trunk, but eventually tears and is in turn replaced by a further layer of cork, which in time shares a similar fate. In the course of time the dead tissue is cast off, and where the cork layer forms evenly producing a smooth bark, it peels off in thin sheets as in the cherry and plane trees, whilst in others with rugged bark, such as the Scots pine, the old bark scales off in quite thick pieces.

The importance of the bark lies mainly in the fact that it forms an impervious skin which prevents transpiration – the evaporation of moisture – from the trunk. The woodworker generally refers to everything outside the cambium layer as the bark.

Rays   These are formed by thin sheets of tissue which stand vertically in the tree and whose cells are elongated radially, unlike those of the wood which are elongated vertically. The sheets or rays extend from the cambium, whence they originate by the normal process of cell division, to the medulla. They vary in height and thickness in different trees, their main work being concerned with the distribution of waste products to various parts of the tree for storage in matured cells.

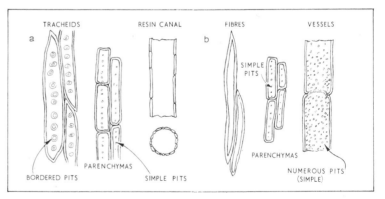

Figure 99 a   Softwood cells
b   Hardwood cells

Softwood structure   The softwood structure is much more primitive than that of the hardwoods. By far the greater number of cells become tracheids which are greatly elongated cells, as seen in Fig. 99, and these form the bulk of the timber. Communication is maintained between the cells for the passage of sap and food through parts of the walls which remain unthickened and unlignified. These areas are known as pits, and are of two main types, viz.: simple and bordered pits, illustrated in Fig. 100. It will be noticed from Fig. 99 that the pitting in the tracheids is of the bordered type. These cells, on ageing, become lignified and harden considerably, giving strength to the tree, and they are formed in very neat rows arranged radially. The remainder of the cells become parenchymas, which are smaller than the tracheids and are furnished with simple-type pits.

The rays in the conifers are usually thin, being only one or two cells in thickness and from twenty to thirty in height, which makes them almost

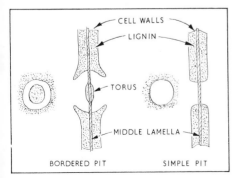

Figure 100   Types of pitting

invisible normally. Under magnification, the rays often serve as a reliable means of identification, together with the precise type of pitting, which, though of one type or the other, varies considerably in minor details between timbers of different species.

Evidence of the functioning of the rays is seen in the resin canals found in most of the conifers, the resins and gums being waste products carried there by the rays.

Hardwood structure   In most cases the bulk of the wood is made up of fibres which correspond to the tracheids in the conifers in that they give mechanical support to the tree, but they differ in that they are sharply pointed at both ends; their pitting is of the simple type and they are not arranged in any form or pattern in the general arrangement.

The vessel or pore is a type of cell peculiar only to hardwoods and is a positive means of identification from softwoods. The vessels are composed of cells formed one over the other making ducts or tubes which run right through the trunk from roots to leaves. They are numerous and are often large enough to be seen comfortably with the naked eye, as for example in oak, as shown in Fig. 101. Their disposition throughout the trunk varies considerably from tree to tree. In some cases, e.g. poplar, sycamore and birch, they

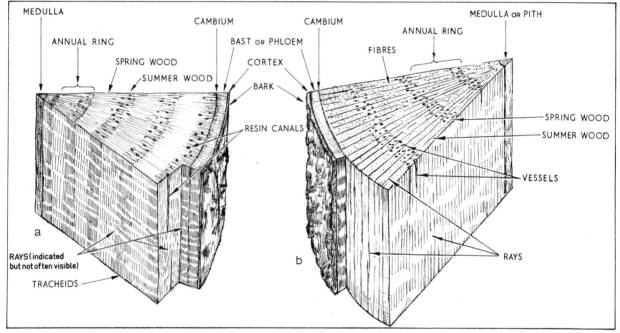

Figure 101a   Structure of pine
b   Structure of oak

are fairly evenly distributed and the wood is known as 'diffuse porous', whilst in others, e.g. oak and elm, the pores formed in spring are large and those formed in summer are very small, the difference forming a clear line of demarcation. These woods are known as 'ring porous'.

Parenchymas are found in the hardwoods also, but they form much more profusely radially in the rays which are often very much more prominent than in the conifers. The layers of cells are quite thick, especially in oak, where they may be from twenty to thirty cells in thickness and several hundreds in height. This makes the rays clearly visible and they produce the silver grain so well known in oak.

Soil, locality and climate   Of particular importance to the formation of good timber are the conditions under which it grows, soil, locality and climate all playing equally important parts.

Thus it is that the beech, a slow grower, always grows at its best on chalk and clay soils, whilst the elm thrives on loamy soils. The Scots pine, which is of a very hardy character, grows well even on poor, sandy or rocky soil, producing a wide range of timbers varying in colour, texture and resin content according to the locality.

The oak is another wood affected greatly by local conditions – sandy soil is said to produce a 'kind' wood, whilst in clay soil the wood is very hard and tough.

The willow need hardly be mentioned as a tree requiring the very wet boggy land found by river banks, growing well in bleak open spots, whilst the plane is well known as a tree which does not object to the smoky atmosphere of large towns and cities. On the other hand we have the lime tree which needs clean air to grow well, and so it has become very popular for bordering the drives found in parks and estates.

The effect of climate on the formation of timber is very noticeable when comparing temperate and tropical zone woods, the lack of a marked variation of seasons in the tropics producing a more evenly formed wood than that of the temperate zones. Any variations from normal climate, such as drought or excessive rainfall, always influence the season's growth rather adversely.

One other important consideration which affects growth and timber is the proximity of other trees. When forest grown, a tree makes no side branches of any size for there is insufficient room or light for it to do so, and in consequence the timber is more free from knots which mark the junctions of branches. Also, in the struggle for light and air the tree is encouraged to produce a very straight trunk.

Felling and conversion

(1) Felling

The felling of timber trees should always take place during the winter months for several very good reasons: (1) The moisture content of the wood is at its lowest and the subsequent seasoning or drying period will be shorter. (2) If extraction from the forest is delayed for any reason there will be no great danger of 'degrade' in the form of end-splitting from rapid drying by the sun. (3) The danger from attack by fungi causing discoloration, and from insects, is reduced in winter time. (4) Lack of foliage makes the stripping of the trunk easier, and the head of the tree is lighter, thus reducing the possibility of damage from felling shakes or splits caused by heavy falls.

The term 'degrade' refers to any condition which reduces the quality and market value of the timber, such as shakes (splits), discoloration or warping which may occur at any time before reaching the consumer.

The importance of the moisture content is readily appreciated from the fact that even when winter-felled, many logs contain between 40 and 50 per cent of their dry weight in moisture. The forester is much concerned with the weight of his logs, especially where rafting is practised in tropical areas, some of the timbers being very heavy. Burma teak presents a case which is dealt with in a rather interesting manner. The problem of weight is solved by 'girdling' the standing tree, a deep notch being chopped to encircle the trunk right through the sapwood. This cuts off the flow of sap but the foliage continues to transpire until most of the moisture in the trunk is evaporated. The weight is reduced so considerably that the logs can be safely floated.

The dry weight of timber The expression 'dry weight' refers to one of the factors used in calculating the percentage moisture content of timber. The dry weight of any timber is found by taking a small sample which is first weighed and then baked in a special oven at 100° centigrade until no further loss in weight occurs. The dry weight is used in the following equation to determine

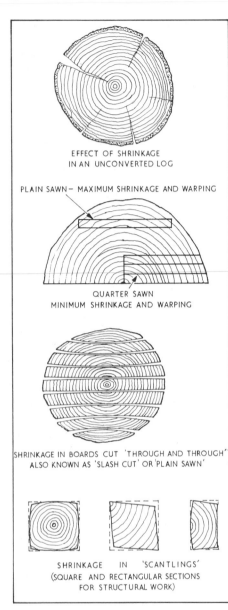

EFFECT OF SHRINKAGE
IN AN UNCONVERTED LOG

PLAIN SAWN – MAXIMUM SHRINKAGE AND WARPING

QUARTER SAWN
MINIMUM SHRINKAGE AND WARPING

SHRINKAGE IN BOARDS CUT 'THROUGH AND THROUGH'
ALSO KNOWN AS 'SLASH CUT' OR 'PLAIN SAWN'

SHRINKAGE   IN   'SCANTLINGS'
(SQUARE AND RECTANGULAR SECTIONS
FOR STRUCTURAL WORK)

Figure 102   The effect of shrinkage in timber

the percentage moisture content:

$$\text{Moisture content} = \frac{\text{wet weight of sample} - \text{dry weight of sample}}{\text{dry weight of sample}} \times 100$$

For example,
if a 60 gram sample weighs 40 grams after drying, then,

$$\text{moisture content} = \frac{60 - 40}{40} \times 100$$

$$= \frac{20}{40} \times 100 = 50\%.$$

References to weight and to moisture content will be found in the section on seasoning.

Shrinkage   The amount of shrinkage which takes place in timber during seasoning as the moisture evaporates is considerable and its effect can be ruinous if logs are left too long in a drying atmosphere between felling and converting, which is the sawing up into planks, boards, battens, etc.

As soon as the moisture content falls, the wood cells contract slightly, the greatest reduction taking place along the annual rings whilst the least amount occurs radially. Shrinkage along the grain is so slight that it can safely be ignored, although Kauri pine is reputed to shrink in this direction. In timbers where the grain wanders from side to side the uneven shrinkage will cause bowing or bending in the length.

The effect of shrinkage in a log is shown in Fig. 102. Splits or shakes occur along the rays which always form a natural line of cleavage and for this reason alone it is always desirable to convert as soon as possible after felling. These splits are properly known as star shakes and heart shakes. See also Fig. 107.

The effect of shrinkage on boards cut tangentially is shown in Fig. 102 and this can be avoided by quarter sawing which is shown more fully in Fig. 103.

The effect of shrinkage in scantlings should be noted. Although perhaps exaggerated in Fig. 102, this movement can be quite considerable.

(2) Conversion

'Conversion' is the trade term for the sawing of logs into marketable timber. It takes place in two stages, the first being the preliminary 'breaking down' of the log, followed at a later date by 're-sawing' in which process the timber is cut more accurately with smaller saws and is planed and machined for the manufacture of flooring boards, mouldings, matched boarding, and so on.

The breaking down of logs involves the use of very large and powerful band and circular saws, with lifting tackle to get logs on to the saw tables which feed into the machines automatically. The band saw is basically a band of thin, flexible steel with rip teeth formed along its edge and stretched over two

Figure 103   Methods of cutting up logs

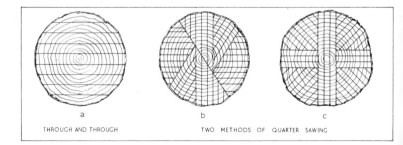

a
THROUGH AND THROUGH

b   c
TWO METHODS OF QUARTER SAWING

pulley wheels set one above the other. Re-sawing is done with smaller machines of the same kind.

Methods of cutting The conversion of timber is no haphazard affair and must be done expertly to avoid the waste of much valuable timber. The methods vary with different woods and according to market requirements.

The through and through method shown in Fig. 103 is the simplest cut and produces boards with uneven edges known as 'waney' unless and until they are trimmed square.

Quarter sawing is the method frequently applied to the cutting of oak so that the rays shall run as nearly as possible parallel to the surfaces to produce figured boards. Timber for good-quality flooring should also be quarter sawn. for in addition to the minimised effect of shrinkage, the best wearing surfaces are presented for use. Ideally, in quarter sawing, *all* boards should be cut radially, but this produces much waste.

Although in this context we are considering the conversion of timber for general purposes, one method of quartering for specialist work is seen in the cutting of pine for sound-boards for guitars, lutes and the viol family.

It is important that sound-boards are cut on the quarter, not only to avoid shrinkage problems but to obtain boards with maximum resonant properties. The finest boards are, in fact, obtained not by sawing but by splitting short lengths of trunk radially. This is done because many trees make a slightly spiral growth and so the wood fibres rarely lay truly in line with the trunk. Quarter sawing will almost certainly produce boards containing 'short' grain which reduces resonance considerably, whereas riven (split) boards will always follow the lay of the grain and will contain long fibres.

The splitting of sound-boards tends to be wasteful and costly but a compromise is reached by first splitting the log radially into quarters, followed by sawing parallel to the split surfaces. Sound-boards are made up in two halves jointed at the centre, the two pieces being cut or split adjacent to each other and opened out like book leaves. Fronts for the viols are made from pairs of split wedges jointed along their wide edges, thus giving extra thickness at the centre for carving the arching of the sound-board.

Marketing

Softwoods Metrication is now established in the timber trade and cross-sections are quoted in millimetres whilst lengths are quoted in metres, beginning

Figure 104 Matched and flooring boards with a selection of stock softwood sizes

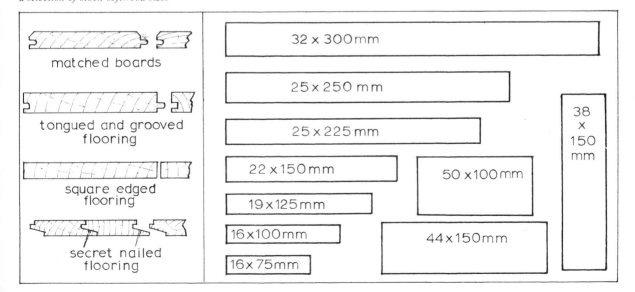

matched boards

tongued and grooved flooring

square edged flooring

secret nailed flooring

| 32 x 300mm |
| 25 x 250 mm |
| 25 x 225 mm |
| 22 x 150mm |
| 19 x 125mm |
| 16 x 100mm |
| 16 x 75mm |

50 x 100mm

44 x 150mm

38 x 150 mm

at 1·8 m and advancing by increments of 0·3 m, viz.: 1·8, 2·1, 2·4, 2·7 and on up to 6·3 m. Large quantities of timber are measured in cubic metres (m³). With timber for covering framework, as in flooring or in matched boards, a superficial measurement in square metres (m²) is used, but these materials can be bought by linear metres when only small amounts are needed.

When ordering prepared (machine planed) timber it is best to give finished sizes, adding a note to that effect, e.g. 'finished sizes after preparation'. When all four surfaces are to be prepared, the abbreviation P.A.R. (planed all round) is used, whilst P.B.S. (planed both sides) indicates that only the sides are to be prepared and the edges left sawn. The actual allowances for reduction in sizes in machine planing differ according to the timber sizes and the class of work, the allowances on timber ordered P.A.R. being 4 mm on surface widths up to 100 mm and 6 mm on widths of over 100 mm.

Hardwoods   These can be obtained with squared edges or as sawn from the log, i.e. with waney edges. The widths of square-edged boards often vary considerably and it is usually less costly to accept board widths as they come rather than to specify definite widths. One orders by the square metre, stating a minimum width which would be acceptable, e.g. '40 m² of 25 mm Japanese oak, P.B.S., finished thickness after preparation: 21 mm, minimum width of boards: 175 mm'.

Whilst small quantities of the thinner hardwood boards are commonly sold by the square metre, large quantities and heavier sections are almost invariably sold by cubic measure.

The seasoning of timber

Seasoning involves the evaporation of excess moisture and is necessary for several reasons: (1) shrinkage, which takes place across the grain as the moisture content falls, takes place when it is of the least consequence, (2) it reduces the risk of decay or attack by the fungi to which green (unseasoned) timber is prone, and (3) green timber cannot be worked satisfactorily by hand or machine, nor will it take finishes, i.e. paint, varnish or polish.

The level to which the moisture content is lowered in seasoning should approximate to that of the atmosphere in which the woodwork is to be installed because the evaporation of more moisture will cause further movement. For example, timber from an out-door stack, taken into a centrally heated building, will almost certainly lose moisture. Conversely, the absorption of moisture will cause swelling.

Shrinkage during seasoning

The shrinkage of timber, which has already been mentioned in connection with conversion, is closely associated with seasoning and is the most common cause of 'degrade' during the process, causing splitting and warping which must be reduced to a minimum by careful control of the drying process. This control involves mainly the prevention of uneven and too rapid drying. Uneven drying is found to take place in stacked boards whose ends are exposed to sunlight or very warm, dry air currents, causing end splitting due to stresses set up in the wood. This can be prevented by sealing up the end grain with a waterproof paint or by shielding from the sun's rays with tarpaulin covers. Too-rapid drying will cause the surfaces of a board to shrink whilst the inside is still wet, producing surface splits or 'checks'.

The methods of seasoning

(1) Air seasoning   This is the oldest method of drying timber, to which the only objections are that: (1) there is little control over the final moisture con-

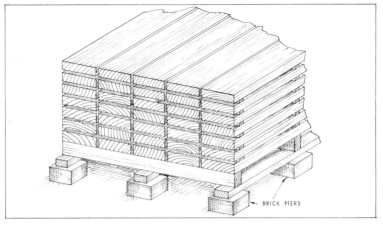

BRICK PIERS

Figure 105   The stacking of timber for air seasoning

tent of the timber, and (2) it is slow. Both these considerations are entirely dependent on the climate, the final moisture content varying between 15% and 20% or more, depending on good or bad seasons.

In air seasoning the timber is stacked in open-sided sheds which afford protection from the sun and rain, but which permit air to circulate freely. The choice of site is important, it must be open and well drained, and the base should be covered with a layer of clinker, or, better, should be concreted to prevent the growth of weed or fungi under the stacks. Scrupulous cleanliness should be observed around the yard, for sawdust and short-ends left lying about could easily rot and spread infection to the timber.

The floor of the seasoning shed consists of a very strong framework of wood treated with a preservative and raised clear of the ground on brick piers to permit of the free circulation of air around the planks which are piled as shown in Fig. 105, spacing or piling sticks separating each piece of timber. These sticks play an important part in the process, for not only do they allow the passage of air over the surfaces, but their thickness permits of some measure of control over the rate of drying. Piling sticks one inch thick are used quite satisfactorily with softwoods as these will stand quicker drying without checking, whilst with hardwoods such as oak, which must be dried more slowly, sticks of half this thickness are employed. The spacing of the sticks is also of considerable importance. With thick softwoods where warping is not expected to be serious, wide spacing is permissible, with intervals up to four or five feet, but where the timber is in the form of thin boards and likely to warp, as larch, elm or birch, a much closer spacing is advisable so that the weight of the pile can help to restrict the movement of the timber.

Seasoning times   With air seasoning the time required to reduce the moisture content to its lowest figure by this method will depend in some measure on when the timber is stacked, as drying is slower in winter time. For 25 mm softwoods stacked in spring, from two to three months will suffice to lower the moisture content to about 20%, and for a thickness of 50 mm, from three to four months.

Hardwoods are best stacked in the autumn or winter so that the initial drying is slower. Boards of 25 mm should be reduced to about 20% moisture content during the following summer, whilst 50 mm timber stacked at the same time will require about a year. These times are approximate only, are for normal conditions of climate, and represent a minimum drying period which can always be extended by a month or two to ensure even distribution of moisture.

Where the timber is to be used for interior work of any quality, the practice in smaller workshops is to store it inside for a period before working, the most convenient place being across the ties of the roof trusses – the warmest part of the building.

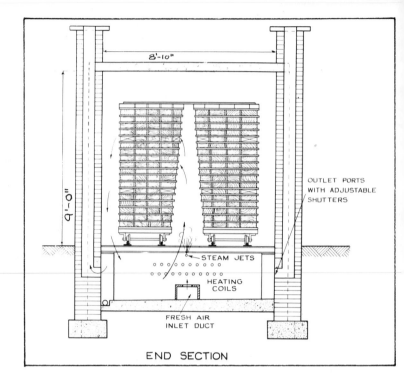

8'-10"

9'-0"

OUTLET PORTS
WITH ADJUSTABLE
SHUTTERS

STEAM JETS

HEATING
COILS

FRESH AIR
INLET DUCT

END SECTION

Figure 106   Natural-draught kiln

(2) Kiln seasoning or conditioning   This method of seasoning or drying timber has been practised for a great many years, but there is much prejudice, summed up in the phrase, 'Nothing good ever came out of a kiln', but rightly or wrongly, it is the method most commonly used today, made necessary by two pressing demands – one for timber of low and controlled moisture content, and the other for a rapid method of drying.

The kiln is often used in conjunction with air seasoning, especially with many of the hardwoods which must not be dried rapidly in the early stages of seasoning. A preliminary period of air seasoning is followed by final drying in the kiln, thus speeding up the process without causing degrade by splitting.

The kiln consists essentially of a brick-built chamber in which the timber is stacked as for air seasoning, and through which air of controlled humidity and temperature can be circulated either naturally, by convection currents, or by the use of powerful electric fans.

There are several different kilns of the forced-draught type, but all apply the principles already explained in different ways, which in their simplest form are as shown in Fig. 106, this being a natural-draught kiln.

The timber is piled on to bogies or trucks which run on tracks for ease in charging the kiln. This operation is done carefully to ensure that the air can circulate freely across all surfaces. The kiln is sealed and the process begun with a preliminary warming up for a very short period, after which the circulating air is made very humid by the injection of steam near the heating coils. This is done to prevent the too-rapid evaporation of moisture from the surfaces which would cause surface splitting by sudden contraction. The humidity is gradually reduced whilst the temperature is increased, finishing up with a flow of hot, dry air. At all times the conditions inside the kiln are under control from outside, humidity and temperature being recorded with the hygrometer and the thermometer which can be seen and read from outside through suitably placed glass panels. The control is operated according to special schedules prepared for various timbers and sizes and based on the original and the final moisture contents. The natural-draught kiln is much slower in operation than the forced-draught kiln, taking about half as long again.

Another type of kiln which is worthy of mention is the 'progressive kiln' which is a long, continuous-operating kiln of the forced-draught type. Green timber enters at one end, and moves slowly along towards a hot and dry air source at the opposite end. Humidity and temperature are self-adjusting as the air passes through, humidity increasing and temperature decreasing as it approaches the new timber entering. It is quite obviously for large-scale operation only.

Other types of kiln have different air-ducting arrangements, with reversible air-flow systems and with other variations, the object of all of them being to speed and equalise the drying rate throughout the kiln.

Degrade in kiln drying is caused through faulty combinations of humidity and temperature, producing warping, surface splits or checks, staining mould growths and a condition known as case-hardening. In this last form of degrade the stresses set up by unequal drying are insufficient to cause splitting, but cause severe warping when the timber is re-sawn. This trouble can be rectified before removal from the kiln if a sample taken from the pile shows case-hardening to have occurred.

Defects and diseases in timber

(1) Defects

The presence of large numbers of knots in timber constitutes the major natural defect as they considerably weaken the stock when sawn up. In this respect the forest-grown tree is always more free from knots as the branching habit is discouraged by the proximity of other trees, and by the removal of side shoots – known by the forester as 'brashing'. Each knot marks the junction of a branch with the trunk and where branches have been broken away or damaged, the knots are found to be decayed and are known as 'dead knots'. They very often fall out of the wood as it is being prepared. Sound, healthy knots are always firmly joined to the surrounding wood.

Spiral, or twisted, grain is caused when the fibres or tracheids form spirally in the trunk. The timber thus formed is always weak and will tend to twist when coverted and seasoned. This defect is usually found in park-grown timber.

The splits which occur during seasoning are known as 'checks', and all follow the lines of the rays. Cup shake is caused through faulty growth, the annual rings failing to cohere. All are illustrated in Fig. 107.

Other defects which may occur in seasoning are warping or curling of boards and bowing (bending) lengthwise.

(2) Diseases

There are many fungi which attack timber, and for growth all require the following: (1) Food in the form of wood cells. (2) Moisture (if less than 20% of the dry weight of the timber, it is insufficient). (3) Oxygen, from the air. (4) A suitable temperature.

A fungus is a parasitic plant which in incapable of manufacturing its own food and must therefore draw its nourishment by living on other organisms. The spore of any fungus deposited on wood, where the necessary conditions prevail, will quickly send down roots (hyphae) which spread rapidly in their search for food, bringing about the collapse of the wood cells, whilst the production of a 'flower' or fruit body ensures further propagation. The spores are produced in vast quantity; they are minute and can be spread unwittingly by the workman, on his boots or clothing and even on tools. Vermin also help in this way.

It should be noted that a moisture content of 20% plus is required for

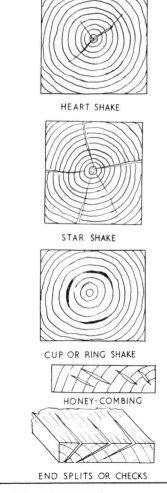

HEART SHAKE

STAR SHAKE

CUP OR RING SHAKE

HONEY-COMBING

END SPLITS OR CHECKS

Figure 107   Defects in timber

germination, and this fact immediately demonstrates the wisdom of using seasoned timber in structural work of any sort which may be hidden. It must also be borne in mind that seasoned timber will absorb moisture if it is available, and can quickly fulfil the conditions needed for the germination of spores.

It will be noticed that posts which are buried in the ground always support fungal growth, and decay first at ground level, this being the point at which the conditions are most suitable. Above ground the wood dries more rapidly after rain, and below ground oxygen is in short supply.

Dry rot (*Merulius lacrymans*)   The worst, and commonest form of dry rot decay in timber is caused by the fungus *Merulius lacrymans*. It thrives in damp, unventilated situations and the decay it produces is known as dry rot because the wood is left in a dry state, breaking into small cubical pieces. It is known as 'lacrymans' or 'weeping' fungus because of the moisture which forms in droplets on the fruit body.

This fungus is particularly dangerous as it can spread by means of fine strands or hyphae which are capable of travelling considerable distances in search of fresh timber for supplies of food. It is possible for the fungus to travel completely through a building in this manner.

The prevention of dry rot depends on the observance of two simple precautions: (1) the use of sound and well seasoned timber, and (2) its installation in dry and well ventilated conditions. The cure is drastic and costly. All affected timber must be cut out and burned at once, whilst the source of dampness and the lack of ventilation must be rectified. Surrounding brickwork must be sterilised with a blow-lamp and the hyphae traced and destroyed. Local and new woodwork should be treated with a preservative or, preferably, sterilised with a 4% solution of sodium fluoride (6 ounces to the gallon), as a precaution against further attack.

Stains in timber   There are a few comparatively harmless fungi which cause disfiguring stains, mainly in the sapwood, which lower the market value of the timber affected. The commonest of these discolorations appear as blue-grey streaks in the softwoods. The lighter-coloured hardwoods are also affected. However, the strength of the timber is not affected as the fungus lives only on the contents of the cells, and not on the actual cell walls, as with the *Merulius lacrymans* and other wood-destroying fungi. The early stages of attack by the wood-rotting fungi are often revealed by reddish- or brown-coloured streaks in the wood, which is always found to be quite soft at these places. The timber is said to be affected by incipient decay, and should be avoided.

Attacks by insects

Most of the damage by insects in Britain is caused by a few members of the beetle family. Certain moths damage the foliage of trees, whilst the larvae of the wood wasp are responsible for a certain amount of damage to felled timber which is left lying unconverted for too long.

(1) The common furniture beetle (*Anobium punctatum*)   This is the most common of the wood-boring beetles and is responsible for much damage to hard and soft woods both in furniture and in structural timbers. Plywood and wicker work are also liable to attack and because old furniture is often stored in lofts or cellars the beetle is easily introduced to those parts of buildings where it can carry on destroying wood undetected for lengthy periods.

The beetle is found from 2·5 to 5·0 mm in length and lays batches of eggs in the crevices in woodwork. Hatching takes place within three or four weeks, when the grubs immediately begin burrowing into the wood, consuming the wood cells for the sake of the cellulose which they contain. They continue boring for from one to two years, after which they hollow out small chambers near the surfaces in which pupation takes place. During pupation, which takes from two to three weeks, the grub assumes the form of the beetle, finally eating its way out through a small round hole of about 1·5 mm in diameter at any time between June and August.

The adult beetles can fly, and soon mate, the female finding a suitable place for her batch of eggs to complete the life cycle. The adult beetles die soon after their mission is complete.

(2) The death watch beetle (*Xestobium rufovillosum*) This beetle is rather similar in shape to the furniture beetle but is larger. The life cycle follows much the same pattern, but the beetles emerge earlier in the summer and the tunnelling period is much longer, lasting often for several years. After pupating in the autumn, the beetle remains hidden until the following spring when it makes its exit through a hole of a little over 3 mm in diameter.

The beetle seems to prefer to attack large structural timbers such as are found in historic buildings and because of this, the attention of the public has, on numerous occasions, been drawn to its activities. Its size makes it readily distinguishable from the furniture beetle and, also, the bore-powder is left in the form of small pellets.

(3) The powder post beetle or lyctus The lyctus beetle as seen in Fig. 108 is a little longer and thinner than the furniture beetle and is responsible for much damage to the sapwood of those hardwoods whose pores are large enough to receive the eggs as they are laid. The grub stays in the sapwood because it is there that it finds the starch which it needs for food. For this reason, the beetle only attacks comparatively newly felled and converted timber, for after about 15 years the starch dries out and has no food value. The lyctus does not bore in tunnels but consumes the wood in thin layers leaving only the shell.

The life cycle is usually of one year's duration, but under warm conditions is much shorter, from which it will be seen that infestations can quickly become out of hand. The timbers which are most susceptible to attack are oak, ash and elm, those with very small pores such as birch, beech and so on, being immune from attack.

(4) The house longhorn beetle This large beetle, at one time rare in Britain, has established itself in recent years and is an avid consumer of softwoods, capable of damaging large-sized timbers such as are found in roof constructions. Like the lyctus beetle, it leaves a shell of sound wood and its presence is not obvious until the wood is tested with a stout knife. The exit holes in infested wood are rather obscure and are oval in shape.

Prevention and remedy It is almost impossible to secure complete immunity from attack by these insects as there is always some unprotected part in any piece of woodwork, especially in old furniture where joints have sprung apart

Figure 108   a   Furniture beetle (× 9)
b   Lyctus beetle (× 6)
c   Death Watch beetle (× 5)
d   House Longhorn beetle (× 1½)

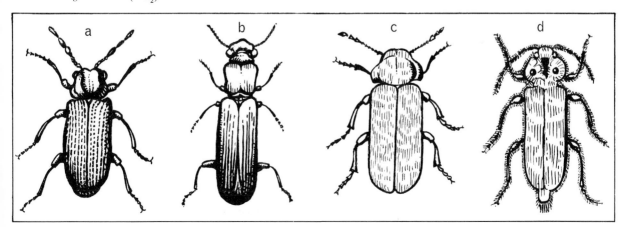

and where unplaned wood is found in backing-boards and the dust-bottoms of drawers. Much can be done, however, by sealing open joints with wax or furniture cream, and by keeping all surfaces well polished. There is little doubt that the aromatic oils in some furniture creams also discourage the attentions of the beetles.

The cabinet maker can, by avoiding the use of the sapwood of oak, prevent attack from the lyctus beetle.

Once an attack has been discovered, an immediate search for the beetles should follow, as they may still be in the vicinity. The affected timbers and any beetles seen should be promptly treated with one of the proprietary solutions to prevent further infestation. Fumigation is another method and is very effective, but it needs special plant and the services of an expert as the chemicals used are of a poisonous nature.

(5) Other wood-boring insects   Other beetles causing damage are the wood-boring weevils and the wharf borers which are associated with water-front timber, whilst the pin-hole borers and the longhorn beetles attack green timber.

The protection and preservation of timber

For whatever purpose timber is used, it always requires a finishing treatment of some sort, whether for inside or outside work. The precise type of finish will depend on the conditions under which the timber is to render service and also on the particular timber being used.

Some timbers are naturally immune to all the destructive agents which so quickly bring others into decay. They may contain aromatic oils or other substances which make them repellent to insects and inhospitable to fungi, whilst others, suitably treated with preservatives will often give service at least equal to these. A list of some of the naturally durable timbers is appended to the glossary of timbers at the end of this chapter.

The majority of the usual finishes can be classed as 'protective' finishes, in the form of polishes, oils, lacquers, enamels, paints and varnishes, all of which form a skin more or less impervious to moisture and attacks by insects and fungi. Their efficiency in keeping out moisture, particularly with outside work, depends entirely on the skin being undamaged, this consideration necessitating periodical inspection and repair to maintain a complete covering.

The preservation of timber involves its impregnation with one of three main types of preservative: (1) oil of tar – creosote, (2) water-soluble chemical preservatives, and (3) those in which the preservative is contained in a solvent; they are not soluble in water.

Creosote is usually forced into the cells of the timber hot and under high pressure whilst sealed in large steel cylinders. This ensures adequate penetration and is the method used for railway sleepers and other outside timbers. Brush application is quite ineffective where the timber has to withstand prolonged immersion as the penetration of the creosote by this method is very superficial.

The water-soluble preservatives are used where the timber is to serve under dry conditions. The chemicals used include sodium fluoride, zinc chloride and mercuric chloride. The last named is very poisonous.

The solvent type of preservative is one in which the chemical is dissolved in a volatile liquid which is then applied to the timber. The solvent – oil of naphtha or spirit – penetrates deeply and then evaporates, leaving the chemical in the wood cells.

Glossary of timbers

It is possible to give only brief notes on a limited number of timbers in this context. The advanced student seeking further information should contact the Publications Department, The Timber Research and Development Association, Stocking Lane, Hughenden Valley, High Wycombe, Buckinghamshire, HP14 4ND from whom a series of nine 'Red Booklets' are obtainable. These booklets give valuable information on 'Timbers of the World'.

Softwoods

Douglas fir (N. America) Also known as Columbian or Oregon pine. A very strong timber which compares strength-wise with pitch pine and is available in great lengths for poles, masts and spars. The heartwood varies in colour from a yellowish to red-brown with clearly defined growth rings, the late growth rings being markedly harder than the early growth. It is not an easy wood to work with hand tools which must be kept sharp. Its other uses are many, including heavy construction work, railway sleepers, flooring, ship building, roof construction, good-quality joinery work and veneers for plywood manufacture. The veneer is usually cut by peeling and this produces a wild and attractive surface figure.

Larch (European) A deciduous tree growing naturally and at its best in mountainous areas at high elevations from the Swiss Alps to the Carpathians. The heartwood is of a reddish-brown colour with growth rings clearly marked. The wood is straight-grained, resinous, heavy and strong. It is used in pit-props, piles, poles, boat planking and in situations demanding strength and durability. Larch grown in the U.K. is generally inferior to the European wood because growth conditions at low altitudes and with short and variable winters do not produce the finest wood.

Scots pine (Europe, N. Asia. Native to Scotland) Also known as red or yellow deal. A commonly used timber in joinery and construction work. It is resinous and strong, and with clearly marked rings, the heartwood varies from a honey colour to red-brown whilst the sapwood is quite light in colour. The wood is sometimes tinged with blue-grey streaks caused by a staining fungus. It is a moderately durable timber, works well with hand or machine tools, glues well and takes stains and varnish or paints.

Pitch pine (N. America) This is the heaviest of the pines and is amongst the strongest. The heartwood is of a red-brown colour with very clearly defined growth rings, the late wood growth being hard and resinous, giving the wood a coarse texture. It is not an easy wood to work, the resin content being trouble-some and picking up on tools unless their working surfaces are kept lightly oiled. The wood is used in heavy constructions, flooring, for masts and spars, decking and other such work. Selected wood is used for good-quality joinery work and is probably best finished by varnishing since the coarse grain tends to show through painted surfaces.

Parana pine (Brazil) A straw-coloured wood with sapwood of a very light colour. The heartwood is often streaked red and pink. This wood is available in wide boards free from defects but there is often a tendency to distortion. It is used for interior joinery work and largely for veneers for plywood manufacture. It lacks toughness and is not suitable for making long ladders or for scaffold boards.

Norway spruce (Europe) Known also as European whitewood and as European spruce. It is recommended that the names white deal, white fir (U.K.) and white pine (Scotland) should no longer be used in order to avoid confusion.

Norway spruce is a light-coloured wood with fairly prominent growth rings,

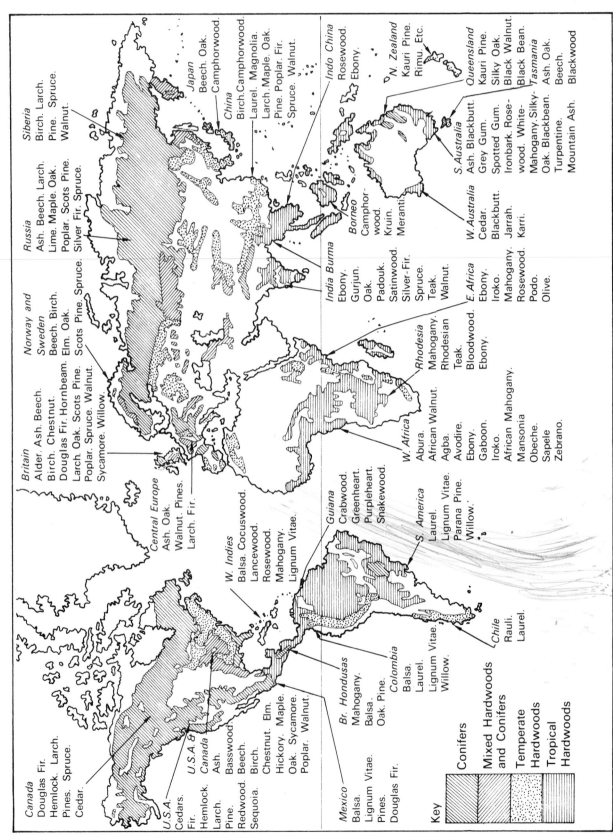

Canada
Douglas Fir.
Hemlock. Larch.
Pines. Spruce.
Cedar.

U.S.A.
Cedars.
Fir.
Hemlock. Larch.
Pine.
Redwood. Beech.
Sequoia.

U.S.A. & Canada
Ash.
Basswood.
Beech.
Birch.
Chestnut. Elm.
Hickory. Maple.
Oak. Sycamore.
Poplar. Walnut.

Mexico
Balsa.
Lignum Vitae.
Pines.
Douglas Fir.

Br. Hondusas
Mahogany.
Balsa.
Oak. Pine.

Colombia
Balsa.
Laurel.
Lignum Vitae.
Willow.

Chile
Rauli.
Laurel.

S. America
Laurel.
Lignum Vitae.
Parana Pine.
Willow.

Guiana
Crabwood.
Greenheart.
Purpleheart.
Snakewood.

W. Indies
Balsa. Cocuswood.
Lancewood.
Rosewood.
Mahogany.
Lignum Vitae.

Central Europe
Ash. Oak.
Walnut. Pines.
Larch. Fir.

Britain
Alder. Ash. Beech.
Birch. Chestnut.
Douglas Fir. Hornbeam.
Larch. Oak. Scots Pine.
Poplar. Spruce. Walnut.
Sycamore. Willow.

Norway and Sweden
Beech. Birch.
Elm. Oak.
Scots Pine. Spruce.

Russia
Ash. Beech. Larch.
Lime. Maple. Oak.
Poplar. Scots Pine.
Silver Fir. Spruce.

Siberia
Birch. Larch.
Pine. Spruce.
Walnut.

Japan
Beech. Oak.
Camphorwood.

China
Birch. Camphorwood.
Laurel. Magnolia.
Larch. Maple. Oak.
Pine. Poplar. Fir.
Spruce. Walnut.

Indo China
Rosewood.
Ebony.

N. Zealand
Kauri Pine.
Rimu. Etc.

Queensland
Kauri Pine.
Silky Oak.
Black Walnut.
Black Bean.

Tasmania
Ash. Oak.
Beech.
Blackwood

S. Australia
Ash. Blackbutt.
Grey Gum.
Spotted Gum.
Ironbark. Rose-
wood. White-
Mahogany. Silky-
Oak. Blackbean.
Turpentine.
Mountain Ash.

W. Australia
Cedar.
Blackbutt.
Jarrah.
Karri.

Borneo
Camphor-
wood.
Kruin.
Meranti.

India Burma.
Ebony.
Gurjun.
Oak.
Padouk.
Satinwood.
Silver-Fir.
Spruce.
Teak.
Walnut.

E. Africa
Ebony.
Iroko.
Mahogany.
Rosewood.
Podo.
Olive.

Rhodesia
Mahogany.
Rhodesian
Teak.
Bloodwood.
Ebony.

W. Africa
Abura.
African Walnut.
Agba.
Avodire.
Ebony.
Gaboon.
Iroko.
African Mahogany.
Mansonia
Obeche.
Sapele
Zebrano.

Key

Conifers	Mixed Hardwoods and Conifers	Temperate Hardwoods	Tropical Hardwoods

it is straight-grained and often of a lustrous appearance and its strength compares favourably with that of Scots pine.

It works readily and is used in a wide range of applications according to its quality gradings which vary as with other timbers due to differing growth conditions. Forest density and high altitudes with the associated slow and even growth produces fine timber, much sought after as tone-wood for piano sound-boards, violin bellies and for other instruments. Among its other uses are packing crates, carcassing, flooring, masts, flag poles and veneers for plywood. Forest thinnings provide our Christmas trees.

Sitka spruce (Canada and U.S.A. west coasts) A creamy coloured wood with a faint pinkish tinge to the heartwood. This is a very clean and straight-grained wood with a high strength–weight ratio. It works very well, finishes cleanly and is used in building, joinery work, masts and spars, gliders, oars and racing sculls. It is also used to some extent in instrument sound-boards.

Western red cedar (Canada) This tree grows to immense heights and gets the name 'red cedar' because the timber when first cut, is of a warm red colour and gives off a strong scent resembling that of the true cedars of Lebanon. It grows in the northern Rocky Mountains from Alaska and southwards as far as California, hence the 'western' in its name.

The timber is light in weight, is soft and straight-grained and its colour matures to a silver-grey on exposure to the atmosphere. It is very durable out of doors and is used extensively in greenhouses, sheds, for posts and fencing and in roofing shingles. Selected wood is used in instrument soundboards.

Hardwoods

Ash (Europe, Britain, N. Africa, W. Asia, also N. America and Canada) Ash, on first cutting, is of a creamy-brown colour which darkens somewhat on drying. The wood is straight-grained and shows an attractive and varied surface figure. It is tough and flexible and because of its strength, finds many uses. It works well and bends readily under steaming. It is used in shafts and handles for hammers, axes, shovels and the like, for bentwood chairs and furniture, in wheelwrighting, vehicle bodies and in sports equipment such as parallel bars, hockey sticks, skis, and for ladder rungs and cart shafts.

Beech (Europe – particularly Central Europe and Britain, also N. America and Canada) European beech is of a pale reddish-brown colour with indistinct growth rings and with fine rays often visible as small brownish flecks. The wood is hard and of a close, even texture, it works well and takes a good finish with stains and polishes. Beech has many applications: in furniture and plywood manufacture and in items of domestic equipment, in shoe heels, brush backs, bobbins, toys, turnery, tool handles, mallets and flooring. Beech was at one time always used in making wooden planes of all kinds.

Birch (Europe, including Britain, also N. America) The birch is a very hardy tree usually producing a rather featureless wood of a pale brown colour with a fine texture, but sometimes very attractive veneers result from grain variations producing curly birch and flamed birch figurations. Large quantities of birch are used in the manufacture of plywood and blockboard and in furniture, dowels and turnery.

Elm (Europe, Britain, W. Asia, also N. America and Japan) Probably the commonest of the trees of Britain until so many were killed in recent years by the ravages of the Dutch elm disease. The wood is of a reddish-brown colour with a wild and coarse grain which makes it difficult to work. It is tough and strong and is essentially a 'country' wood, much used in farm buildings and equipment, not only for its qualities but also because of its (one time) ready availability locally. Its uses include weather boarding, waggon building, wheelwrighting, wharf construction, piling, coffins and chairs. Wych elm has a much straighter grain and is considered to be the superior timber.

Figure 109   Forest regions of the world

Greenheart (*S. America*)   A very heavy and exceptionally strong and tough wood. The heartwood varies in colour from a greenish-yellow to olive, brown and black. It is exceedingly durable, especially in marine situations – in piers, docks, locks, decking, groynes, in ship construction and so on. In addition to its usefulness in heavy construction work such as bridges, platforms, etc., it is also used for fishing rods and for billiard-cue butts.

Lime (*Europe, Britain*)   The lime grows freely in the British Isles and is often used as an ornamental tree. The wood is a pale brown colour and of a soft, compact and uniform texture. Its strength properties are good but it is used more for its resistance to splitting and its softness, qualities which make it ideal for carving. It is used in piano keys, in harps, in turnery, for artificial limbs and hat blocks.

Mahogany (*Honduras*)   This mahogany, used so extensively in the past in high-quality cabinet making, joinery, boat building and pattern making, is now in short supply. Importers have had to find other sources and many species from Africa are now in general use (see under African woods). However, mahoganies from Central America and the West Indies have not entirely disappeared and are often named according to the country of origin, e.g. Brazilian, Mexican and Peruvian mahoganies.

Maple (*Europe, Asia, N. Africa, N. America, Canada*)   Many species of the maple are found over these continents. The wood is of a light brownish colour with dark rings often giving it an attractive figure and sometimes it is found with a ripple grain which produces 'flamed' or 'fiddle back' maple which is highly prized for musical instrument bodies. Maple is not easy to work and has a 'leathery' feel under hand planes whilst the ripples in fiddle back wood will tear out readily under a coarse plane setting. Such wood is best worked very lightly across grain and finished by scraping.

General uses are in turnery, domestic woodware, brush backs and other small items.

Rock maple (*Canada and Eastern U.S.A.*)   is heavy and hard, straight grained and of even texture and is used in preference to the 'soft' maples in dance and gymnasia flooring. Other uses include furniture, turnery, piano actions, sports goods, dairy and laundry equipment, butchers' blocks, etc. In addition to the fiddle back maple mentioned, other figured woods include the well-known bird's eye, curly and blister maple.

Oak (*Europe, N. America, N. Asia*)   There are numerous species of oak, most of which flourish in woodlands in the temperate zones whilst in warmer climes, they grow best in mountainous areas.

The oak has many historical associations and traditional uses. In England it was (and still is to some extent) the principal ship-building timber, it provided naturally curved and very strong timbers (knees) for forming hulls, it was also almost the only timber used in building in Western Europe. It is extremely durable and strong and can be seen in the roof beams of large cathedrals and other buildings of great age. The cooper uses cleft (split) oak in making wooden barrels which are still needed for the proper maturing of wines and spirits.

European oak is mostly of a golden-brown colour with very pale sapwood. It is a timber needing careful and slow seasoning, being intolerant of rapid drying especially in the early stages. English oak is not an easy wood to work because of its coarse grain and hardness but it does finish well and is especially beautiful when quarter sawn, its prominent rays enriching surfaces with the well-known silver grain.

Other uses of this adaptable timber include waggon building, bridges and staging, mining, window sills, door steps, gate posts and in other situations demanding a timber to withstand contact with the earth and the elements. Oak is not confined only to constructional work, it is a prominent wood in furniture making, in panelling, it is a 'traditional' wood in church furnishings, e.g. pews, pulpits, rood screens (often beautifully carved), flooring, ladder rungs and high-quality joinery work.

Oak glues well and takes stains and polishes, a pleasant dark brown finish being obtained by fuming (with ammonia vapour) followed by wax polishing. Unprotected iron fittings, screws or nails should not be used in oak exposed to the weather for they will quickly corrode away and leave ugly, dark stains. It is better to use non-ferrous metals in such situations.

Sycamore (Europe, W. Asia, Britain) A very light coloured wood – almost white when first cut and showing slightly darker growth rings. It is sometimes found with attractive curly grain or ripples and then requires great care in planing. It is quite a hard wood with a compact texture, it is strong and can be worked to a very fine and smooth finish.

The wood is used a lot in turnery, bobbins, textile rollers, handles and for veneers which are often dyed in various colours including grey, the veneer then being known as harewood.

Teak (Burma, India) A greenish-brown wood when first cut but darkens on maturing. It is an oily wood sometimes of great beauty in its grain markings. It is very durable and is acid and fire resisting, and resistant to the ravages of the white ant. It is a moderately hard wood of considerable strength and is used in ship building and constructional work and is useful in bench tops for chemical laboratories since it is resistant to acids and chemicals.

Walnut (Europe) Walnut is known by its country of origin, e.g. English, French, Italian, Turkish. The tree was introduced into Britain in the fifteenth century. The sapwood is of a pale straw colour and quite distinct from the heartwood which is mostly of a grey-brown colour and often with dark streaks in a wavy grain formation which makes the wood very attractive. Colours and markings vary considerably according to locality. Burrs, crotches and stumps are valuable for veneer cutting. Walnut is used in furniture, in veneers, fancy goods, turnery and for rifle butts.

African timbers

Abura This wood is a light pink-brown colour, of medium weight with a fine texture and straight grain. It has no great strength nor is it durable out of doors but it does work cleanly and is particularly useful in handicraft and for furniture and cabinet making.

Agba A yellowish-pink wood, resembling mahogany in some respects, grain and working properties being similar. It is a fairly hard and straight-grained wood which works very nicely, although it is sometimes rather sticky due to the presence of a gum. The wood is very resistant to decay and is used in joinery work, shop fittings, flooring, turnery, furniture, coach building, veneer and plywood.

Ebony A very hard and dense wood, the most sought after kinds being the jet black wood used in decorative work and in musical instruments. Other kinds show attractive black and brown stripes. The ebonies are all difficult to work.

Gaboon Of a pink-brown colour, straight-grained and showing very little figure, this wood is used extensively in plywood, blockboard and laminboard. It is also used to some extent as a substitute for mahogany.

Mahogany The West African mahoganies are widely used nowadays and include a number of species, many of which are named according to the port or country of origin. These timbers are in good supply and can be obtained in wide boards. They are mostly of a coarser texture than the American woods and show considerable variations in texture, colour and weight. Grain is often interlocked and there is sometimes a tendency to distortion in drying but, in spite of these things, these mahoganies give satisfactory results in good-quality joinery work, in staircases, flooring, boat building and as veneers.

Mansonia   A yellowish to grey-brown wood often tinged with a dark purple. The colour varies considerably, but the darker mansonia is not unlike American black walnut. It is a durable timber and it works easily with hand or machine tools. It is used in cabinet making, in joinery work and in turnery.

Obeche   A comparatively soft timber of a pale yellow colour. The grain is often interlocked but it is not difficult to work provided that tools are kept sharp. The wood is light in weight, is not durable and its uses are confined to indoor work in cupboards, small furniture and such items. It is used as a core stock for plywood.

Sapele   This is a red-brown coloured wood which shows a characteristic and evenly spaced stripe, especially on quarter-sawn surfaces, making an interesting feature. It has an interlocking grain which makes planing and moulding rather difficult but it can be worked to a good finish with care, taking stains and polish well. Sapele is used in furniture, cabinet making, boat building, joinery work and flooring. It also makes very attractive veneers.

Utile   Widely distributed in tropical Africa, the heartwood is a pale pink on cutting but darkens to a red-brown later. Its interlocking grain produces a broad stripe resembling that in sapele, to which it is related. The wood works quite well apart from the extra care in dealing with interlocked grain. Utile takes glues, stains and polishes well and is used for the same purposes as with sapele.

Walnut   African walnut is so called because of a semblance in colour and grain markings to true walnut. Of a golden-brown colour, it is marked with very dark streaks, the sapwood being of a light colour and very clearly defined. Interlocking grain shows in a stripe effect on quarter-sawn surfaces. This wood is not difficult to work by hand or machine but some care must be taken to prevent picking up on interlocking grain. It is used in cabinet making, furniture and in joinery work, panelling and veneers.

Naturally durable timbers   Some timbers are more resistant to decay than others and the following are quoted. *Softwoods*: western red cedar, sequoia, yellow cedar, southern cypress. *Hardwoods*: Burma and Rhodesian teaks, Borneo camphorwood, English oak and iroko.

Full information on uses, durability, resistance to marine borers and termites can be found in the 'Red Booklets' previously mentioned.

Questions

(1) Describe the characteristic features of four of the following timbers: redwood, ash, oak, mahogany, teak and balsa.

(L)

(2) Very highly figured wood, e.g. burr walnut, is usually cut to make veneers. If such wood was cut into boards and used for purposes such as the frame of a door, the top of a box or table, what would be the probable result, and why?

(O and C)

(3) Wood varies considerably in weight, texture, colour, degrees of hardness and durability. Bearing these factors in mind, state which woods you would recommend for making the following items: (a) a model yacht, (b) a model aircraft, (c) a garden wheelbarrow, (d) a ladder, (e) a new handle for a garden hoe, (f) a deck chair, (g) a drawing board. Give reasons for your choice in each case, bearing in mind the points enumerated above.

(SU)

(4) Name the timbers which are most suitable for the following purposes: (a) outdoor structures, e.g. greenhouses, (b) tall poles for outdoor use, (c) radio cabinets, (d) garden barrows, (e) food utensils. Give reasons for your selections.

(OL)

(5) Describe with the aid of sketches: (a) the structure of a hardwood and a softwood, (b) the difference between heartwood and sapwood cells.

(N Counties Tech)

(6) Name two insect borers which attack timber and the type and condition of timber they are most likely to attack. Suggest ways of: (a) preventing insect borer damage, and (b) eliminating the pest from timber already affected.
Describe the life cycle of one of these insect borers.

(N Counties Tech)

(7) Name one softwood and one hardwood and compare their characteristics.
For each wood named suggest an article for which the wood is suitable, giving reasons. In each case name a suitable method of finishing the article.

(JMB)

(8) What are the advantages of: (a) natural timber seasoning, (b) kiln seasoning?
Why is it desirable to know the moisture content of timber to be used for internal doors and frames? Illustrate your answer by using actual figures.

(N Counties Tech)

4

Timber products

Although many new and wonderful materials are becoming available to industry and to the small user, wood is still very much in demand. It is one of the materials most readily adaptable to the many and varied needs of man, it is comparatively easy to work and, if properly cared for, is certainly as durable as any other material in common use.

Today, timber is used very extensively in its manufactured forms, firstly for economic reasons and secondly because its physical properties are greatly improved by scientific processing.

The economic reasons have become important largely because of the heavy demands which have been made on the sources of supply of prime quality timber. In recent years much research has been carried out with a view to making use of the wood waste from mills and lumber camps, the efforts made by the scientists having met with some very considerable success in various directions so far.

The total wastage of timber has been estimated as high as 30% of the total volume extracted from the forests. This is a high figure, but much of the waste is now used in the manufacture of pulp for various types of boards which serve admirably as timber substitutes.

The manufacture of plywood is the oldest of the processes by which the physical properties of timber are improved. By this means boards of great sizes are obtained free from defects and unaffected by shrinkage or splitting. They can be made so thin that they can be rolled up or so thick that they are self-supporting and of very great strength.

The cutting of veneers
Two methods of veneer cutting are commonly employed today, viz.: rotary and slice cutting, the old method of saw cutting having disappeared.

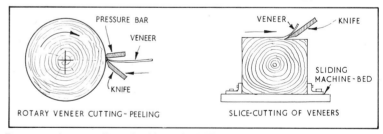

Figure 110 Veneer cutting

Rotary cutting or peeling In this method, illustrated in Fig. 110, the log, which has been previously softened by steaming, is rotated slowly between centres in a peeling lathe. A very strong and sharp knife is fed automatically into the log and as soon as the timber has been reduced to a true cylinder, a continuous sheet of veneer is peeled from the log until it is reduced to about 125 mm in diameter when it can no longer withstand the pressure from the knife. The veneer is cut to size as it leaves the lathe and is then passed through a drying machine.

Rotary-cut veneers are used almost exclusively for plywood manufacture, and in the case of Douglas fir, a most attractive and rather wild grain effect is produced as the peeling knife follows the annual rings very closely. This wood makes very handsome panels suitable for staining and varnishing.

Slice cutting The rather exaggerated grain formation produced by rotary cutting would rob many hardwoods of their natural beauty and in some cases would be wasteful in the early stages of truing up the log. The beautiful effect of the rays in oak, for example, would be lost completely whilst a mahogany 'crotch', which is a portion of the trunk at the junction of a large branch, could not be set up in the peeling machine because of its shape and because rotary cutting – if it were possible – would spoil the beauty of the grain formation. Another case which might well be quoted here concerns 'burrs' – the huge wart-like growths which sometimes form to cover wounds on the trunks of many trees. These are often highly prized for veneers but could not be cut in the lathe because of their irregular shapes and because of their peculiar texture.

In all these cases the veneers are produced by slice cutting as shown in Fig. 110. After steaming to soften it, the timber is secured to the machine bed and the leaves of veneer are sliced by the knife passing back and forth, the depth of cut being set after each stroke. In some machines the knife is stationary whilst the log moves across it. One important point about slice-cut veneers is that each successive leaf matches its neighbours very closely in its grain markings and they can be used in pairs to very good effect.

Plywood, laminboard and blockboard

Plywood   Plywood consists of veneers, referred to as laminations, which are glued or cemented together with the grain of each at right angles to its neighbour. It is always made up in odd numbers so that the outer layers run in the same direction, thus ensuring balanced stresses within the board. If made up with more than three laminations it is known as multi-plywood. The thickness of the veneers is varied considerably and the total number gives no accurate indication of the thickness of the plywood. A plywood known as 'stoutheart' is made up with a very thick core lamination and two quite thin facing veneers.

A great variety of timbers is used in the manufacture of plywood, often depending on the timbers available in the country in which it is made. Among the woods used are birch, alder, beech, gaboon, Parana pine, Douglas fir, etc. and also in common supply is plywood with an extra facing veneer of hardwood, oak, mahogany, walnut and so on.

The special properties of plywood which make it so invaluable to the wood worker are: (1) its stability, for it does not expand or contract as solid wood will, although it will absorb moisture and may tend to curl as the surface veneers expand, (2) its flexibility, for it lends itself admirably to curved work, particularly in the thinner gauges, and (3) its strength which comes from the crossing of the grains in the laminations. Even the thinnest plywood cannot be split.

Laminboard and blockboard   These are types of built-up boards of greater thickness with all the qualities of plywood except, of course, that they cannot be bent.

Laminboard consists of a core of wood strips glued together and faced on both sides with one or more veneers. Blockboard is of a similar construction, but the core is made of larger strips, usually square in section, to produce boards which are thick and strong enough to make such items as flush doors in one piece and for other large pieces of joinery work. Both types of board make excellent grounds for veneered work and are very strong and stable. They are obtainable in thicknesses from 13 mm upwards.

Plywood manufacture   The rotary-cut veneers, after cutting to size and drying, are patched where knot holes appear and are then graded either as core or facing veneers.

They are then ready for gluing or bonding and here the manufacturer has a wide choice of adhesives. Liquid glues are spread evenly by passing the veneers through metal rollers which pick up the glue from a trough underneath, after which the sheets of plywood are held in powerful presses until set. For weather-resisting plywoods the laminations are bonded with synthetic resin glues of various types, some of which are applied in the form of thin sheets laid between each pair of veneers. All require great pressure in a hot platen press to 'cure' the resin and effect the bonding.

Insulation board (*fibre board*) A soft and porous board, marketed for the purpose indicated by its name. It is made from wood waste, which after shredding and pulping is rolled under some pressure to thicknesses of 12 and 19 mm.

Hardboard This is also made from pulped wood waste, but with hardeners and bonding agents added. It is formed in very powerful presses and at some considerable temperature, being produced in two grades, 'medium' or 'semi-hardboards' and 'standard' hardboards, according to their densities. Standard hardboard is also obtainable in a specially strong and water-resistant form known as 'tempered' hardboard. A wide range of sizes is available. Before fixing, hardboards should be conditioned to prevent distortion, the textured side being damped and the boards left for 24 hours before fixing with rustless 'hardboard' nails.

Chipboard In this type of board, wood chips of a uniform size are bonded, usually with a urea formaldehyde glue, at high temperature and under great pressure. The most popular thicknesses are 12 and 19 mm boards of up to 1220 by 2440 mm. Many uses are found for chipboard and a number of 'manufactured' forms are available, e.g. with veneered surfaces, boards sealed ready for painting and cut sizes suitable for cabinet work or book shelving, with sides veneered and edges lipped with hardwood. Veneered boards are faced on both sides, each veneer balancing the other and giving stability.

Plastic laminates The decorative plastic laminates – such as Formica – provide attractive surfaces which are hard wearing, heat resistant and hygienic. They are formed from three types of paper, each impregnated with a thermo-setting resin. A number of sheets of kraft paper, impregnated with phenolic resin form the base or filler, giving the laminate its strength and flexibility. Over these is placed a sheet on which the pattern is printed and this is impregnated with a melamine resin. A top layer of pure alpha cellulose paper, impregnated with melamine resin, becomes transparent during the curing process which follows and forms a tough, protective skin. In curing, the layers (laminations) are subjected to great pressure at high temperature between highly polished stainless steel plates and they fuse together in a rigid, homogenous sheet.

In the school workshop, the laminates (1·6 mm thick), are best cut with a sharp, finely set saw with 12 points per 25 mm and the sheet supported over its whole area – especially along the cutting line. Excessive pressure with

Figure 111 a   Manufactured boards

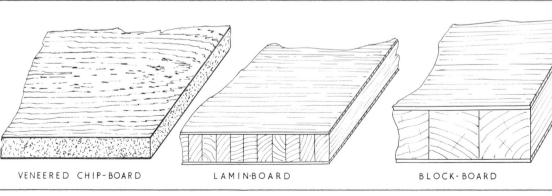

VENEERED CHIP-BOARD   LAMIN·BOARD   BLOCK-BOARD

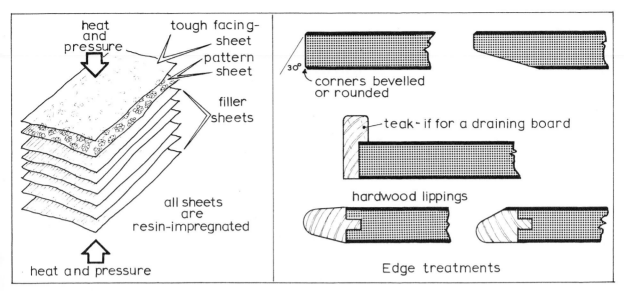

Figure 111b   Diagram showing manufacture of plastic laminate. Edge treatments

a dull saw might cause the sheet to split. Alternatively, a Stanley knife with a blade specially for this purpose can be used. Edges can be trimmed effectively with a block plane and after finishing with a fine file or cabinet scraper, they can be polished with fine steel wool.

The laminates can be bonded to almost any material, provided that a suitable adhesive is used and for fixing to wood surfaces, the synthetic resin adhesives give good results whilst allowing of some movement after positioning. The impact glues give an immediate bond, but accurate location is essential. It is advisable to use a manufactured board, i.e. plywood, chipboard, as a solid wood is always liable to move with temperature and humidity changes.

5

Practical work

Bench work

Although this book has been prepared for the student who has presumably had some previous training at the bench, a section devoted to the fundamentals of good practice will be more than justified. A clear understanding and a mastery of the basic tool manipulations pave the road to success in craftwork and in this respect the preparation of timber accurately to sizes and with all faces square to one another is probably the most difficult and frustrating task to the beginner. A sound knowledge of the principles and diligent practice will help to overcome these and other difficulties as they are encountered.

Cutting out

In marking out with pencil for cutting from the board, ample allowances for planing and the squaring of ends must be made. The amount of these allowances will depend to some extent on the skill of the operator in sawing accurately, the beginner needing to remember his or her lack of experience. About 4 mm on width and thickness and about 12 mm on the length should be allowed for planing and for squaring of the ends. The types and the uses of the various hand saws have been discussed in Chapter 2 and it only remains to study the details given in Fig. 112.

The preparation of timber (*planing*)

This is detailed in tabular form:

(1) Select the face side and the face edge. These are the two adjacent faces most completely free from knots and other blemishes.

(2) Plane the face side and as soon as all the saw marks have disappeared test it with the straight-edge along the length and across the width as in Fig. 113. The wood can be tested for winding (twisting) by sighting across a pair of wood strips placed on edge across the surface, one at each end and parallel to each other. Any twisting will easily be seen.

Put on the face mark very clearly, adjoining the face edge.

Figure 112   Using the saw

TWO FAULTS TO BE AVOIDED

CORRECT GRIP - FORE-ARM AND SAW IN LINE

EYES, SHOULDER, ELBOW, WRIST AND SAW TIP IN SAME PLANE

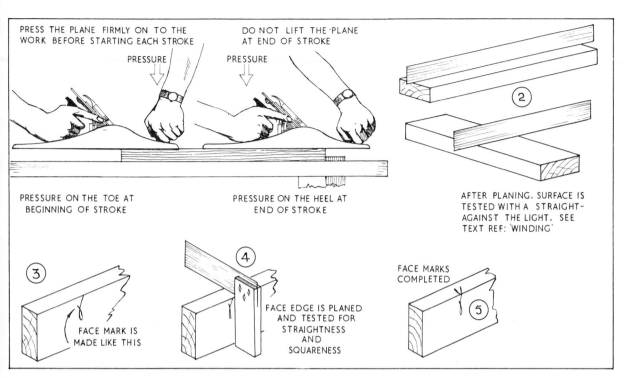

PRESS THE PLANE FIRMLY ON TO THE WORK BEFORE STARTING EACH STROKE

PRESSURE

DO NOT LIFT THE PLANE AT END OF STROKE

PRESSURE

PRESSURE ON THE TOE AT BEGINNING OF STROKE

PRESSURE ON THE HEEL AT END OF STROKE

AFTER PLANING, SURFACE IS TESTED WITH A STRAIGHT-AGAINST THE LIGHT. SEE TEXT REF: 'WINDING'

③ FACE MARK IS MADE LIKE THIS

④ FACE EDGE IS PLANED AND TESTED FOR STRAIGHTNESS AND SQUARENESS

FACE MARKS COMPLETED

⑤

Figure 113   Preparing face side and face edge

Figure 114   Using the marking gauge

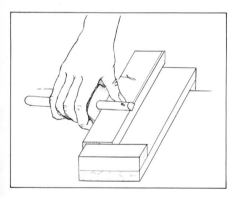

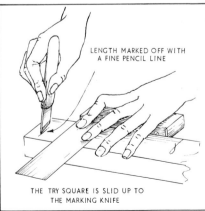

LENGTH MARKED OFF WITH A FINE PENCIL LINE

THE TRY SQUARE IS SLID UP TO THE MARKING KNIFE

Figure 115   Marking out

(3) Plane the face edge, test it with the straight-edge along the length and also with the square.

Put on the face edge mark clearly, adjoining the face side mark.

(4) Gauge the wood to width as in Fig. 114 both on the face side and on the back.

(5) Plane off the waste wood taking care not to pass the gauge lines.

(6) Gauge the wood to thickness along both edges.

(7) Plane off the waste wood.

Marking out

The marking or striking knife is generally used in marking out for joint constructions and for squaring off the ends of timber. The knife gives a clear-cut line and also gives a cleaner finish to corners because the top layers of fibres are severed. Its use in conjunction with the try square is shown in Fig. 115.

Sawing at the bench

The tenon and dovetail saws are used at the bench; in Fig. 116 the tenon saw is shown cutting the sides of a trenching. Sawing is started at the far side on the waste side of the line and the saw is lowered to the horizontal as cutting proceeds. The stance is important, the left foot pointing in the direction of sawing with the knee flexed whilst the right leg is braced firmly with the foot towards the right. This causes the weight to be transferred by the left arm to the work, holding it firmly in place. The saw point, wrist, elbow, shoulder and the eyes should all be in the same vertical plane, otherwise the saw will quickly wander off course.

Planing end grain

This can be done on the shooting board or in the vice. If the plane is taken straight across, some means must be found to prevent the grain from breaking away at the far side. The shooting board is useful also in making edge-to-edge

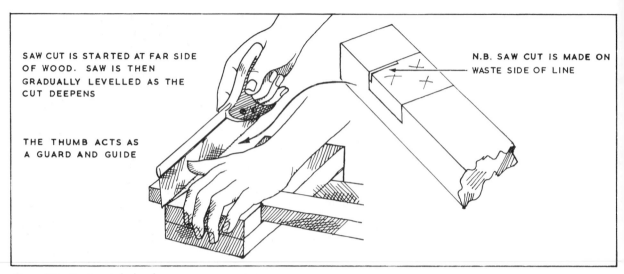

SAW CUT IS STARTED AT FAR SIDE
OF WOOD. SAW IS THEN
GRADUALLY LEVELLED AS THE
CUT DEEPENS

N.B. SAW CUT IS MADE ON
WASTE SIDE OF LINE

THE THUMB ACTS AS
A GUARD AND GUIDE

Figure 116   Sawing at the bench

joints, one edge being planed face side up and the other, face side down to compensate for any lack of squareness in the plane or shooting board.

Using chisels

In using chisels for paring – as opposed to 'chopping' when the mallet is used – care must be taken to keep the left hand from straying in front of the cutting edge. This can happen almost unconsciously, especially when the work is not held securely and needs steadying. For horizontal paring the work should be held in the vice whilst the chisel is held safely with *both* hands. The paring of the waste wood in a simple trenching is shown in Fig. 121 whilst other uses of the chisel are illustrated later in the chapter. Vertical paring is shown in Fig. 120.

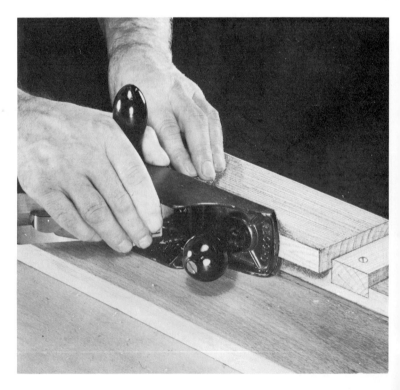

Figure 117 a   Using the shooting board

Figure 117b   Chamfering with the block plane

HOLDING PLANE
SLIGHTLY ASKEW GIVES
A SLICING CUT

Figure 118   Planing end grain

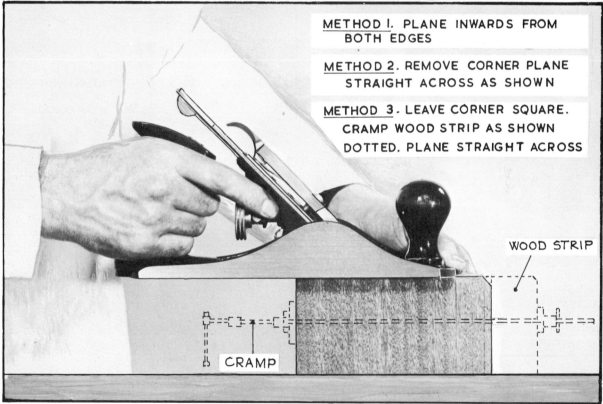

METHOD I. PLANE INWARDS FROM
    BOTH EDGES

METHOD 2. REMOVE CORNER PLANE
    STRAIGHT ACROSS AS SHOWN

METHOD 3. LEAVE CORNER SQUARE.
    CRAMP WOOD STRIP AS SHOWN
    DOTTED. PLANE STRAIGHT ACROSS

WOOD STRIP

CRAMP

Joints and construction

The halved joint

This joint can be used in framing where members lap or cross over, a part
of each being cut away. Cross halving would be used, e.g. in a table underframe
with diagonal stretchers.

Figure 119 a   Using planes

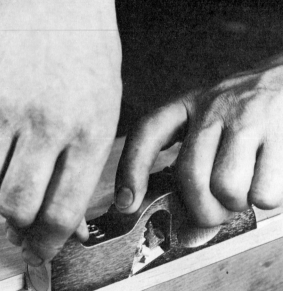

TYPICAL USE OF THE BULL-
NOSE SHOULDER PLANE

*Figure 119 b (below left)   Typical use of the
shoulder plane*

Figure 120 (below right)   Vertical paring

Figure 121   Horizontal paring

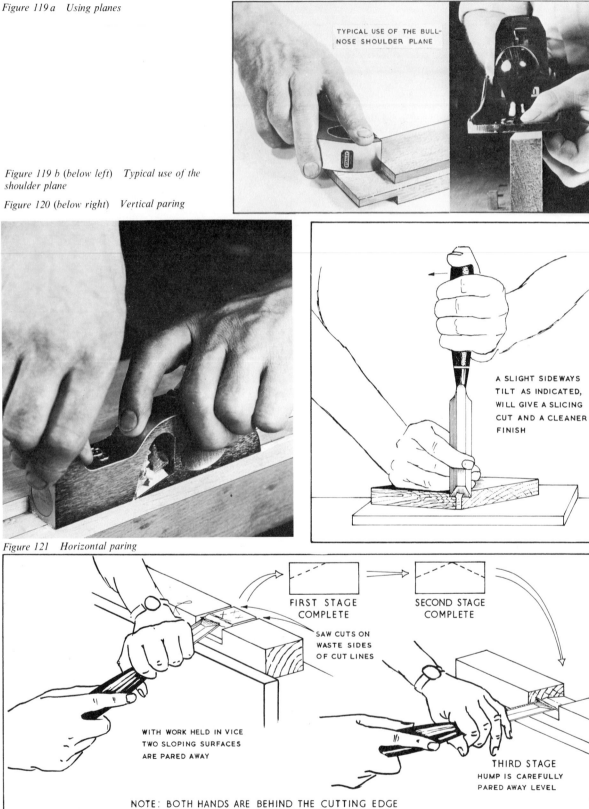

A SLIGHT SIDEWAYS
TILT AS INDICATED,
WILL GIVE A SLICING
CUT AND A CLEANER
FINISH

FIRST STAGE
COMPLETE

SECOND STAGE
COMPLETE

SAW CUTS ON
WASTE SIDES
OF CUT LINES

WITH WORK HELD IN VICE
TWO SLOPING SURFACES
ARE PARED AWAY

THIRD STAGE
HUMP IS CAREFULLY
PARED AWAY LEVEL

NOTE: BOTH HANDS ARE BEHIND THE CUTTING EDGE

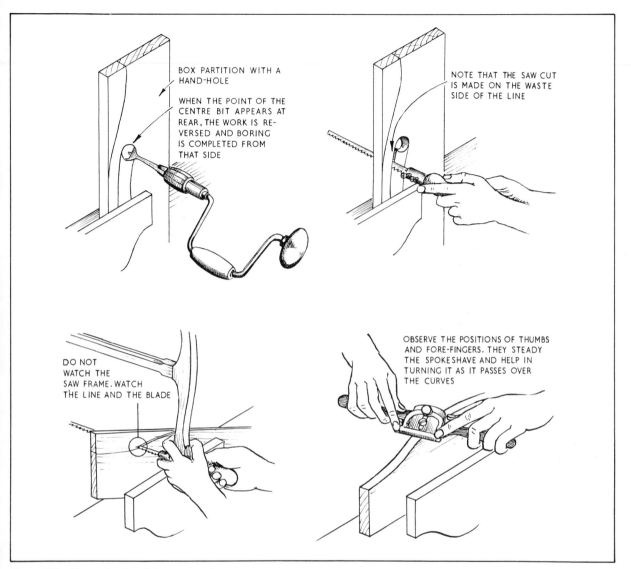

BOX PARTITION WITH A HAND-HOLE

WHEN THE POINT OF THE CENTRE BIT APPEARS AT REAR, THE WORK IS REVERSED AND BORING IS COMPLETED FROM THAT SIDE

NOTE THAT THE SAW CUT IS MADE ON THE WASTE SIDE OF THE LINE

DO NOT WATCH THE SAW FRAME. WATCH THE LINE AND THE BLADE

OBSERVE THE POSITIONS OF THUMBS AND FORE-FINGERS. THEY STEADY THE SPOKESHAVE AND HELP IN TURNING IT AS IT PASSES OVER THE CURVES

Figure 122 Above: piercing. Below: contouring

The angle and the tee halvings are not used very often as they have no great strength and always need some form of fixing with either screws or nails in addition to being glued. This makes them unsightly.

The dovetailed halving appears in various forms in light work, examples of which may be seen in Chapter 1, Fig. 9. In the form shown in Fig. 123 it is regarded as a good introductory exercise to dovetailing proper.

The bridle joint

This joint is used in light framing, but the objection to it is that a large part of the wood is cut away from the through member (A in the plain bridle joint drawing), thus weakening it considerably. This is not so apparent in the angle bridles and they are sometimes used as substitutes for haunched mortise and tenon joints where appearance is not important.

The mitred bridles form a useful group of joints provided there is no objection to revealing the end grain.

The mortise and tenon joint

This is certainly the most common on all joints and is used in many different

Figure 123   Halved joints

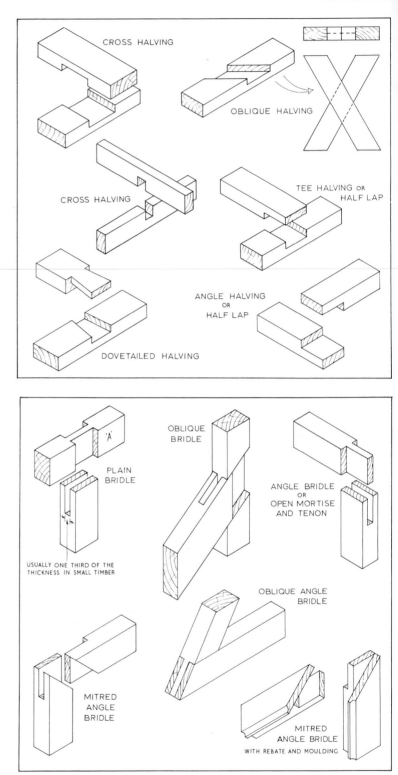

Figure 124   Bridle joints

forms by wheelwrights, boat builders, carpenters, joiners and cabinet makers.

It appears at its simplest in Fig. 125 as a plain mortise and tenon joint. The tenon is one third of the total thickness, dividing the strength up equally

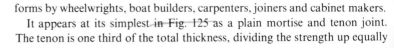

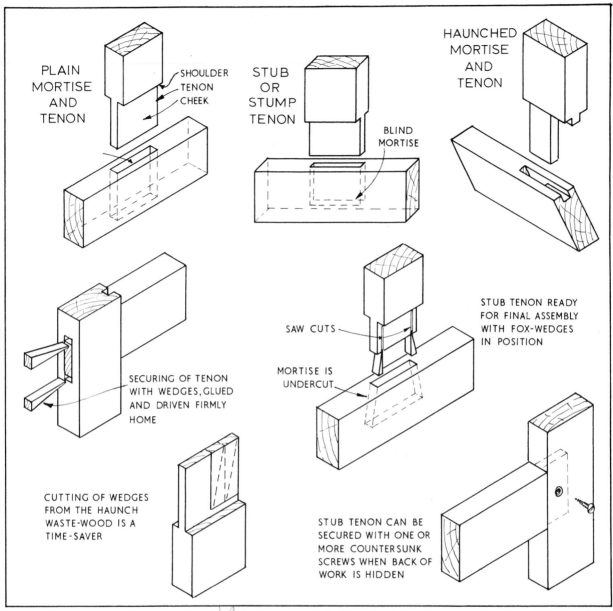

PLAIN
MORTISE
AND
TENON

SHOULDER
TENON
CHEEK

STUB
OR
STUMP
TENON

BLIND
MORTISE

HAUNCHED
MORTISE
AND
TENON

SECURING OF TENON
WITH WEDGES, GLUED
AND DRIVEN FIRMLY
HOME

SAW CUTS

MORTISE IS
UNDERCUT

STUB TENON READY
FOR FINAL ASSEMBLY
WITH FOX-WEDGES
IN POSITION

CUTTING OF WEDGES
FROM THE HAUNCH
WASTE-WOOD IS A
TIME-SAVER

STUB TENON CAN BE
SECURED WITH ONE OR
MORE COUNTERSUNK
SCREWS WHEN BACK OF
WORK IS HIDDEN

*Figure 125 The mortise and tenon in light
frame construction*

for work in small timber and although one cannot always apply the 'one third'
rule strictly, it is always possible to get a close approximation. The weakest
part of the joint is at the root of the tenon and on this point, attention is
directed to Fig. 128.

The stub tenon (also called 'blind' or 'stump' tenon) is used where no end
grain may show outside. It is secured after gluing by inserting a countersunk
screw or dowel pin or by the fox wedging method shown.

When the mortise and tenon joint is used at the corner of a frame, a portion
of the tenon is cut away leaving a short haunching which is accommodated
in a groove extending from the mortise. The haunching gives extra gluing surface and prevents the tenon from twisting in the mortise. If it is desired to
conceal the haunching it can be diminished (tapered) as in Fig. 133, centre
drawing.

These joints as in Fig. 125 are all used in framing with square edges, i.e.
no grooves or rebates, an example of such a frame being given in Fig. 130.

Figure 126 (right)   Mortising

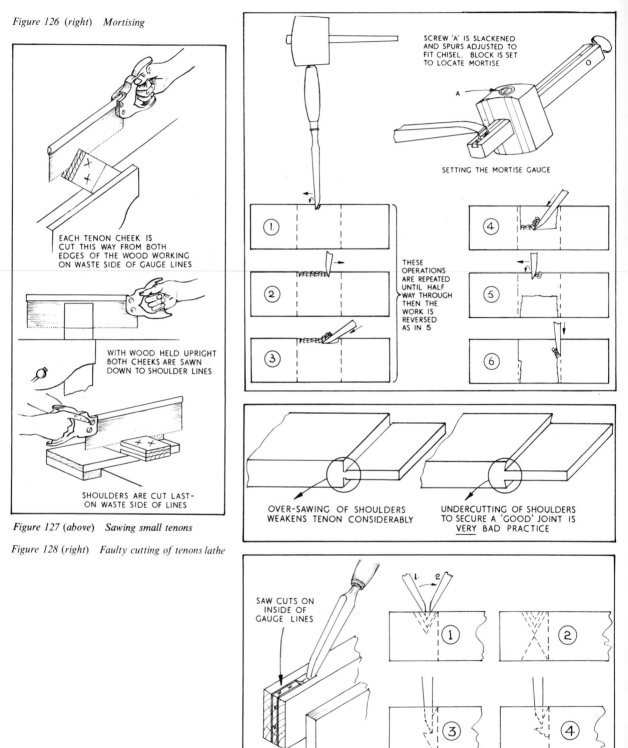

EACH TENON CHEEK IS
CUT THIS WAY FROM BOTH
EDGES OF THE WOOD WORKING
ON WASTE SIDE OF GAUGE LINES

WITH WOOD HELD UPRIGHT
BOTH CHEEKS ARE SAWN
DOWN TO SHOULDER LINES

SHOULDERS ARE CUT LAST-
ON WASTE SIDE OF LINES

Figure 127 (above)   Sawing small tenons

Figure 128 (right)   Faulty cutting of tenons lathe

*Figure 129   Cutting the open mortise or bridle
for a bridle joint*

SCREW 'A' IS SLACKENED
AND SPURS ADJUSTED TO
FIT CHISEL. BLOCK IS SET
TO LOCATE MORTISE

A

SETTING THE MORTISE GAUGE

1.   4.

THESE
OPERATIONS
ARE REPEATED
UNTIL HALF
WAY THROUGH
THEN THE
WORK IS
REVERSED
AS IN 5

2.   5.

3.   6.

OVER-SAWING OF SHOULDERS
WEAKENS TENON CONSIDERABLY

UNDERCUTTING OF SHOULDERS
TO SECURE A 'GOOD' JOINT IS
VERY BAD PRACTICE

SAW CUTS ON
INSIDE OF
GAUGE LINES

1. 2.

①   ②

③   ④

The setting of the mortise gauge and the 'chopping' of a mortise are illustrated in Fig. 126. The cheeks (sides) of tenons should always be sawn and
should not be smoothed in any way as the roughness forms a good key for
the glue.

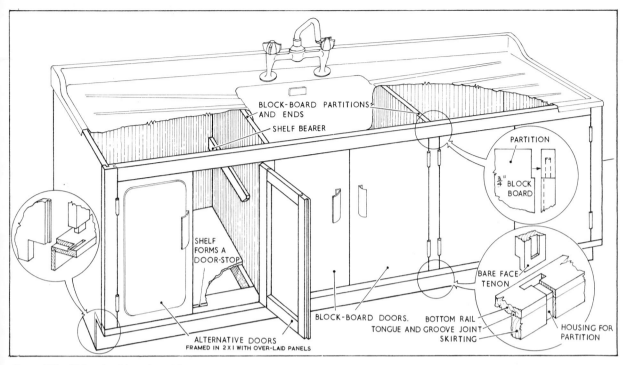

BLOCK-BOARD PARTITIONS AND ENDS
SHELF BEARER
BLOCK BOARD
PARTITION
¾" BLOCK BOARD
SHELF FORMS A DOOR-STOP
BARE FACE TENON
HOUSING FOR PARTITION
SHELF FORMS A DOOR-STOP
BLOCK-BOARD DOORS. TONGUE AND GROOVE JOINT
BOTTOM RAIL
SKIRTING
ALTERNATIVE DOORS FRAMED IN 2 X 1 WITH OVER-LAID PANELS

Figure 130   Sink unit with cupboard front

In Fig. 131 the mortise and tenon is shown in the form used for panelled frames, doors and for glazed work. In the first case the face edge of the timber is ploughed to receive a panel of solid or plywood. The groove takes away part of the tenon and the size and position of the mortise must be adjusted accordingly. As a guide for assembly the position of the rail is indicated on the stile by a short pencil line known as a 'sight line' (see Fig. 136).

In the case of glazed work provision must be made for the replacement of broken glass and the pane is rebated into the frame as shown in Fig. 131, being held in place by means of a small beading or fillet mitred and pinned in place. As with the wood panel, the edge of the tenon is set back from the face edge of the rail and a sight line is marked on the stile for assembly purposes.

The fitting of a mirror in a rebate is shown in Fig. 132.

The mortise and tenon for glazed work

The long and short shoulder mortise and tenon is not suitable for all types of glazed work and the best practice is illustrated in Fig. 133.

All rails and stiles are prepared with rebates and 'struck' mouldings, i.e. worked out of the solid wood, those which are fixed with glue and pins being known as 'planted' mouldings. The shoulders are of equal lengths and from the drawing it will be noticed that a portion of the moulding by the mortise is cut away and mitred at 45° to 'mate' with a similar mitre on the rail moulding.

As an alternative to the mitred mouldings, the rail moulding is sometimes 'scribed' (shaped) to fit over the stile moulding giving an appearance almost identical with that of a mitre. This method is used by joiners when fitting up doors which often have wide rails of 200 mm plus. If a plain mitre were used between rail and stile mouldings, any shrinkage of the rail would at once reveal a gaping mitre, but with the scribed joint the rail is free to move a little over the stile moulding without showing any gap.

The struck moulding is also used on one or both sides with a plough groove

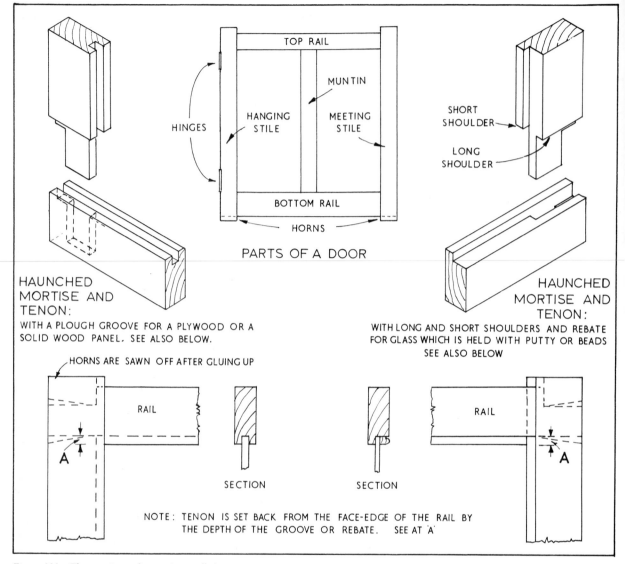

PARTS OF A DOOR

HAUNCHED MORTISE AND TENON:
WITH A PLOUGH GROOVE FOR A PLYWOOD OR A SOLID WOOD PANEL. SEE ALSO BELOW.

HAUNCHED MORTISE AND TENON:
WITH LONG AND SHORT SHOULDERS AND REBATE FOR GLASS WHICH IS HELD WITH PUTTY OR BEADS SEE ALSO BELOW

HORNS ARE SAWN OFF AFTER GLUING UP

RAIL

A

RAIL

A

SECTION   SECTION

NOTE: TENON IS SET BACK FROM THE FACE-EDGE OF THE RAIL BY THE DEPTH OF THE GROOVE OR REBATE. SEE AT 'A'

Figure 131   The mortise and tenon in panelled frames and doors

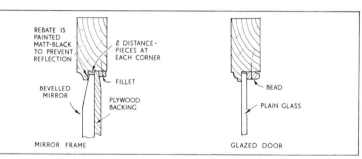

Figure 132   The fitting of glass panels

for panelled doors and when used on one side only the joint will require a long and short shoulder joint.

The wedging of tenons   The fitting of wedges to tenons is clearly explained in Fig. 134 to which may be added a 'rider' – the wider the stile the more important the fitting of the wedges becomes.

Wedges should be driven evenly after checking that rails are correctly at

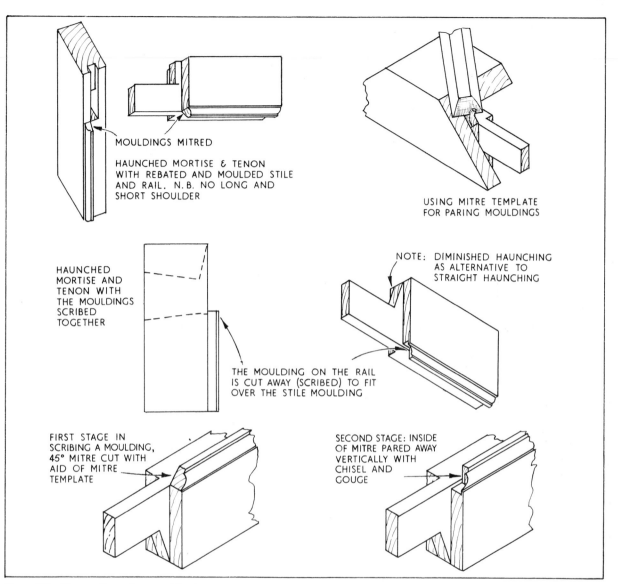

MOULDINGS MITRED

HAUNCHED MORTISE & TENON
WITH REBATED AND MOULDED STILE
AND RAIL. N.B. NO LONG AND
SHORT SHOULDER

USING MITRE TEMPLATE
FOR PARING MOULDINGS

HAUNCHED
MORTISE AND
TENON WITH
THE MOULDINGS
SCRIBED
TOGETHER

NOTE: DIMINISHED HAUNCHING
AS ALTERNATIVE TO
STRAIGHT HAUNCHING

THE MOULDING ON THE RAIL
IS CUT AWAY (SCRIBED) TO FIT
OVER THE STILE MOULDING

FIRST STAGE IN
SCRIBING A MOULDING,
45° MITRE CUT WITH
AID OF MITRE
TEMPLATE

SECOND STAGE: INSIDE
OF MITRE PARED AWAY
VERTICALLY WITH
CHISEL AND
GOUGE

*Figure 133   The mortise and tenon with rebate
and moulding*

their sight lines. Driving one wedge too hard may move the rail along or pull
the frame out of square; also, care must be taken not to over drive the wedges
or they will do more harm than good.

The pinning of tenons   The securing of tenons with dowels by draw-boring
is an excellent method of holding provided that is no objection to the pins
showing – they are not easily concealed. They are generally used in the heavier
types of woodwork such as door frames, staircases, and so on. Draw-boring
is explained in Fig. 135.

Making a small door

The manufacture of small doors or frames of various types is a job which
recurs frequently and although there is nothing especially difficult about such
work, it is one of the many tasks which must be tackled methodically to avoid
making mistakes. The process is set out in tabular form:

(1) Prepare the timber to finished sizes leaving a little extra on all lengths.
Prominently mark face sides and edges.

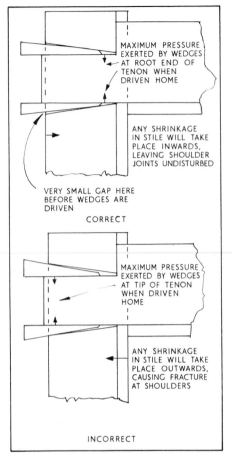

Figure 134   The wedging of tenons

(Labels within Figure 134:)

MAXIMUM PRESSURE EXERTED BY WEDGES AT ROOT END OF TENON WHEN DRIVEN HOME

ANY SHRINKAGE IN STILE WILL TAKE PLACE INWARDS, LEAVING SHOULDER JOINTS UNDISTURBED

VERY SMALL GAP HERE BEFORE WEDGES ARE DRIVEN

CORRECT

MAXIMUM PRESSURE EXERTED BY WEDGES AT TIP OF TENON WHEN DRIVEN HOME

ANY SHRINKAGE IN STILE WILL TAKE PLACE OUTWARDS, CAUSING FRACTURE AT SHOULDERS

INCORRECT

(2) Mark each piece clearly in large block letters as follows: T.R. (top rail), B.R. (bottom rail), M.R. (middle rail), St. (stile).

(3) Mark out the parts in pairs or groups as in Fig. 136.

(4) Prepare all mortises, not forgetting to allow for wedge room.

(5) Saw down the cheeks *only* on the tenons. If the shoulders are cut at this stage it will be difficult to work with the plough or rebate plane from the face side.

(6) Work all rebates, grooves or mouldings.

(7) Cut the shoulders on all tenons.

(8) Assemble each joint separately, testing for the fitting of the shoulder joints, squareness and for alignment (see Fig. 137).

(9) Cut the panel to size. If it is in solid wood it must be cut slightly undersize *across* the grain to allow for any expansion which may take place. This allowance should be not less than 3 mm per foot width. Even if the panel is made from plywood, a small clearance should be left on both width and height. Check that the panel will enter all plough grooves with hand pressure only.

(10) Assemble door. Check for fitting and winding (see Fig. 138).

(11) Glue all joints, but not the panel; cramp immediately and wedge the tenons, removing surplus glue with a wet rag. Check again for winding, and squareness as in Fig. 139 and leave overnight for the glue to set.

(12) Saw off protruding tenons and wedges.

(13) Flush off both sides with the smoothing plane and clean off with glass-paper in the manner suited to the type of finish required. See Chapter 7, Finishes, for further information on this point.

(14) Saw off the bottom horns and shoot the door to size, working in the following order: (a) Straighten the hanging stile. (b) Offer the door up to the carcase and then shoot off the bottom edge of the door to make a good fit. (c) Repeat the last stage working on the top edge of the door. (d) Shoot the meeting stile making an even joint all round. Attention is directed to Fig. 159 regarding meeting stiles. The joint should be quite fine for polished work and a little easier for a painted finish.

(15) Fit the hinges to the door, keeping the ends in line with the top and bottom rails and hang the door in its frame.

Gluing and cramping a small door   The final assembly of a small door or frame requires a little preparation and care if the job is not to be spoiled in its last stages. Three main points must be borne in mind:

(1) The joints must be pulled together tightly so as not to show a line of glue afterwards.

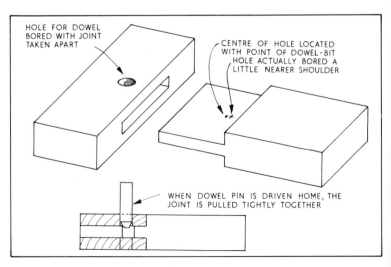

(Labels within Figure 135:)

HOLE FOR DOWEL BORED WITH JOINT TAKEN APART

CENTRE OF HOLE LOCATED WITH POINT OF DOWEL-BIT HOLE ACTUALLY BORED A LITTLE NEARER SHOULDER

WHEN DOWEL PIN IS DRIVEN HOME, THE JOINT IS PULLED TIGHTLY TOGETHER

Figure 135   Draw-bore pinning

Figure 136 The marking out of door stiles and rails for plough grooves or rebates

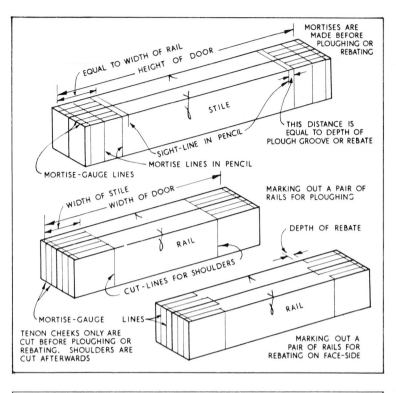

Figure 136 The marking out of door stiles and rails for plough grooves or rebates

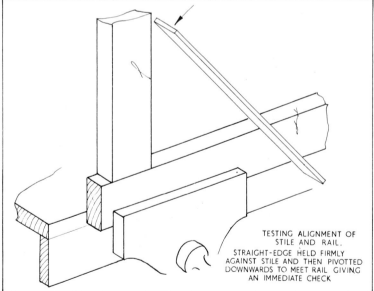

Figure 137 Checking the fitting of joints

(2) The door must be square.

(3) The door must be out of winding, i.e. flat.

Before gluing up, the bench should be cleared of all tools and two stout and straight pieces of timber laid out as shown in Fig. 139. These must be checked for winding by 'boning' with one eye closed. Wedges should be prepared and two sash cramps adjusted for length, allowing room for small protecting pieces to be included under the cramp shoes. The mortises in one stile are glued first, using a thin stick, then one of the appropriate tenons is glued and inserted at once. The panel is then entered and slid home and is followed

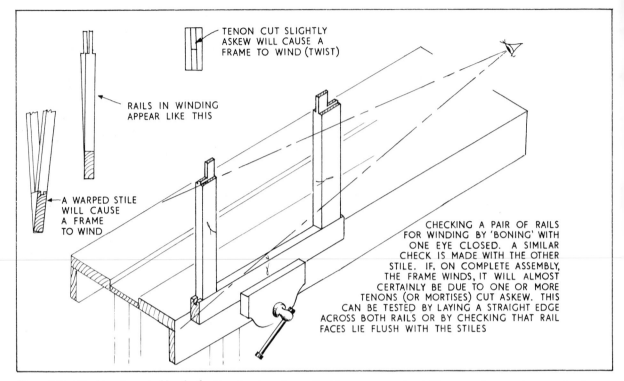

TENON CUT SLIGHTLY
ASKEW WILL CAUSE A
FRAME TO WIND (TWIST)

RAILS IN WINDING
APPEAR LIKE THIS

A WARPED STILE
WILL CAUSE
A FRAME
TO WIND

CHECKING A PAIR OF RAILS
FOR WINDING BY 'BONING' WITH
ONE EYE CLOSED. A SIMILAR
CHECK IS MADE WITH THE OTHER
STILE. IF, ON COMPLETE ASSEMBLY,
THE FRAME WINDS, IT WILL ALMOST
CERTAINLY BE DUE TO ONE OR MORE
TENONS (OR MORTISES) CUT ASKEW. THIS
CAN BE TESTED BY LAYING A STRAIGHT EDGE
ACROSS BOTH RAILS OR BY CHECKING THAT RAIL
FACES LIE FLUSH WITH THE STILES

Figure 138   Checking the assembly of a frame

by the other rail with one tenon glued. The opposite mortises are glued next, then the tenons, and the door is pushed together by hand pressure.

With the door on the gluing up strips, the cramps and the wood protecting pieces are positioned and enough pressure applied to close the joints and squeeze out the surplus glue. The cramps should be kept clear of the door

Figure 139   The use of cramps and squaring lath

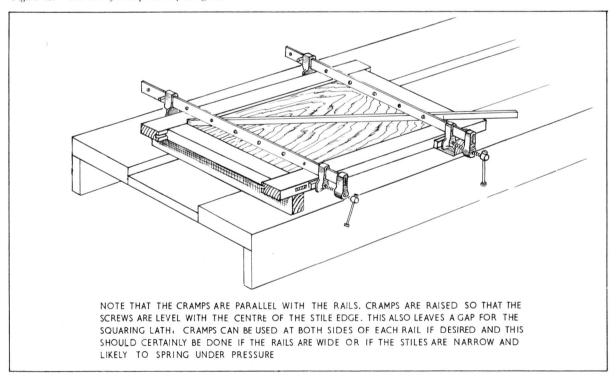

NOTE THAT THE CRAMPS ARE PARALLEL WITH THE RAILS. CRAMPS ARE RAISED SO THAT THE
SCREWS ARE LEVEL WITH THE CENTRE OF THE STILE EDGE. THIS ALSO LEAVES A GAP FOR THE
SQUARING LATH. CRAMPS CAN BE USED AT BOTH SIDES OF EACH RAIL IF DESIRED AND THIS
SHOULD CERTAINLY BE DONE IF THE RAILS ARE WIDE OR IF THE STILES ARE NARROW AND
LIKELY TO SPRING UNDER PRESSURE

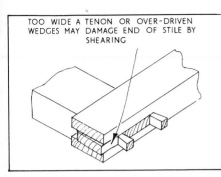

TOO WIDE A TENON OR OVER-DRIVEN
WEDGES MAY DAMAGE END OF STILE BY
SHEARING

Figure 140   Faulty wedging

Figure 141   The bare-faced tenon

by about 12 mm, for a reason to be explained later, and they must be parallel to the rails whose positioning is checked from the sight lines. The door will be pulled out of square if the cramps are not properly placed, whilst the use of excessive pressure may cause bruising and distortion.

A check for squareness is made next, using a squaring lath to compare the diagonals of the frame as in Fig. 139. It is for the insertion of this lath that the cramps are kept raised from the face of the door. The point of the lath is pressed into one corner of the frame and the length of the diagonal is marked on the lath with a pencil line. This is repeated for the opposite diagonal and any discrepancy will be shown by the two lengths on the lath. The correct diagonal length is mid-way between these two and should be clearly marked by measuring, the frame being adjusted by tapping the end of the appropriate stile until the diagonals are equal. The glued wedges can now be driven home

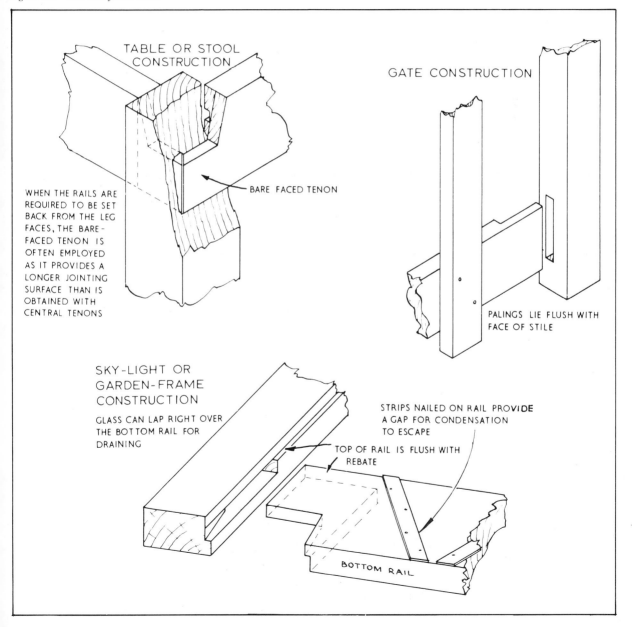

TABLE OR STOOL
CONSTRUCTION

WHEN THE RAILS ARE
REQUIRED TO BE SET
BACK FROM THE LEG
FACES, THE BARE-
FACED TENON IS
OFTEN EMPLOYED
AS IT PROVIDES A
LONGER JOINTING
SURFACE THAN IS
OBTAINED WITH
CENTRAL TENONS

BARE FACED TENON

GATE CONSTRUCTION

PALINGS LIE FLUSH WITH
FACE OF STILE

SKY-LIGHT OR
GARDEN-FRAME
CONSTRUCTION

GLASS CAN LAP RIGHT OVER
THE BOTTOM RAIL FOR
DRAINING

STRIPS NAILED ON RAIL PROVIDE
A GAP FOR CONDENSATION
TO ESCAPE

TOP OF RAIL IS FLUSH WITH
REBATE

BOTTOM RAIL

firmly but with care, surplus glue removed with a clean wet rag and the door
set aside to dry after being checked for winding.

The bare-faced tenon
The bare-faced tenon which has one shoulder only is illustrated in Fig. 141
which shows three examples of its application. In addition to the information
given in the illustrations it is only necessary to add that some care is needed
when cramping these joints, for with only one shoulder to bear upon, the stiles
will readily twist on the tenons. Only light pressure should be applied.

Housing joints
Fig. 142 shows the housing joints which are commonly used for shelving and
carcase work. The making of a stopped housing is shown in five sketches which
are self-explanatory. The double stopped housing is made with mallet and

Figure 142   The housing joint

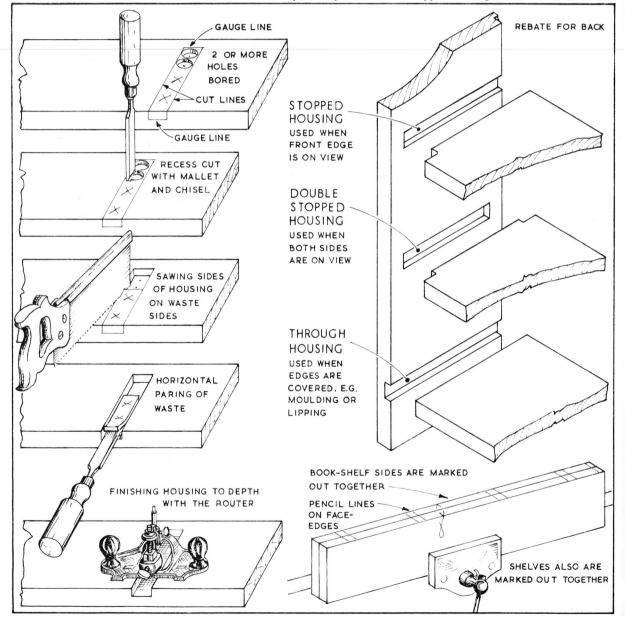

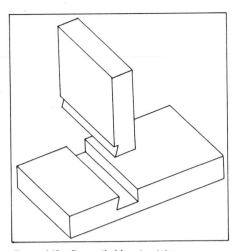

Figure 143   Dovetailed housing joint

chisel after boring a complete row of holes with the centre bit. Waste wood is removed by paring with the chisel reversed and the housing is finished to depth with the router.

Fig. 143 shows a dovetailed housing which requires no nails or other fixing in addition to gluing. It can also be made as a stopped dovetailed housing and requires some care in its preparation if it is to make a good joint. It is tapered slightly to facilitate assembly.

Dovetailing

Dovetailing, which makes a very strong joint, is a method of keying pieces of timber together by engaging one or more tapered pins or tails cut on one piece with corresponding sockets cut on the other. This joint is particularly suitable for joining wide boards as the tails and sockets can be repeated *ad lib* to any limit within reason.

Among experienced craftsmen it is almost a point of honour to cut dovetails which fit accurately straight from the saw with no paring or easing of the sides of the tails or pins to get the joint assembled. Such skill comes only with diligent practice. Dovetailing will always be a challenge to the craftsman of any calibre, and all woodworkers will set out to do their best with this joint. This is true pride in craftsmanship, born in the knowledge that a fine piece of work will remain as mute testimony to his or her skill long after the person has been forgotten.

For dovetailing at its finest we must look to the cabinet makers, especially to the work of the pre-machine-dovetail era, and for dovetailing at its strongest we must look to the joiners and carpenters.

Fig. 144 shows dovetailing in two of its simplest forms, a single dovetail, and common dovetailing, also known as through dovetailing.

The setting out of a dovetail is shown in Fig. 145 together with one of the more common templates which can be bought ready-made or can be made at home from sheet brass.

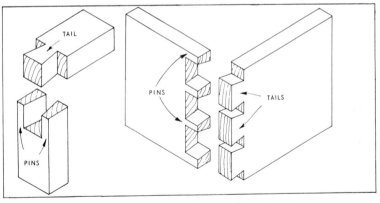

Figure 144   Single and common dovetailing

Common dovetailing is shown, step by step, in Fig. 146 in the making of a box. In the first sketch the four sides are shown cut to length and with ends accurately squared. They are laid out in order and numbered to avoid confusion later on. A sharp marking gauge or a cutting gauge is set to the thickness of the wood and each piece is gauged on both sides – at both ends. Sketches 4, 5 and 6 show the marking out and cutting of the sides which are placed together with face sides outwards and face edges the same way. In sketch 7 the tip of the tenon saw is being used to mark out the pins from the tails, the saw teeth giving the exact location of the tails on the box end. In Fig. 150 is shown a scriber which is made quite easily from a piece of round silver steel; it is much more manageable than the saw and is well worth the trouble of making. In sketch 8 the pins are being cut and it should be noted that the

Figure 145   Dovetail proportions.
A 'gallows' shelf bracket

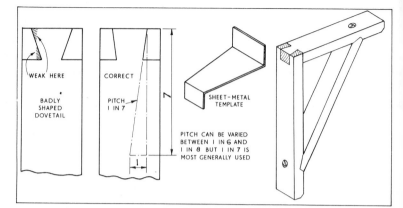

Figure 146   Making a dovetailed box

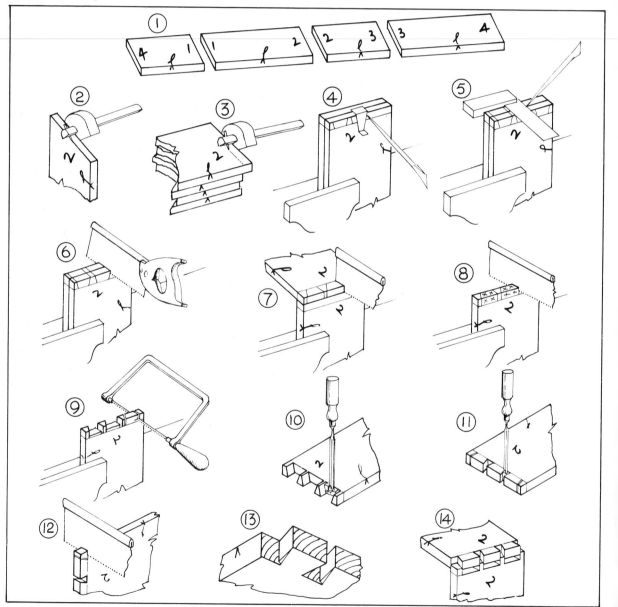

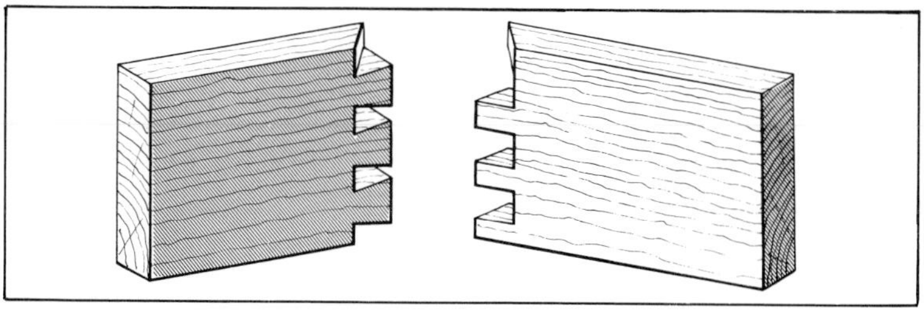

Figure 147   Common dovetail with mitre (essential if top edge is moulded)

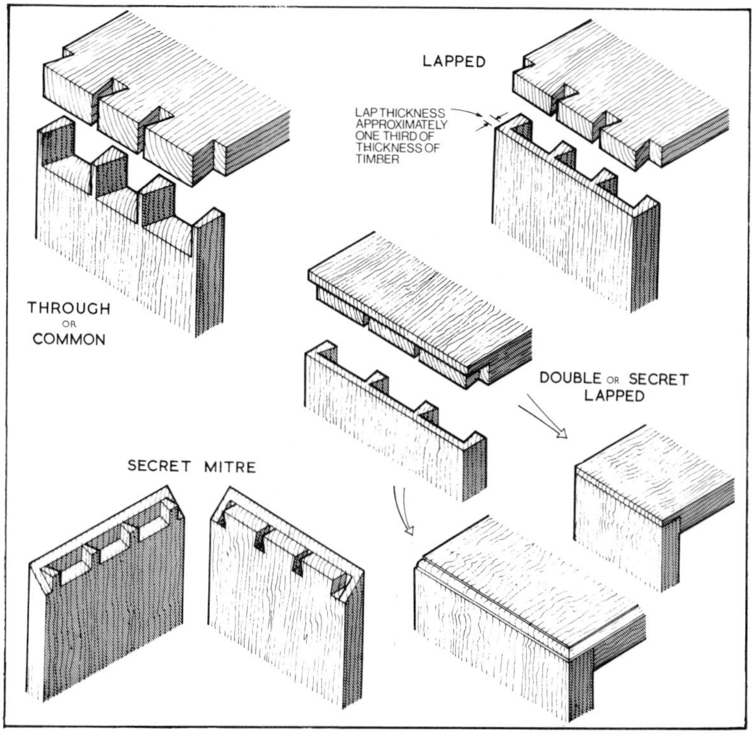

Figure 148   Various types of dovetailing

waste wood is clearly marked, with the saw cuts being made on that side of the line. A coping saw or a bow saw is used to remove the bulk of the waste, finishing off accurately with a bevel-edged chisel as in sketches 10 and 11.

Attention is directed to sketch 13 which shows a very small paring taken off the inside corner of each tail to assist assembly and to obviate the danger of breaking away the fibres when this is done.

Fig. 147 shows a common dovetail with the top edge mitred, a useful joint for shallow trays where the edge may be required with a moulding.

Lapped dovetailing is seen in Figs. 148, 149 and 150. This is the joint used in drawer making and it should be observed that the plough groove for the bottom is so placed that it comes in the bottom tail on the drawer side and so does not show on the outside.

The secret or mitred dovetail is a strong and useful joint which finds applications in box carcassing for contemporary style furniture. The joint is completely hidden, giving a clean appearance.

Double or secret lapped dovetailing is also illustrated and this can be used effectively in cabinet work of all kinds.

Drawer construction is dealt with in Fig. 149, the front and sides being lap dovetailed and the back common dovetailed. Lap dovetailing is further illustrated in Fig. 150.

Figure 149   Drawer construction

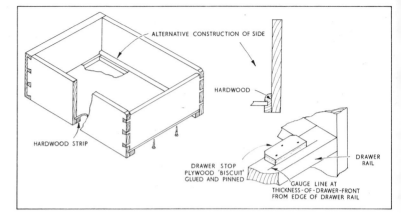

Figure 150   Marking out and cutting lapped dovetails

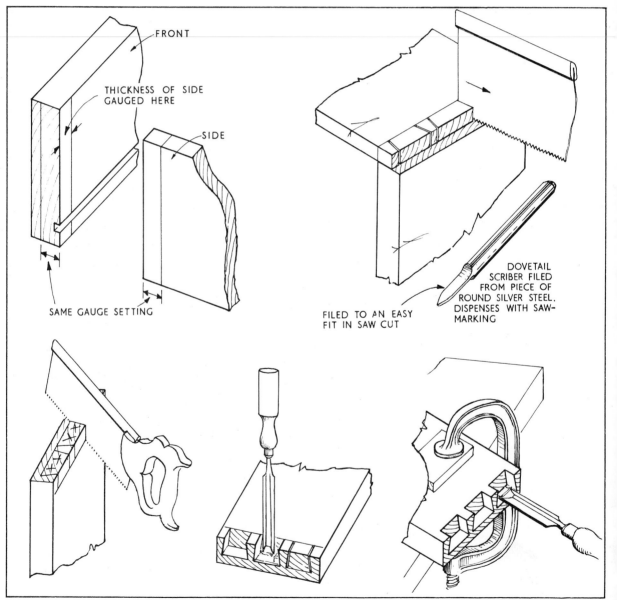

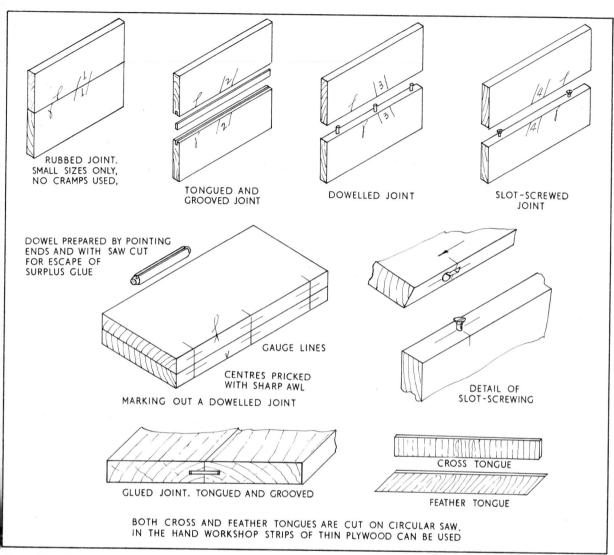

Figure 151   Glued joints for increasing width

Figure 152   Assembly of glued joint

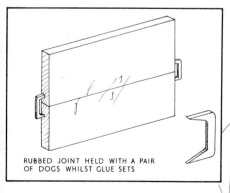

RUBBED JOINT HELD WITH A PAIR
OF DOGS WHILST GLUE SETS

Glued joints for increasing width

Various types of edge-to-edge joints are illustrated in Fig. 151.

The rubbed joint is made in small sizes only and is assembled with bone glue. The edges are shot with the trying plane in the usual way. With one piece held in the vice the joint is glued and immediately assembled, the top piece being rubbed to squeeze out the surplus glue which is wiped away with a wet rag. The joint is carefully leaned against a sloping support and left to set.

The tongued and grooved joint is very much more commonly used and gives a strong joint. At the bottom of Fig. 151 two types of tongue are shown, but both require cutting on a circular saw and would be very awkward to cut by hand. However, a plywood strip is quite a satisfactory substitute and this is the method used in most hand workshops. These joints are usually put under pressure whilst the glue sets using cramps for this purpose. On small joints it is possible to use a pair of joiners' dogs as shown in Fig. 152.

Dowelling makes a good strong joint if some care is taken over the marking out and with the preparation of the dowels. The saw cut is made for the escape of glue when the dowel pin is driven home and the point facilities its entry into the prepared hole.

Slot screwing is a method of jointing used quite commonly for secret fixings of various kinds. From the detail in Fig. 151 it will be seen that the screw is first driven partly home into one of the pieces of the joint. A keyhole opening is made in the other part, the round portion to receive the head of the screw and the slotted portion to accommodate the screw shank. The joint is assembled and the screw-head cuts a small dovetailed slot inside when the top member of the joint is driven along in the direction of the arrow. Having been assembled without glue, the joint is taken apart and the screws tightened one half turn each. On gluing and final assembly, the extra half turn on the screws gives a much tighter joint. This joint is more fully known as secret slot screwing.

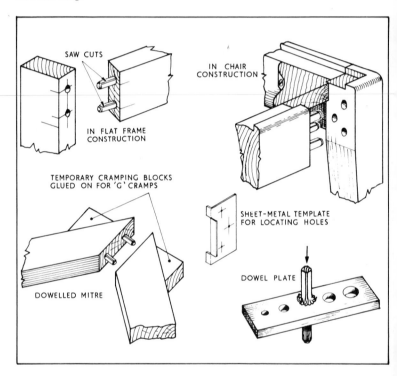

Figure 153   Other dowelled joints

The use of dowels

Dowels are used quite extensively for making joints and for the purpose of locating parts of assemblies, a well-known example of the latter being found on the meeting edges of the old type of draw-leaf table. Ramin is the wood commonly used for the manufacture of dowel rods nowadays.

If a dowelled joint is to have any strength it is essential that the holes be placed accurately, for any easing of the dowels with chisel or rasp to obtain a correct location or 'register' of the parts will result in a serious weakening of the joint. To this end, it is probably safer to use a thin sheet-metal template as shown in Fig. 153 through which the centres can be pricked with a fine, sharp awl.

A special dowel bit is manufactured for this work. It is a short twist bit of the Jennings' pattern and is illustrated in Chapter 2, Fig. 78. Dowel bits are made very accurately to size.

The dowel plate, once very commonly used, is a hard steel plate with reamed holes of standard sizes through which roughly shaped and pointed sticks are driven, producing quite clean dowels. The plate is never struck with the hammer, one dowel being driven out with the next. It is not possible to make very long sticks by this method.

Clamps

Clamps are used in holding wide boards flat by fixing battens (clamps) to them with screws or nails. The tongued and grooved clamps shown in Fig. 155 are effective but make no allowance for any movement in the board. In the clamping of good-quality drawing boards in solid wood – usually of Sitka spruce nowadays – provision is made for movement as shown in Fig. 155. The deep slots in the back eliminate any tendency to curling in the board and the saw cuts across the ebony strip help to prevent any loosening if the board should move. The clamps on the matched boarded door are known as ledges.

Hinges

The hanging of a door, whatever its size, calls for careful fitting of door to frame with suitable clearances all round. Hinges are then fitted and screwed in place on the 'hanging stile' after which, with the door supported in position, exact locations for hinge recesses can be marked on the frame. Since it is possible that some adjustment to the frame recesses might be needed, it is wise to drive only one screw in each hinge for testing, the rest being driven when door action is satisfactory.

Gauges for recessing are set as shown in Fig. 156, great care being taken to set them accurately and if a very close joint is required the gauge should not be set to the thickness of the leaf of the hinge, but to the centre of the pin. A few other types of hinges are shown in Fig. 185, Chapter 8, and in Fig. 158 are shown the common faults which may be caused through inaccurate work. These should be studied carefully together with Fig. 159.

Figure 154   Tongue and groove. Carcassing joints

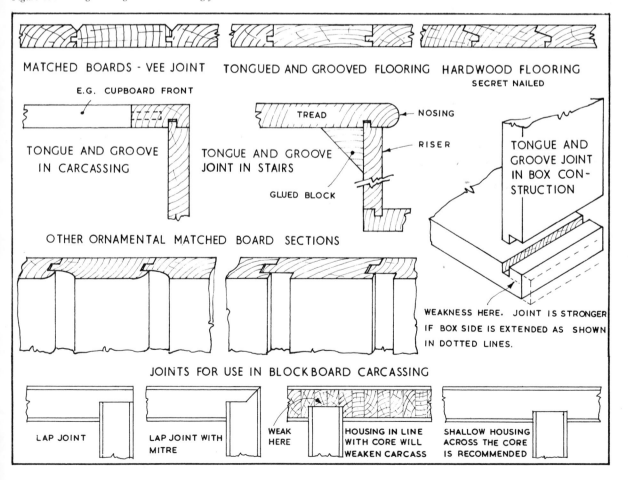

MATCHED BOARDS - VEE JOINT   TONGUED AND GROOVED FLOORING   HARDWOOD FLOORING
SECRET NAILED

E.G. CUPBOARD FRONT

TONGUE AND GROOVE IN CARCASSING

TREAD — NOSING

RISER

TONGUE AND GROOVE JOINT IN STAIRS

GLUED BLOCK

TONGUE AND GROOVE JOINT IN BOX CONSTRUCTION

OTHER ORNAMENTAL MATCHED BOARD SECTIONS

WEAKNESS HERE. JOINT IS STRONGER IF BOX SIDE IS EXTENDED AS SHOWN IN DOTTED LINES.

JOINTS FOR USE IN BLOCKBOARD CARCASSING

LAP JOINT   LAP JOINT WITH MITRE   WEAK HERE   HOUSING IN LINE WITH CORE WILL WEAKEN CARCASS   SHALLOW HOUSING ACROSS THE CORE IS RECOMMENDED

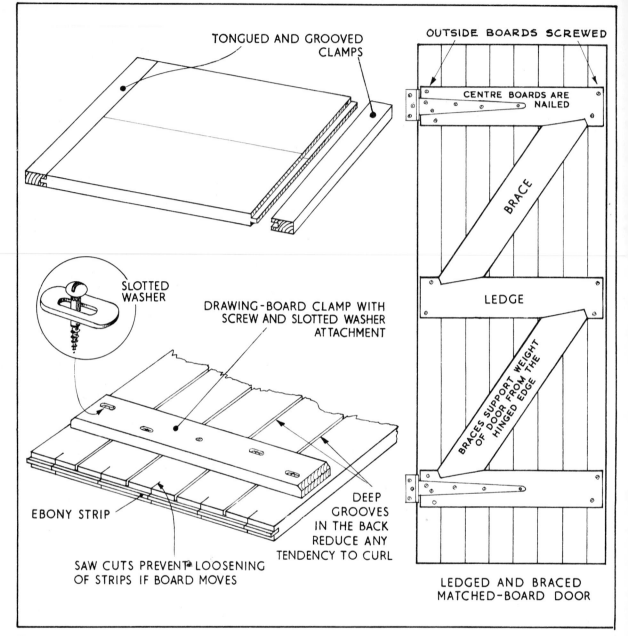

Figure 155 Clamps

Cutting lists

In any cabinet or joinery works the cutting list forms an important link in the progress of each job through the factory and is one of the first items prepared after the setting out (drawing) of the job.

The cutting list is equally important to the lone worker in his small workshop, ensuring that each piece of work is commenced in an orderly manner, without omissions or duplications of component parts.

Each item is identified by name on the list, with its finished (planed) sizes stated together with any remarks which may be necessary. The allowances for planing, which have already been discussed in Chapter 3, are added when the timber is sawn from stock and in addition to these, extra length should always be allowed for squaring off the ends accurately at the bench.

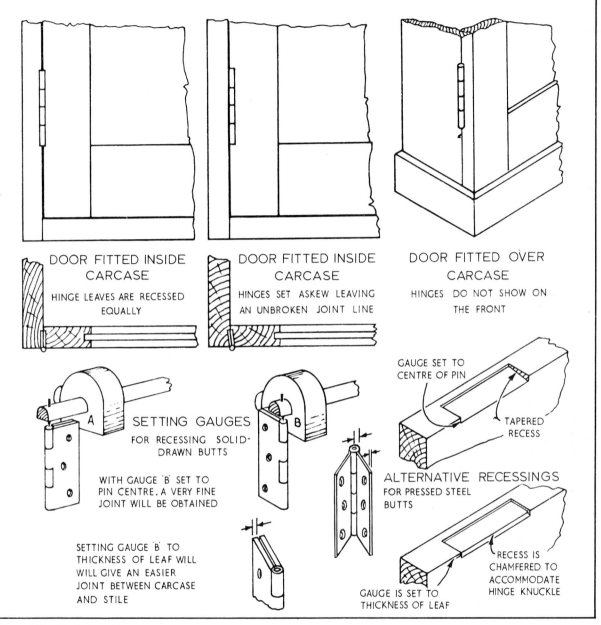

DOOR FITTED INSIDE CARCASE

HINGE LEAVES ARE RECESSED EQUALLY

DOOR FITTED INSIDE CARCASE

HINGES SET ASKEW LEAVING AN UNBROKEN JOINT LINE

DOOR FITTED OVER CARCASE

HINGES DO NOT SHOW ON THE FRONT

SETTING GAUGES

FOR RECESSING SOLID-DRAWN BUTTS

WITH GAUGE 'B' SET TO PIN CENTRE. A VERY FINE JOINT WILL BE OBTAINED

SETTING GAUGE 'B' TO THICKNESS OF LEAF WILL WILL GIVE AN EASIER JOINT BETWEEN CARCASE AND STILE

GAUGE SET TO CENTRE OF PIN

TAPERED RECESS

ALTERNATIVE RECESSINGS

FOR PRESSED STEEL BUTTS

GAUGE IS SET TO THICKNESS OF LEAF

RECESS IS CHAMFERED TO ACCOMMODATE HINGE KNUCKLE

Figure 156   The fitting of hinges

When ordering material from the timber merchant it is important to state that the sizes are 'finished sizes' for prepared timber, or 'sawn sizes' for unplaned timber.

A sample cutting list is given for a small two-panelled cupboard door, 1000 mm in height and 750 mm wide with a muntin and plywood panels.

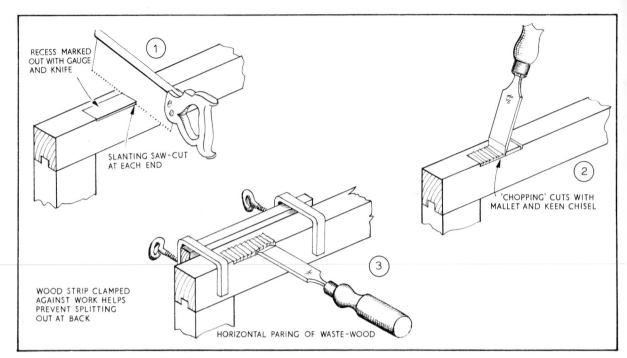

Figure 157   Recessing a door stile for hinges

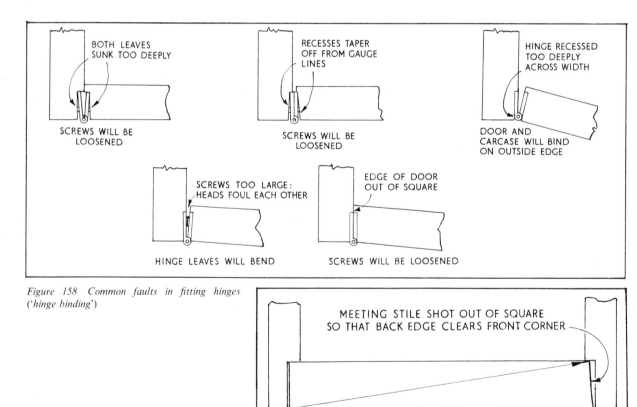

Figure 158   Common faults in fitting hinges ('hinge binding')

Figure 159   Fitting of narrow or thick doors

CUTTING LIST

Job No: _37_   *Cupboard door . 1 off Y. Deal Painted*

ITEM	No. off	Finished Sizes			Sawn Sizes		
		L	W	T	L	W	T
Stiles	2	1000 mm	71 mm	21 mm	1020 mm	75 mm	25 mm
muntin	1	945 "	62 "	21 "	945 "	66 "	25 "
Top Rail	1	750 "	62 "	21 "	770 "	66 "	25 "
B. Rail	1	750 "	71 "	21 "	770 "	75 "	25 "
Panel	2	872 "	290 "	9 "	—	—	—

Questions

(1) Show by sketches the joints you would use for:
(a) the corners of a small box,
(b) a foot stool,
(c) a fixed shelf in a bookcase.
Give reasons for choosing the joints you have sketched.

(L)

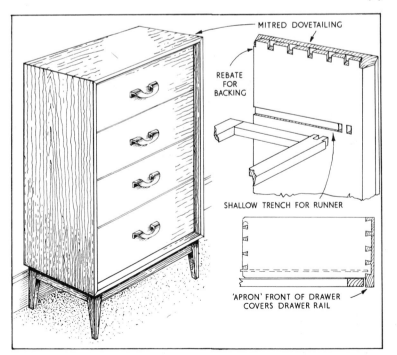

Figure 160   Chest

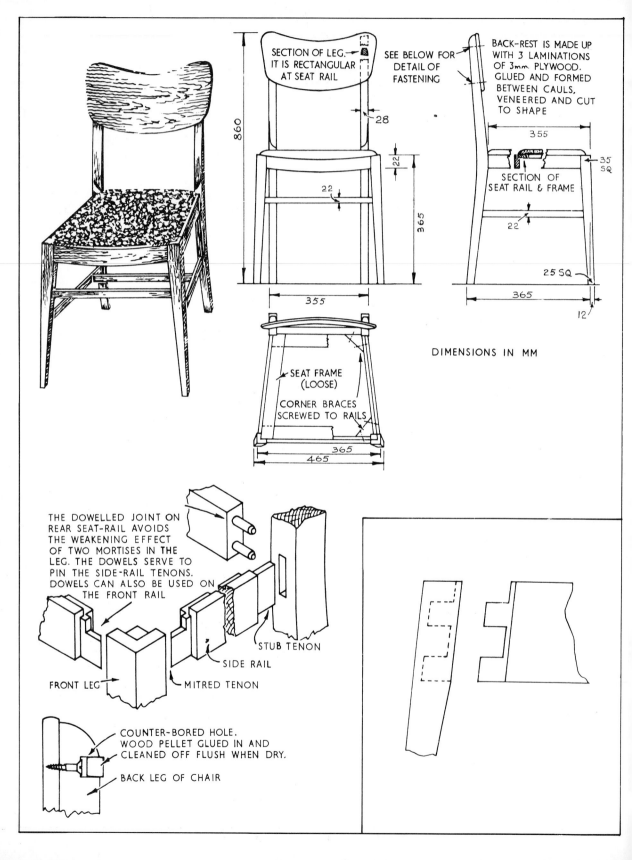

SECTION OF LEG.
IT IS RECTANGULAR
AT SEAT RAIL

SEE BELOW FOR
DETAIL OF
FASTENING

BACK-REST IS MADE UP
WITH 3 LAMINATIONS
OF 3mm. PLYWOOD.
GLUED AND FORMED
BETWEEN CAULS,
VENEERED AND CUT
TO SHAPE

860

28

22

22

365

355

355

SECTION OF
SEAT RAIL & FRAME

35
SQ

22

25 SQ

365

12

SEAT FRAME
(LOOSE)

CORNER BRACES
SCREWED TO RAILS

DIMENSIONS IN MM

365

465

THE DOWELLED JOINT ON
REAR SEAT-RAIL AVOIDS
THE WEAKENING EFFECT
OF TWO MORTISES IN THE
LEG. THE DOWELS SERVE TO
PIN THE SIDE-RAIL TENONS.
DOWELS CAN ALSO BE USED ON
THE FRONT RAIL

STUB TENON

SIDE RAIL

FRONT LEG

MITRED TENON

COUNTER-BORED HOLE.
WOOD PELLET GLUED IN AND
CLEANED OFF FLUSH WHEN DRY.

BACK LEG OF CHAIR

Figure 161 (opposite)   Design and details for dining chair (see also Fig. 176)

Figure 162 (opposite inset)   A wide rail with 'twin' or double tenon in a stool construction

(2) Make neat freehand sketches of three kinds of dovetail joint and give several examples of their application.

(OL)

(3) By means of notes and sketches explain the different methods employed to fix the following into a cabinet door: (a) a wooden panel, (b) plain glass, (c) a mirror.

(JMB)

(4) Sketch three types of woodwork joint where dowels could be used. Explain how to make a 9 mm dowel 100 mm long.

(JMB)

(5) Tabulate the steps in planing a piece of rough sawn timber 250 mm by 50 mm by 22 mm to 250 mm by 45 mm by 15 mm. Make a list of all the tools you would require.

(AEB)

Figure 163   Small table construction

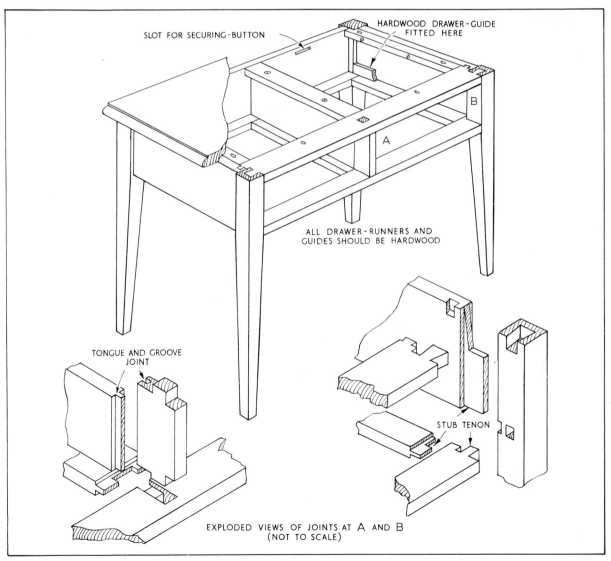

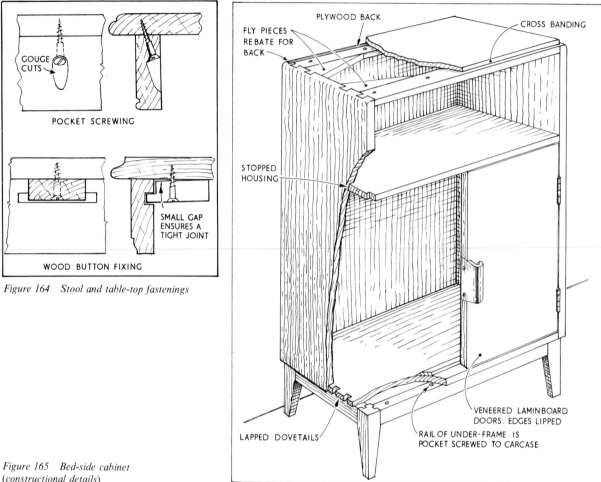

POCKET SCREWING

GOUGE CUTS

WOOD BUTTON FIXING

SMALL GAP ENSURES A TIGHT JOINT

Figure 164   Stool and table-top fastenings

PLYWOOD BACK

CROSS BANDING

FLY PIECES
REBATE FOR
BACK

STOPPED
HOUSING

LAPPED DOVETAILS

VENEERED LAMINBOARD
DOORS. EDGES LIPPED

RAIL OF UNDER-FRAME IS
POCKET SCREWED TO CARCASE

Figure 165   Bed-side cabinet
(constructional details)

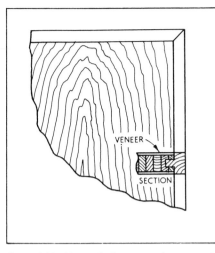

Figure 166 Tongued edging-strip for veneered laminboard door

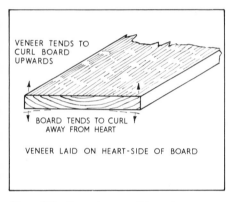

Figure 167 Veneering on solid wood

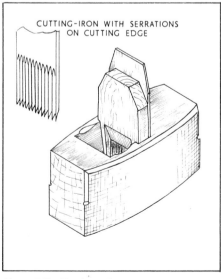

Figure 168 Toothing plane

6

Veneering

Introduction

In veneering, articles made in the common timbers are faced with thin leaves of choice and often rare hardwoods. The practice goes back to antiquity and came to Britain in the seventeenth century.

In the early days veneers had to be sawn and so were quite thick, considerable skill being needed to cut and lay them successfully. Today they may be as thin as 0·25 mm and glued to cloth or paper backings for strength, but generally thicknesses vary between 0·6 and 0·8 mm.

Before the days of 'man-made timbers' veneers were laid on solid wood. In wide panels this created problems, for in drying and shrinking a veneer can quite easily cause a wide board to curl across its width when grains run in the same direction. This problem was overcome to some extent by veneering on the heart side of slash-sawn boards (see Fig. 167), but the results must have been somewhat unpredictable, even for the experienced craftsman. Much veneered work was done on soft pine or Honduras mahogany, wide boards being veneered on both sides for stability.

Surfaces for veneering are known as 'grounds' and today, block-, laminand chipboards have replaced the solid woods for this purpose. Even so, the problem of curling when veneering on one side only must still be considered – large boards for good-quality work being veneered on both sides, usually with a selected facing veneer and one of inferior quality on the back to act as a 'balancer'.

Apart from the fact that pleasing effects can be obtained by the judicious use and combinations of different woods, the use of veneers plays an obvious part in the conservation of rare and costly hardwoods. Some woods are quite unsuitable for use in the solid for constructional work and can be used only as veneers, one example being the burrs (see p. 67) in which the grain formation is very wild and often quite beautiful in colour and texture. The cutting of veneers is shown in Fig. 110.

In industrial veneering for cabinet and furniture making, presses of various kinds are used to hold veneers during glue setting, shaped work often being dealt with by the inflation of flexible bags which mould themselves to the curvatures of the grounds. Where liquid glue is used, spreading is usually done mechanically, rollers picking up and quickly spreading the correct amount of adhesive over the work.

In these and many other ways, manufacturers have made the business of veneering into a 'fine art' and whilst such technology cannot readily be used in the small workshop, it is still possible to undertake many interesting projects without the use of a press. Veneers are simply laid 'by hand', using the veneer hammer or a small roller to lay the veneer and to squeeze out surplus glue.

The limitations in the small workshop will be found in the size of leaves which can be laid and in the kinds of wood in the veneer, some of which show prominent rippling whilst others are of necessity cut thicker, both kinds usually needing a press.

Hints on veneering

The beginner need find no great difficulty in veneering provided that he makes his early attempts on small articles, the problems of curling being of little consequence in items such as trinket boxes, chess boards and the like. He should avoid laying large veneers until he has gained confidence and experience and is well advised to use only straight-grained woods. Many veneers show a slight curling across the width and these should be laid hollow side down when the edges will be less inclined to lift after gluing. If the work can be held in a press, this problem will not arise.

A few general rules are offered for guidance:

(1) Veneers should not be laid over structural joints, for however well made, they might move at some later date and show through the veneer.

(2) Veneering on the edges of plywood or blockboard and on end grain should be avoided, but if this must be done then the surfaces should first be well sized with glue. The laminations on plywood and blockboard may show through later whilst adhesion on end grain may not be really permanent.

The edge treatment of flush doors in blockboard is best done with hardwood strips, tongued and grooved to the door. The strips are mitred at the corners and cleaned off flush with the face veneer (see Fig. 166).

(3) With regard to the use of balancer veneers on plywood panels, one cannot quote precise widths and thicknesses at which balancers become necessary, but as an approximate guide it may be taken that 9 mm plywood up to about 225 mm wide, will remain flat with only one side veneered. With thinner plywood, widths will of course become proportionately smaller. Balancer veneers should be laid at the same time as the face veneers and with the same grain direction.

(4) Having ensured that surfaces for veneering are quite flat and cleanly finished, one other process must be given some thought. Until recent times, it was always considered important to provide a 'key' in gluing by scoring surfaces with a toothing plane (Fig. 168) or by scraping with a saw. This keying of wood surfaces is now often regarded as a superfluous process and its mention here might be considered as of mere historical interest. However, if keying serves no useful purpose, at least it can cause no harm, always provided that it is done *along* the grain. Any scoring across the grain will leave short, loosened fibres, thus weakening instead of strengthening the bond.

Adhesives

The animal glues (bone and hide or 'Scotch' glues) are not commonly used nowadays and have been largely superseded for general purposes by the modern cold glues or 'adhesives'. Apart from the several good features of these adhesives in matters of strength, durability and range of applications, the fact that they are used cold is of importance in the laying of veneers, enabling work to proceed at a reasonable pace and without taking precautions against the chilling of hot glue in a cool or draughty workshop.

The white PVA glues are probably the most suitable for school use, notable amongst these being the Evostik Resin W woodworkers' glue. These glues are perhaps a little too stiff for spreading over large areas by brushing, but a small roller or plastic spreader with serrated edge can be used effectively to give an even and thin spread of glue.

Laying veneers

Let us assume that we are to veneer a small panel, 450×300 mm, on one side only, with sycamore and a cross banding of walnut, 25 mm wide all round as in Fig. 169.

It will be necessary to use a very sharp, thin knife and a straight-edge to cut and trim the veneers and if the straight-edge is of wood, then care must be taken to hold the knife firmly and in line with the edge, otherwise it may 'nick' into the wood and then ride up over the top and injure one's fingers. It is perhaps safer to use a steel straight-edge, holding it down at the ends with small G cramps.

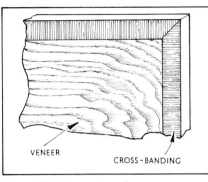

Figure 169   Veneered panel

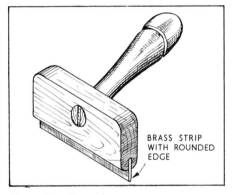

Figure 170   Veneer hammer

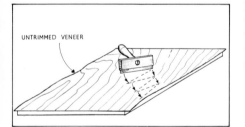

Figure 171   The veneer hammer in use

Figure 172 (left)   Cutting cross bandings

Figure 173 (right)   Trimming waste veneer

Veneers will be found to split easily if cut when bone dry but cutting is much easier if the veneer is moistened on both sides. Moistening on one side only will make it curl and become unmanageable.

(1) With the sycamore veneer cut a little larger than finished sizes, mark its location on the panel.

(2) Spread the PVA glue evenly on the panel using a roller or plastic spreader.

(3) The veneer, which should be quite damp, may show some curling and if so, it should be laid hollow side down, otherwise the edges may lift.

(4) The veneer hammer can be used as in Fig. 171 to press the veneer down and to squeeze out surplus glue towards the edges. A small roller will do this job equally well. A fair pressure will be needed and if the veneer tends to lift in the middle, work with the roller or veneer hammer towards the edges again.

(5) Wipe the surface over with a clean, damp cloth and run the fingers across the surface to feel for any glue pockets or air bubbles which may need squeezing out.

(6) This is not a large area of veneer to lay and if it showed no marked rippling when dry, there is no reason why it should not remain flat whilst drying. If any edges lift, they can be held down with strips of paper glued over them.

(7) Stand the panel aside for the glue to set overnight.

(8) The walnut cross bandings can now be prepared. Damp a piece of veneer large enough to cut all the cross bandings and trim one end cleanly. Then, using a parallel strip of wood 25 mm wide as a gauge from this edge, cut enough bandings to go right round with 50 mm or so to spare. Put these aside for the time being.

(9) Returning to the panel, the sycamore veneer can be trimmed to size. The straight-edge is positioned using the 25 mm strip as a gauge from the edge. It is best to trim the two ends first so that any splitting at the edges of the veneer can be included in the waste when trimming the sides to width.

The straight-edge should be held firmly in place with two small G cramps. Do not try to cut through the veneer in one cut, make several light cuts and with the straight-edge still in place, waste veneer can be lifted away, paring with a sharp chisel, bevel downwards. The sides can be trimmed in the same way.

(10) The cross bandings can now be laid. Starting at a corner, glue the panel and press down a strip of walnut banding, damping the top at the same time to prevent it from curling upwards. The banding must be pressed firmly but remembering that it will split if the veneer hammer is used too heavily along the length. A small roller is probably more suitable for this job. The next strip of banding is laid at once, overlapping the first by 5 or 6 mm. With a short straight-edge held across the overlap, both strips are cut through as in Fig. 174.

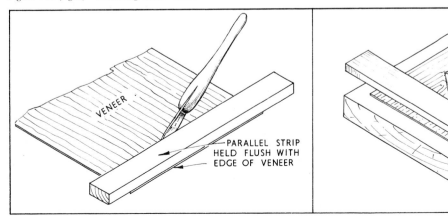

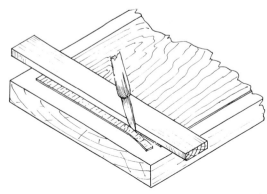

Discard the top piece of waste, lift the end of the other strip, extract the trapped piece of waste and press the banding back into place. A strip of paper glued over the joint will hold the ends together whilst the glue sets.

(11) When the whole length is laid, both ends can be mitred at 45° with the knife and the next banding can be started at the mitre, working along as before and gluing strips of paper over each joint as it is made. Avoid using too much moisture on the bandings as shrinkage on drying may pull joints open.

Wipe away surplus glue and stand the panel aside for 24 hours before scraping and finishing with fine glasspaper.

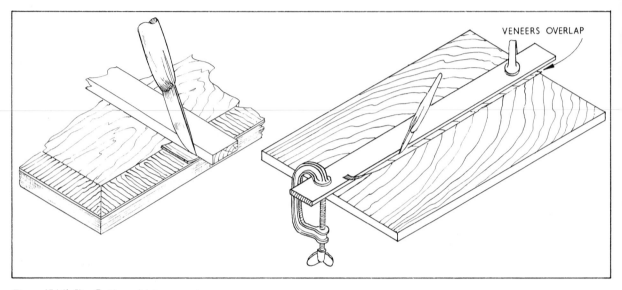

Figure 174 (*left*)   *Cutting a joint on a cross banding*

Figure 175 (*right*)   *Cutting the joint between two matching veneers*

Laying a pair of matched veneers
It often happens that two or more leaves must be used to cover wide panels or perhaps a pair of matching veneers are to be laid side by side. The leaves must be wide enough to allow a small overlap at each joint and with one veneer laid as previously described, its 'mate' is then laid, overlapping the first by a few mm. Both veneers are then trimmed at the same time as shown in Fig. 175, the underneath strip of waste being lifted out after raising the other veneer edge. The joint is then covered with a strip of paper glued in place.

Veneering curved work
Although it is possible to lay mild, straight-grained veneers on gentle sweeps (curves) simply by hammering, it is usually advisable to use a caul to hold the veneer in close contact while the glue sets. A caul may simply be a piece of wood shaped to the curve, or perhaps some kind of built-up structure for large surfaces. Sometimes a caul is needed when laying wild, strong-grained veneers on flat surfaces. In all cases, arrangements must be made to apply some pressure on the work by means of cramps.

It should be mentioned in passing that cauls are not generally used in industrial practice, veneer being formed over a curved surface by the inflation of a strong, flexible bag within a closed chamber. As the flexible container inflates, it follows the contour of the ground, exerting an even pressure over the whole surface.

In Fig. 176 is shown the kind of mould and caul which were used in making the curved chair back-rests seen in Fig. 161. The plywood laminations in the caul will retain the curve of the mould once the glue has set. Glue is best applied with a roller to ensure an even spread and for speed, since even a cold glue

Figure 176 Forming curved back for chair illustrated in Fig. 161. (A small geometric error will result from forming the caul directly on the mould as shown, but will be of little consequence on such a flat curve.)

may become tacky if too much time is taken in spreading. It is not at all important to glue the veneers at the same time as the plywood laminations – they can be laid later by the same method if one feels there are too many surfaces to glue in one operation.

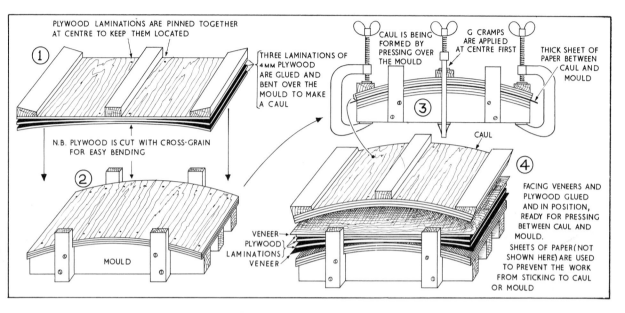

Laying quartered veneers

Figures 177 a and b show two quartered panels which are especially attractive if made up with fairly straight-grained veneers. Matching veneers can be made up as shown at c.

In preparation the panel is marked out in quarters and then veneer No. 1 is laid with a small overlap on the two mating edges. Veneer No. 2 is laid next overlapping No. 1 and the joint is cut in the manner already described, the cut being made with the grain, i.e. from the centre outwards to avoid splitting off the short-grained corners. Both veneers are now trimmed right across the panel at the centre line, then No. 3 veneer is trimmed and fitted up to No. 2, and is laid overlapping the centre line. No. 4 veneer is next trimmed and fitted up to No. 1 and is laid overlapping No. 3, after which the joint is cut in the usual way and in line with that already cut at the top, veneer trimmings are removed, surplus glue wiped away and all joints covered with paper strips.

Blisters   Sometimes small air bubbles are trapped under a veneer when it is laid, forming blisters. If the veneer is of any size it is well nigh impossible to work them out towards the edge. Any that form must be dealt with at once by slitting the veneer cleanly with a sharp knife, a little thin glue is worked underneath, and the veneer pressed down again.

Inlaying

This is the art of shaping thin pieces of any suitable material and inserting them into corresponding recesses cut into a solid wood background. The art is as old as mankind and throughout the ages all sorts of materials have been used, including all the common and valuable materials, ivory, mother-of-pearl, enamels and many different kinds of wood.

Although the craft has been practised universally, some of the finest examples are of oriental origin, both the Japanese and the Chinese being masters of the craft.

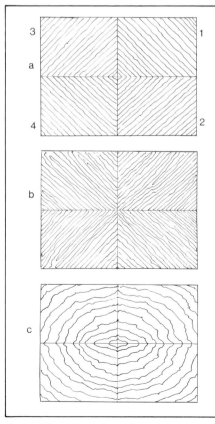

Figure 177   Quartered panels

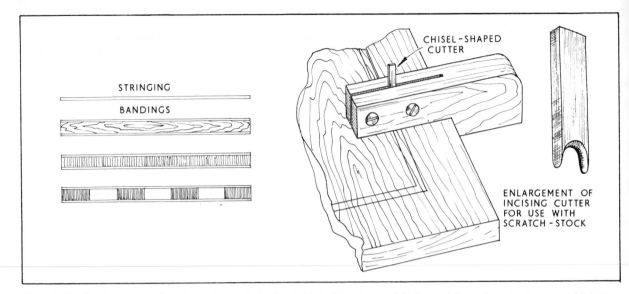

Figure 178 (left)   Decorations for inlaying

Figure 179 (right)   Inlaying a banding

Intarsia   This is the name – of Italian origin – given to the type of inlaying in which designs are sawn or cut from different woods and inlaid into solid wood backgrounds. The inlay is cut from veneer or much thicker wood and its contour traced on to the background. The waste in the recess is then cut away, the edges being very neatly cut with chisels and gouges. The inlay is glued and pressed home in a vice or tapped down with a softwood block and mallet.

Where several pieces of inlay form one part of a design they are glued to a paper backing, marked out and inserted in one piece.

Marquetry   The French were at one time great exponents of the art of inlaying, decorating their cabinet work with the most exquisite floral designs, and to Pierre Boulle is accredited the 'invention' of marquetry work which is really a development of intarsia. Marquetry is not inlaying in the proper sense as a complete design is built up piece by piece to cover the entire background. Vari-coloured veneers are used for this work which is becoming increasingly popular today, being used frequently as a mural decoration in the form of large panels, whilst the amateur practises at home on the table making small pictures. He cuts his veneers with fine knives and uses tube glue or cement.

The professional marquetry worker uses a very fine saw held in a frame and cuts several veneers at once, the insert and its corresponding recess being cut at the same time.

The word 'marquetry' should not be confused with 'parquetry' which is the name given to inlaying in geometrical patterns most commonly seen in wood-block floors.

Figure 180 a   Examples of veneered panels

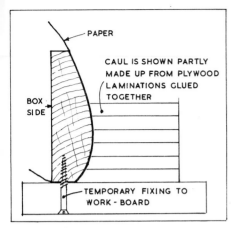

Figure 180 b   Veneering the box side (see photograph below)

Figure 180 c   Casket veneered in amboyna and ripple-cut ash with ebony feet and edgings. Ripple-cut veneer is slightly corrugated and can only be laid with cauls (Photograph: Colin D. Marshall)

Stringings and bandings

These are ornamental strips bought ready-made in many different woods and in a great range of sizes, a few of which are illustrated in Fig. 178. Stringings are plain strips of wood, the smallest about 1 mm square and commonly made from ebony (black), box (creamy white) and rosewood (red-brown). Bandings are composite strips made up from two or more contrasting woods and obtainable in an almost infinite variety of patterns. They are made by sawing strips from the edges of slabs made up of strips of coloured woods sandwiched between veneers.

These strips can be used by inlaying them either on solid or veneered surfaces. If used in a veneered surface they can be included as veneering proceeds, but otherwise they are inlaid after the surface has been finished. This form of decoration is not used very much nowadays, the tendency being to rely more on the arrangement and the quality of plain veneers.

7

Finishes

Paints

Oil paints consist of a base, often of lead, zinc or iron oxide, together with a pigment to colour the paint and these are mixed in with linseed oil which acts as a binder. Turpentine is used in thinning the paint to a workable consistency and on exposure to the atmosphere the linseed oil oxidises and hardens, forming a tough, glossy and weather-resistant coating. Oxidation of the linseed oil is accelerated by the addition of certain metallic oxides which are known as 'driers'. A mixture of red and white lead oxides is used in the well-known pink primer used in the priming of bare wood, for which purpose, aluminium primer is also used.

Although oil paints are still used to some extent, the synthetic resins have made available a wide range of flat, egg shell and gloss paints and varnishes which are in general use today. The advantages which they offer are: ease of application, good opacity (obliterating power), good durability, good weather resistance and quick-drying properties.

Preparation of surfaces for painting

All nails must be punched below the surface and the work is then cleaned off with the smoothing plane, finishing with M2 glass paper folded over a cork block. Working diagonally to the grain in both directions, any plane stops are removed and the scoring of the wood provides a good 'key' for the paint. After dusting down, all knots are coated with 'knotting' (shellac in naphtha) to prevent resins from weeping through the paint and this is followed by a coat of primer, used fairly thin and worked well into all nail holes and any other surface defects. When quite hard, all holes are stopped with linseed oil putty, the primer in the holes preventing absorption of the oil into the wood which would leave only whiting in the holes. After rubbing down with glass paper, an undercoat of an appropriate colour is applied and this should be of a kind recommended by the manufacturer if any of the synthetic paints are being used. When hard, the work is rubbed down again, followed if necessary by a second under-coat which must also be rubbed down before the finishing coat is applied. This rubbing down with glass paper between coats is important if clean, smooth surfaces are to be obtained.

Oiling

Boiled linseed oil is used in preference to the raw oil as it hardens much more rapidly. On small articles, a mellow finish can be obtained by rubbing in a little oil every day or so, but the process is rather protracted.

Stains

The staining of wood prior to varnishing or polishing is not very fashionable today, the trend being for natural colours with clear finishes. Nevertheless, the woodworker should know of the various media employed as fashions change, and in any case it is sometimes necessary to colour parts of jobs where very obvious colour variations may be undesirable. Four kinds of stains are used:

Chemical stains Included among these are: lime water, dilute ammonia (ammonia vapour is used in the fuming of oak), and bichromate of potash which was at one time always used on the mahoganies. The first mentioned are used on oak and walnut.

Water stains Obtainable in a range of colours in powder form for dissolving in hot water. Included are the alkaline dyes, permanganate of potash, vandyke crystals, mahogany lake, raw and burnt sienna.

Spirit stains These are the aniline dyes, soluble in methylated spirit and giving a wide range of very intense colours. Spirit stains dry out very rapidly and have one big advantage over water stains in that they do not raise the grain. This is discussed under the next main heading.

Oil stains The pigments are dissolved in turpentine or other volatile oils (e.g. naphtha) and produce powerful and penetrating stains. As with the spirit stains, these do not raise the grain.

Preparation of surfaces for staining

The utmost care is needed in cleaning off surfaces for staining and polishing or varnishing as poor workmanship simply cannot be hidden. Especial care must be taken at changes of grain direction, e.g. where rails meet stiles, as cross-grain planing may cause tearing which is well nigh irreparable and even though it may appear to have been rectified, such damage will often cause very dark patches to appear when the work is stained. The smoothing plane must be finely sharpened and set and care taken not to leave any stops or ridges which tend to show through the polish, however much rubbing with glass paper might be done.

Surfaces should be tested for flatness as light reflected from a polished surface will not fail to reveal undulations and dubbed-off edges. Glass papering should be done *with* the grain only, although this is not always easy with the softwoods which tend to clog the paper quickly. With the hardwoods, shoulders can be traversed with a cabinet scraper held aslant to the grain and then finished with No. $1\frac{1}{2}$ paper.

If water stain is to be used, then damping-off is advisable, the surfaces being wiped over with a wet cloth. Fibres which have been pressed down will swell and lift, leaving the surface quite rough to the touch. When quite dry, the surface is gently cut down with fine paper until smooth again and on staining, there will be little or no lifting of the grain. Water stains should be applied quite liberally, flushing the liquid over entire surfaces (or the whole job) with a large swab as quickly as possible. The swab is then wrung out and the surplus stain mopped off, beginning at the place where staining commenced. Spirit stains are best applied with a large polishers' mop, working very quickly and taking care not to overlap anywhere in order to avoid dark patches. Oil stains can be applied with a brush or rag.

Varnishes

Varnishes are made from resins dissolved in oils or spirit and they produce a brilliant and durable finish for inside or outside work. Before varnishing bare or stained wood, surfaces should be sized (sealed) with glue-water or a proprietary sealer to prevent complete absorption of the first coat of varnish. Nowadays, the polyurethane varnishes are used extensively and with these it is possible to secure a finish comparable with polished work which, in addition, is very hard and durable.

Wax polishing

Wax polish is made by dissolving shredded beeswax in turpentine or turps substitute. The resultant paste is rubbed firmly into the wood with a fairly coarse rag, the turps dries out leaving a film of wax which is polished with a dry cloth or a stiff brush. Further applications can be made, producing a dull polish which is much favoured. A superior wax finish can be obtained after first French polishing to a full shine. When this is hard, the surface is cut down with a wad of very fine steel wool (grade 000) charged with a matt polishing wax and working evenly over the whole surface. Surplus wax is wiped away and later, the work is burnished with a soft cloth. Polishing wax can be obtained from F.T. Movvell & Co. Ltd., 214 Acton Lane, London NW10 7NH.

French polishing

This is the process of applying a film of shellac, usually on hardwoods, giving a hard surface with a high gloss which is more or less transparent, according to the type of polish used.

French polish is made by dissolving shellac in methylated spirit and is made in a variety of colours ranging from white and clear polishes for fancy veneers or marquetry work, through a range of browns and reds to black. Clear polish can be tinted quite satisfactorily with spirit stain.

The process of polishing can be divided into three stages: (1) staining, (2) filling of the grain, and (3) polishing.

Staining has already been dealt with, and the next consideration is grain filling. When the stain is quite dry, one coat of polish is laid on with a large camel hair mop to act as a sealer for the stain. When dry, the surface is ready for filling in and for this purpose a paste made from powdered whiting, turps and a little gold size is used. It can be purchased ready mixed in various colours or can be coloured at home by mixing in any of the powdered pigments. The paste is rubbed well into the grain with a coarse rag and just before it is dry, any surplus filler is removed with a clean rag. The work is set aside overnight to harden properly. If at all rough, it is then cut down lightly with No. 0 paper and is ready for polishing.

Polishing is done with a rubber which is made up with a centre of unbleached wadding enclosed in a soft linen cover. It is moulded into a pear shape which can be gripped comfortably. When not in use the rubber is kept in an airtight container to prevent it from drying out.

Before commencing work some attention should be given to the conditions under which it is to be done. The room should be warm and draught free as any dampness or cold air currents will cause discoloration of the polish. There should be plenty of light so that the operator can see clearly what he is doing and can judge the progress of his work from the reflections.

The rubber is charged by removing the cover and pouring the polish into the cotton wool, taking care not to overload it. This can be checked by pressing the rubber with the fingers, a little polish should appear at the sides but there should not be sufficient to run out. The cover is first pulled up over the tip of the rubber and then the sides are drawn up and gripped by the fingers taking care not to leave any wrinkles on the rubbing face. Polish is worked into the surface with long strokes along the grain, the rubber being recharged as often as necessary to keep the polish moving on to the surface. This 'fadding in' as it is known, should be kept up until the polish begins to pull on the rubber and the work can then be set aside for some hours to harden off.

After cutting down once more to a smooth surface, the next stage known as 'bodying in' can begin. The rubber is used with a circular motion and a fair pressure, working over the surface evenly and never staying in one spot. At this stage a little linseed oil will be needed to lubricate the rubber and prevent it from sticking, but only the smallest quantity may be used, a few spots on the surface being sufficient. These will be picked up by the rubber and distributed evenly. The rubber can be plied to the work with a circular, elliptical and figure of eight motion, recharging moderately as the rubber works out dry and eventually the entire surface will have received an even body of shellac. A slightly thinner polish is now used for recharging, diluted with a little spirit, and when the surface assumes a fair shine with a rather misty appearance the rubber is worked out dry and the job set aside to harden ready for the finishing stage.

Having been left overnight, the surface is cut down very gently with a piece of used No. 0 paper and work recommences with the slightly thinner polish. The rubber is worked out dry and any oil smears are removed by changing the cover cloth and working with long sweeping strokes.

When the rubber is bone dry the work can be spirited as follows. Three or four spots of spirit are placed in the palm of the hand, just enough to moisten it, and the rubber placed face down on this. The hand is closed and held for a few moments whilst the spirit evaporates, then the rubber, loaded with the vapour, is quickly drawn along the surface from end to end in straight lines until the whole surface is left clear of rubber marks.

The beginner is advised to practise polishing on as many different woods as possible to gain experience. He will find, among other things, that some woods polish more readily than others, woods with very compact grains such as beech and sycamore polishing satisfactorily without resorting to the use of grain filler.

Questions

(1) Explain, in detail, how you would proceed to clean up and:
(a) French polish an oak table, and
(b) paint a whitewood kitchen cabinet.
What are the ingredients in the polish and the paint?

(L)

(2) The appearance of various woods used in furniture making may be changed by means of staining, fumigating, painting, polishing, oiling. In what circumstances would you use these processes either singly or in combination? Give reasons for your choice.

(OL)

8

Materials

Glues and adhesives

In recent times the word 'adhesive' has come more into general use along with 'glue' and although these two terms have much the same meaning, 'adhesive' is perhaps used to describe the widening range of modern, sophisticated materials, but not exclusively since some of these are still described as 'glues'.

Dictionary definitions of glue usually describe what was once known as 'Scotch' glue, an animal glue made from bones and hides. Although it has largely fallen out of use in general woodworking, it is still in demand and supply, usually in the form of small beads and known as 'pearl' glue.

Formerly, all glues were of animal or vegetable origin with one or two mineral glues which are of no concern here. Bone and hide and the fish glues are examples of *animal* glues whilst flour paste, cellulose, dextrin, gum resins and rubber solutions are *vegetable* glues. These are all still in use but many other adhesives, based mainly on the synthetic resins, are now available. Some are used for special purposes and others produce the ultimate in bonding strengths to the point where it is possible to dispense with mechanical fastenings such as screws, bolts and rivets in structural work.

An interesting development of the rubber based adhesives is found in the contact glues – so useful to the woodworker in facing articles with plastic laminates such as Formica. These adhesives are applied to both joint faces and give immediate bonds under moderate pressure, allowing work to continue without delay.

Notable among the high performance adhesives are the epoxy resins which give bonding at least as strong and often stronger than the jointing materials. These will bond almost any materials provided that the joint faces are quite clean and free from grease; and they work equally well on dead-smooth surfaces as on non-porous materials.

(1) Bone and hide glue

Used correctly, this kind of glue gives good, strong joints and is still deemed worthy of mention. It requires some preparation, must be used hot, is not water proof and quickly deteriorates if over heated during melting. These conditions of use have obviously brought it into some disfavour now that cold glues, conveniently packed and ready for instant use, are so readily available.

The glue beads are first soaked in water and then, with water in the outer pot (see Fig. 181), is simmered gently until the glue is melted, not forgetting that boiling will spoil the glue. Consistency is tested by raising a full brush above the pot when the stream of glue should break into droplets at 75 to 100 mm. Water can be added to thin the glue whilst further simmering will evaporate water and make the glue thicker.

This glue will quickly gel on cooling and once this initial setting has taken place, no amount of pressure will squeeze surplus glue from a joint. In a cold or draughty workshop, this means that work must be done rapidly. All kinds of joints must be close fitting, for apart from looking ugly, a thick layer of glue does not make for strong joints.

For good work, the following requirements should be noted: (1) hot glue of the right consistency, (2) close fitting joints, (3) glue which has not turned a dark colour from over heating, and (4) rapid spreading of glue and assembly.

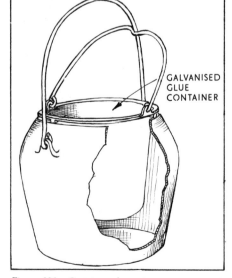

GALVANISED GLUE CONTAINER

Figure 181   Cast iron glue-pot

Except in the case of small rubbed joints (see Chapter 5), joints should be closed under pressure and although this kind of glue is reckoned to have set after 5 or 6 hours at room temperature, it is good practice to leave glued work overnight.

(2) Casein glue

Casein glue is made from the curds obtained after skimmed milk has been allowed to sour. The curd is pressed, dried and ground to a fine powder to which is added an alkaline substance which makes it soluble in cold water, viscous and durable.

The glue is prepared for use by mixing in cold water to a fairly stiff consistency by measuring the quantities and is allowed to stand for a short time, after which it remains fit for use for some hours. Joints made with casein glue are not rubbed and require to remain under pressure until set, the time required varying with the grade of glue used, but wherever possible, joints are left to set overnight.

The casein glues give very strong joints which are resistant to heat and damp, the only objection to them being that the alkaline content causes deep staining of woods with high tannin contents, as for example oak. This type of glue is also suitable for paper, cardboard, linoleum, asbestos, plaster board and certain types of plastics used for table tops.

(3) Synthetic resin glues

(*1*) *Urea-formaldehyde resin*   This is the most commonly used of the UF resin glues, giving joints of high strength and waterproof qualities. The chemical reaction involved in the setting begins when resin and hardener are brought together and this can be done in several ways, the glues being available in two forms, either as 'one-shot' powder or as two-part mixtures.

In the one-shot powder both resin and hardener are ready mixed in powder form, and provided that this mixture is kept quite dry the hardener will remain inactive. When required for use the glue is prepared by mixing with water, converting the powder to a liquid and activating the hardener. With the reaction promoted, the glue then has a limited pot-life and cannot be stored. For this reason only enough for immediate use should be prepared.

In the two-part mixtures, the resin and hardener are supplied separately, the resin being in either powder or liquid form, powdered resin being prepared by mixing with water. In some cases, hardener is mixed with the resin with the consequent limitation on pot life and sometimes the resin is applied to one joint-face and liquid hardener to the other, no reaction taking place until the two are brought together.

(*2*) *Phenol-formaldehyde glues*   The use of this type of glue is really restricted to industrial workshops as the setting temperatures are rather critical and need careful control.

This glue is used in the manufacture of waterproof plywood under high pressure and produces a joint which is quite unbreakable. The glue is completely unaffected by exposure to weathering or even to boiling water.

(*3*) *Resorcinol resin glues*   These glues represent an improvement over the phenol-formaldehyde glues. They posses properties of strength and resistance to weathering, they are water-soluble until 'cured' (set) but are very much less sensitive to temperature variations, this latter point being a big advantage.

These glues are used extensively in boat building, the only objection to them being the high cost.

(4) PVA (Polyvinyl acetate) glues

PVA glues represent the latest development in the woodworking glues and are becoming increasingly popular because no preparation is required and because they are so easy to use.

The glue is supplied ready for use straight from its container. White in colour and non-staining, it has an indefinite store life, is very clean in use and is water-soluble. It is commonly used in the furniture trade and is suitable for handi-craft and for domestic use. It is not a waterproof glue.

Nails

Fig. 182 shows the various types of nail in common use. They are mainly used for simple constructions with butt joints as in the sketch in Fig. 183, which shows how nails should be 'dovetailed'. The smaller oval brads, panel pins and veneer pins are used for securing small mouldings, etc. It should be noted that the long axes of oval and cut nails lie with the grain to avoid splitting. The larger sizes of wire and cut nails are used by carpenters and builders in roof and other constructional work. Oval brads are used largely by joiners for assembly work as they leave comparatively small holes when punched down. The bradawl should be used before driving nails near edges to prevent splitting, the blade always being entered *across* the grain.

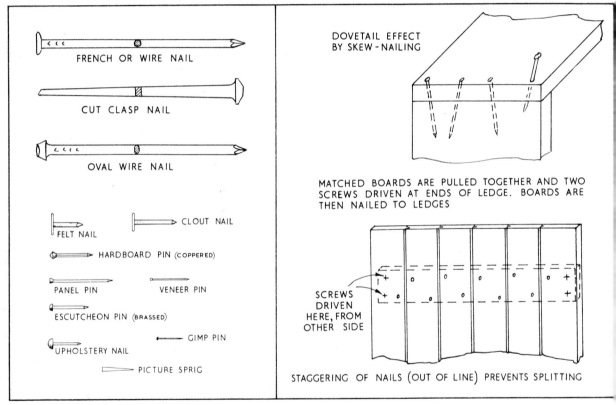

Figure 182 (*left*) *Types of nails*

Figure 183 (*right*) *The use of nails*

Screws

The various types of wood screw used in woodworking are shown in Fig. 184. The countersunk or flat head screw is used where the head is to lie flush or is to be sunk below the surface, whilst the other two types with round and raised heads are used for securing metal fittings or for ornamental work. The round-headed screw is generally supplied ready painted with black Japan as it is frequently used for securing latches and strap hinges on outside work.

Wood screws are usually stocked in steel or brass, but different finishes and metals are available, blued or Japanned steel, nickel and chromium plated

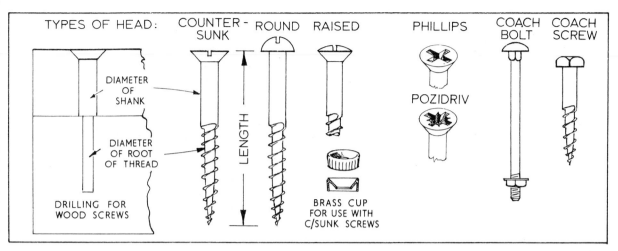

Figure 184   Fastenings

brass in a wide range of sizes. The method of measuring length should be noted from the sketch, the diameters being graded by numbers, from No. 4/0, the smallest made, then No. 3/0, No. 2/0, No. 0, then Nos. 1, 2, 3, and so on, up to No. 32. Lengths vary between 3 mm and 175 mm.

Screws should never be driven without first drilling the correct-sized holes as shown in Fig. 184. This is especially important when working on hard-

Figure 185   Hinges, locks and bolts

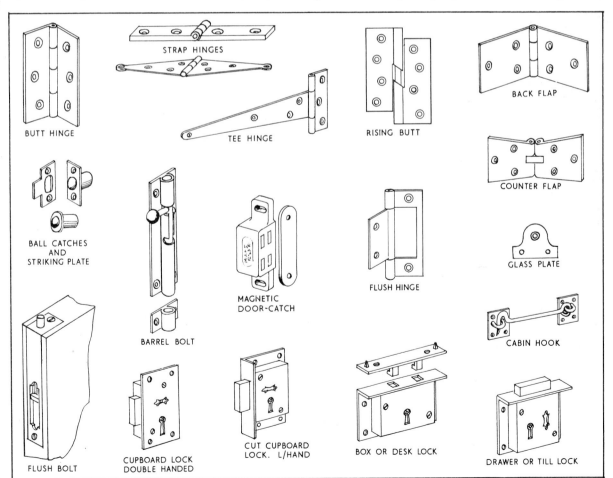

woods, where under-sized holes make heavy work, or when using brass screws which break very easily. Wherever possible, brass screws should be used in oak which quickly corrodes iron or steel, the rusting being even more rapid when exposed to the weather.

Where it is expected that the work will occasionally have to be removed, as in inspection panels, pipe casings and so on in buildings, brass cups are fitted as shown so that the screw heads and drivers shall not damage the face of the work.

Glasspaper

For the finishing of wood by hand or machine the woodworker can choose from a wide range of abrasives. Glasspaper and glass cloth, still in general use, are made from crushed glass coated on to the appropriate backing. The following grades are available:

Very fine	*Fine*	*Medium*	*Coarse*
Flour	2/0, 0, 1	1, F.2, M.2	S.2, 2, 3

Of special interest in hand finishing are the garnet papers, made from the mineral garnet, in a wide range of gradings. The density of the coating is carefully controlled to minimize 'filling in' or clogging, thus giving the paper a longer life.

From the long list of abrasives, reference should be made to flint paper which is suitable for soft resinous woods, Coralum cabinet paper for use on hardwoods, and lastly, silicon carbide waterproof paper for the wet 'sanding' of paint, cellulose or other materials likely to be injurious to the operator.

Glasspaper should always be used folded tightly over a cork block; if used in the fingers there is always a tendency to 'dubb off' the edges and to make slight dips in the flat surfaces.

9

Wood turning

Most look forward eagerly to the time when they can work on the lathe and the realisation of this ambition always gives pleasure, for wood turning is indeed a satisfying craft. Nowadays, the school workshop is considered incomplete without a lathe and with the advent of small power tools, wood turning, albeit in a limited fashion, has become an established home hobby.

There are several tool techniques which need some practice, but with careful instruction and demonstrations, most pupils are able to achieve quite reasonable results in a fairly short time, beginning with modest, but useful articles. It is pleasing to watch the desired form taking shape as the waste wood comes away cleanly and with so little effort and, undeniably, a contributing factor is the feeling of 'having power at one's elbow'; but this was not always so. Before the days of the electric motor and where no other power source was available, the lathe was often operated by means of a foot-motor in which a large fly-wheel was turned with a treadle and connecting rod, a belt drive to a small pulley on the lathe spindle giving the required speed increase. However well such a mechanism was made and maintained, any large turnery job must have entailed much hard work at the treadle.

In ancient times, lathes were crudely made and in the pole lathe, the work was turned by means of a leather belt or cord passed around the work two or three times. One end was attached to a treadle and the other to a springy pole or lath which when bent down over the lathe, pulled the belt tight. On depressing the treadle, the work rotated towards the operator and then backwards as the belt was pulled up again, cutting taking place only on the forward rotation. Pole lathes were in use until quite recent years, mainly by the bodgers of Buckinghamshire who specialised in turning chair legs and spindles from locally-felled and riven (split) timber. Setting up his shed and lathe in the woods, the bodger would lop the branches from a suitable young tree and pull the trunk over to serve as a pole for his lathe.

The modern lathe

In Fig. 186 is seen a modern, motorised lathe, the structural parts of which are iron castings designed to make a robust machine capable of dealing with quite large work. The styling of the machine gives the turner clear access to his work and with a freedom from odd corners and dust traps, cleaning down is not a lengthy chore. The wood-turning lathe is an uncomplicated machine, the main components being: (1) the headstock, (2) the bed, (3) the tailstock, (4) the tool rest body and tool rest, and (5) the power unit.

Headstock and spindle   In the machine illustrated, the headstock is embodied in a large pedestal casting which encloses the motor, all electrical controls and the vee-belt drive to the spindle, stepped pulleys giving a range of speeds, viz. 425, 790, 1330, and 2250 r.p.m. Access doors which must be opened to change the belt from one pair of pulleys to another, are fitted with microswitches which prevent the machine from running or starting whilst either door is open. This is a very desirable feature in lathes for school use. In bench lathes, i.e. with no pedestal casting, the headstock is usually a separate component which is bolted to the bed.

The headstock is a strong casting and the spindle, passing right through, runs in ball- or roller-bearings. Bowls or discs are mounted on face plates

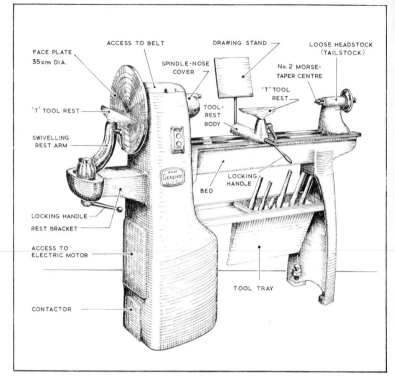

FACE PLATE
35cm DIA.

ACCESS TO BELT

DRAWING STAND

LOOSE HEADSTOCK
(TAILSTOCK)

SPINDLE-NOSE
COVER

No. 2 MORSE-
TAPER CENTRE

'T' TOOL
REST

'T' TOOL REST

TOOL-
REST
BODY

SWIVELLING
REST ARM

LOCKING
HANDLE

BED

LOCKING HANDLE

REST BRACKET

ACCESS TO
ELECTRIC MOTOR

TOOL TRAY

CONTACTOR

Figure 186   A modern wood turning lathe with provision for large bowl turning

screwed to the spindle whilst small items are held in a chuck of one kind or another. In addition to the screw thread for holding chucks and face plates, the spindle nose is taper bored to receive a live centre for driving work which needs supporting at both ends. The lathe spindle is hollow, i.e. in the form of a very stiff tube which not only facilitates the removal of the centre with a bar passed through the bore, but would also permit the holding of any special job on the face plate by means of a draw bolt passed right through the spindle. Long and slender work, e.g. dowel rods, could if necessary be passed through the spindle and gripped in a three-jaw chuck for turning or parting off short lengths.

The live centre (so called because it is the one which does the driving) is usually made with two or four spurs for driving the work, a cone centre in the tailstock supporting the outer end. This method of holding the work is known as 'turning on centres'. The left-hand end of the spindle is threaded to take a face plate for very large work, the thread being left handed so that the plate winds on against the lathe rotation. An adjustable bracket and post are provided for the tool rests. The lathe shown is equipped with domed covers, one for each end of the spindle, and whichever is not in use should have its cover in place to prevent accidents from clothing getting caught and wound in. It is considered dangerous for two people to work together on the same lathe, one at each side of the headstock, one obvious risk being the probability of a misunderstanding about starting the machine.

The bed   This is usually a deep, U-sectioned casting with large ports to allow waste wood to fall through. Top and side faces are machined to provide accurate ways on which tailstock and tool-rest body can slide.

The tailstock   This is used mainly in supporting work on centres but is also used in drilling, with taper-shank drills held in the barrel or with straight-shank drills in a chuck with a taper adaptor. The tailstock can be locked any-where along the bed by means of a cam device which pulls a small steel plate

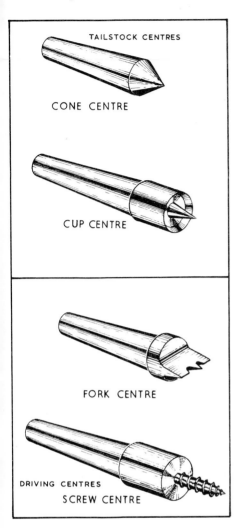

Figure 187   Lathe centres

Figure 188   Wood turning tools

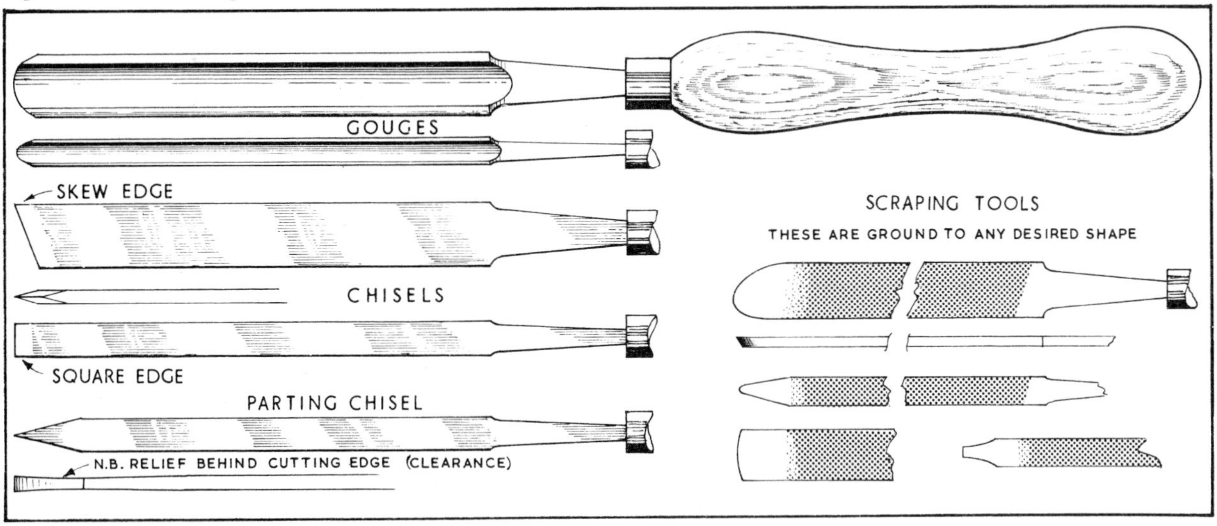

tightly up against the underside of the bed. The centre is adjusted up to the work by means of a hand wheel and screw which moves the barrel in either direction. A locking device is provided so that when adjusted, the tailstock barrel will not slacken off.

Tool-rest body and tool rests   Machined on its under face, the rest body can be slid along the bed, swivelling round for convenience in working and can be locked at any point. The locking device is similar to that in the tailstock. The tool rest is rotated and set for height before locking.

Centres   In turning between centres, the fork centre seen in Fig. 187 is commonly used in driving, four-prong centres being more suitable for heavy jobs. The cone centre, used in the tailstock is for general use whilst the cup centre is more suitable for light work.

Tools   Gouges and chisels of various kinds are used and whilst these are mostly intended for cutting in its true sense, i.e. with a slicing action which removes the waste in the form of shavings, a few shaped tools are used in scraping which results from the tool being held more or less horizontally. Whilst it is possible to produce almost any form by scraping, this method should only be adopted where it is not possible or is very difficult to employ tools in cutting with a slicing action, explained later. Scraping does, of course, provide an easy way of doing things as no particular skill is required, but in many cases it gives unsatisfactory results, especially on softwoods. It is much more satisfying if tools are used correctly in cutting wood. A selection of tools is seen in Fig. 188. These include gouges in various widths and sweeps and chisels bevelled on both faces with square or skew cutting edges. Those tools used in scraping are made with a flat top face, are ground to any required curve and are frequently made from worn flat files. Gouges are used in making roughing cuts, i.e. removing the bulk of the waste, to bring the work to its approximate shape and also in turning hollow contours. Chisels are used in a variety of operations including taking finishing cuts and in turning decorative features.

Gouges and chisels are made in 'standard' sizes and also as 'long and strong' tools for use on heavy work. The standard tools are themselves much longer and stronger than bench chisels and gouges, the extra length enabling the turner to hold them steady against the leverage from the work and to manipulate them with some precision.

Turning between centres

Setting up the work   As a first example let us assume we are to make a roller for the towel rack seen in Fig. 10. A piece of sawn timber, 50 by 50 mm, is cut to length with an allowance of about 40 mm for centring. The centre point at each end is located with diagonals and a small drill hole is made at each centre to help in mounting the work.

There is no great difficulty in turning work of this size straight from the square, but for the beginner it is perhaps wiser to remove the corners, laying the wood in a trough, as in Fig. 189, whilst planing. In preparing work for mounting on a fork centre, a shallow saw cut can be made across the end grain and the centre tapped well home with a mallet before inserting the centre in the headstock. A hammer must not be used for tapping a centre. With the work held against the centre, the tailstock is moved in and locked, then the back centre, lightly oiled, is adjusted up to the work and locked. Some care is needed in making this last adjustment, for although some pressure is needed to hold the work against the live centre, it must not be excessive or the centre will quickly heat up and scorch the wood. The cone will collect a charred deposit and unless this is removed, it will soon heat up again. High speeds will also induce rapid heating of the centre.

With the work set up, the large tee rest is fitted and adjusted to a little above centre height with a gap to the work of about 5 or 6 mm. The work should be turned by hand to check for clearance all round. Locking devices on all adjustable parts of the machine must be checked before starting up and on the question of speed, the guiding principle is that the larger the diameter of the work, the more slowly it should turn and vice versa. For a 50 mm diameter job in softwood, the professional turner would select a high speed, completing the work in an incredibly short time, but the beginner is well advised to stick to moderate speeds in the region of 1000 r.p.m. for a job of this size.

Turning a cylinder   The first roughing cuts are made with a wide gouge and with the left hand on the rest, the fingers lay over the gouge, holding it firmly down on the rest. The right hand is at the end of the handle, holding the gouge at an upward inclination, but before attempting one's first ever cut at the lathe, there is a warning for the uninitiated. The gouge *must* be in contact with the tool rest *before* it touches the work otherwise it will be snatched and put very

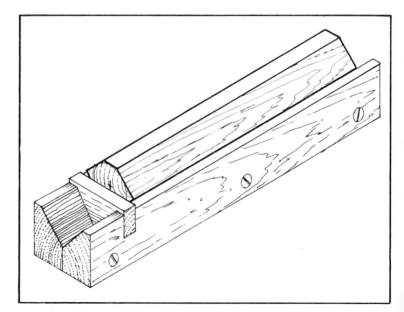

Figure 189   Chamfering square timber in a trough

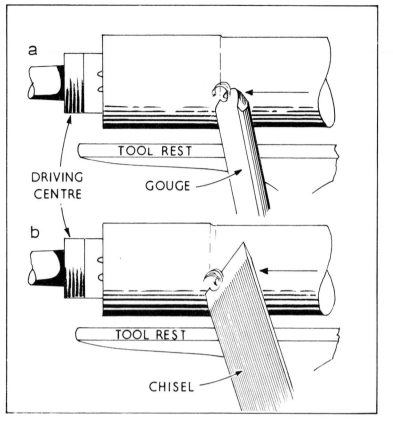

Figure 190 a Turning a cylinder with the gouge
b Taking a finishing cut with a chisel

firmly in its place and although there is no real danger in this, such a happening can be disconcerting, to say the least.

The wood must be brought to a circular form and this is perhaps best done with a succession of light but quite firm approaches with the gouge over the whole length, the lathe being stopped for moving the rest along. This will leave a series of ridges and a rough surface from the coarse scraping action and a slicing cut can now be taken with the gouge turned over sideways as in Fig. 190. It is not easy to start this cut at the very end, but it can be started a little way in, or, alternatively, at the centre and working outwards. The gouge is first presented to the work at such an angle that the bevel rubs the surface without any cutting being done and it is then moved around slowly until, with the bevel still rubbing, the edge begins to cut. The gouge is then traversed slowly along, the hand rubbing along the rest which acts as a guide. This slicing cut will leave a smooth surface but there will be a slight ridge from the gouge shape and a finishing cut can now be taken with the skew chisel.

The diameter should be checked at the ends and middle and any local humps or tapers can be rectified with the gouge. Plenty of wood should be left for the chisel as one is hardly likely to turn a true cylinder at his first attempt and several passes may be needed. The chisel is presented as in Fig. 190, supported on the rest and pressing on the work with the bevel rubbing with no cutting being done. Raising the right hand slowly, a point will be found at which the chisel starts cutting and this angle must be maintained as the tool is traversed along, taking a fine, continuous shaving as it passes over the surface. Any variation of this angle will cause the chisel to run in or out and it must be carefully controlled to produce a true cylinder. Cuts can be taken in either direction and can be started and stopped at any point. Note that

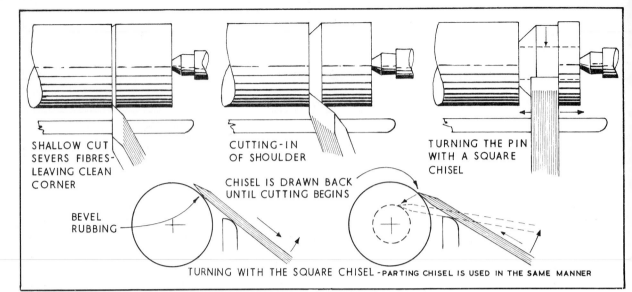

SHALLOW CUT
SEVERS FIBRES-
LEAVING CLEAN
CORNER

CUTTING-IN
OF SHOULDER

TURNING THE PIN
WITH A SQUARE
CHISEL

CHISEL IS DRAWN BACK
UNTIL CUTTING BEGINS

BEVEL
RUBBING

TURNING WITH THE SQUARE CHISEL -PARTING CHISEL IS USED IN THE SAME MANNER

Figure 191   Turning a pin

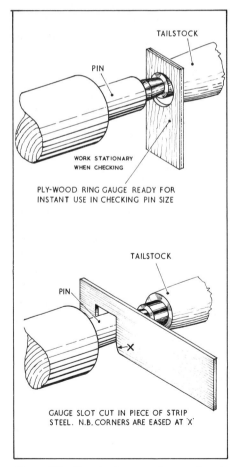

TAILSTOCK

PIN

WORK STATIONARY
WHEN CHECKING

PLY-WOOD RING GAUGE READY FOR
INSTANT USE IN CHECKING PIN SIZE

TAILSTOCK

PIN

X

GAUGE SLOT CUT IN PIECE OF STRIP
STEEL. N.B. CORNERS ARE EASED AT 'X'

*Figure 192   Two simple gauges for use when
turning a number of identical pins*

the point of the chisel does not touch or cut the wood at any time; if it does, it will surely be snatched and will dig in, spoiling the work. Only the middle or the heel should cut and always with the bevel rubbing. Little or no glass-paper should be needed as the chisel produces very clean surfaces when properly handled, but if glasspaper is used, it should be a fine grade and folded over a cork block. The tool rest should be moved away to avoid getting the fingers nipped.

Turning a pin   The steps in turning the pins on the roller are shown in Fig. 191. Since they are required to rotate in a hole, they are made slightly under size, but when pins are used in stools and other constructions, they must be made accurately to be of any use. If a number of identical pins are to be turned, it is quicker to check them for size with some kind of a gauge instead of using callipers each time, one method being to use a strip of metal slotted to the required size to be passed over each pin. Made of mild steel, of a good size and with sharp corners eased off, such a gauge can be used with the work turning when the pin is nearly to size. The gauge will then slide over and leave a small channel, indicating the precise size. Alternatively, a hole can be bored through a strip of 5 mm plywood, using the bit which will bore the holes in the job itself. This gauge can then be slipped over the tailstock centre and left there, being readily available for trying on each pin as it nears the finished size. The lathe should be stopped each time the gauge is used or it will quickly be rubbed over size.

Going back to our roller, note that whilst the right-hand pin is turned right at the end of the work, at the headstock end it must be made within a recess, leaving enough wood to take the drive from the fork centre without splitting. The turning of the beads is shown in Fig. 193 and when both are done, a V cut can be made in each pin, as shown and the ends sawn off at the bench. The pins can, of course, be brought to length by parting.

Parting   Work turned on centres requires extra length for mounting and the final operation involves parting off to length in the lathe unless the nature of the job permits of its being sawn off to length. The parting chisel is used in the same manner as for turning with the square chisel and this is shown in Fig. 191. To ensure a clean corner on the work, a shallow cut can be made with the skew chisel to sever the outer fibres. Where both ends of a job are to be parted, both cuts can be worked along together in the beginning, but the driven end must not be reduced too far in advance of the outer end in

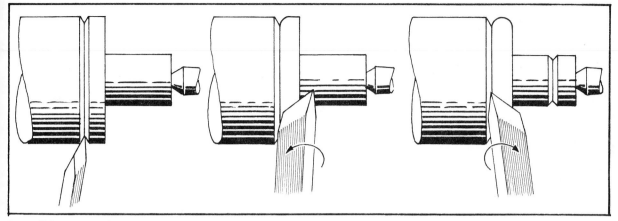

Figure 193   Turning a bead. The 'v' cut in the pin is in preparation for sawing to length

case the torque loading causes it to break unexpectedly. In any case, it is safer for the beginner to leave quite sizeable 'core' portions at the ends, finishing the parting with the saw after taking the work out of the lathe.

The parting chisel will leave rough surfaces because the wood fibres are broken and not cut and if a smooth surface is required, the work must be parted with the skew chisel as shown in Fig. 194. Again, the question of the depth of cut arises and whilst the experienced turner will take the cut almost through, the learner must use discretion, leaving a good portion at the centre for finishing by sawing, paring and glasspapering. The adjustment of the tail-stock centre is important in parting, for too much pressure may crush the fibres endways when their bulk has been reduced. There is not much fear of this happening when a stout core is left, but the adjustment ought to be checked.

Table and chair legs   Whilst it is unlikely that the amateur will go in for turning cabriole legs and other advanced work involving the use of offset centres, one job he is almost sure to come across is the turning of legs with square portions left for the joining of rails and stretchers. The cutting in at the ends of the cylindrical part is done with the skew chisel as in Fig. 194. The squares are sometimes finished with straight ends, but they are more usu-ally rounded as in the drawing. The shoulders are marked in clearly and accu-rately in pencil so that the lines show clearly when the work is turning and without giving a blurred impression. Locating of the centres must be done quite accurately so that the turned portion comes in the middle of each square part and with the work set up in the lathe, the rest is brought in close and the work is turned by hand to check that all four corners clear. Even at low speeds, the four corners will show only as a blurred outline and not only must one be careful in placing his hand on the rest to avoid bruises, but the utmost

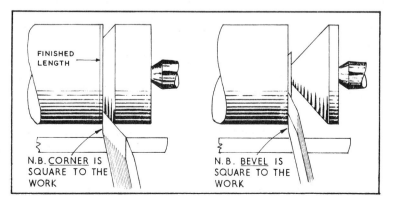

Figure 194   Parting and end facing with the skew chisel

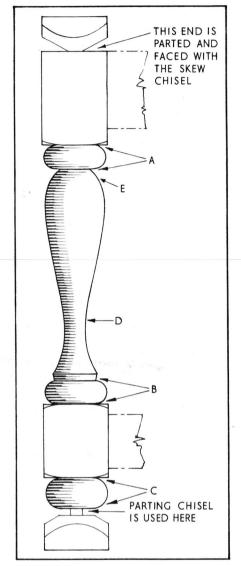

Figure 195   A turning example

THIS END IS
PARTED AND
FACED WITH
THE SKEW
CHISEL

A

E

D

B

C

PARTING CHISEL
IS USED HERE

caution is needed in placing the chisel there. A momentary slip with the chisel will instantly result in all four corners being nicked and, somehow, this sort of thing only ever happens to the square portion and the job is spoiled before it is even started. Note that the chisel is used long point downwards and that it must be really sharp if we want a clean job.

With the shoulders cut in, the cylindrical part is turned with the gouge to the size of the largest diameter in the contour and with a reasonable finish, there is no need to go over this with the chisel. It should be borne in mind that since the squares will need cleaning up afterwards with the smoothing plane, the turned portion should be made a shade smaller than the square so that high parts are not touched by the plane.

The 'traditional' shape in Fig. 195 will serve as an example for looking at some other operations. We can now cut narrow Vs in at A, B and C, but at B, the very short taper or bevel is cut when all else is finished and so the cut should not be so deep here. The large bead at A is turned with the skew chisel, starting at the crest and turning the chisel around until it begins to

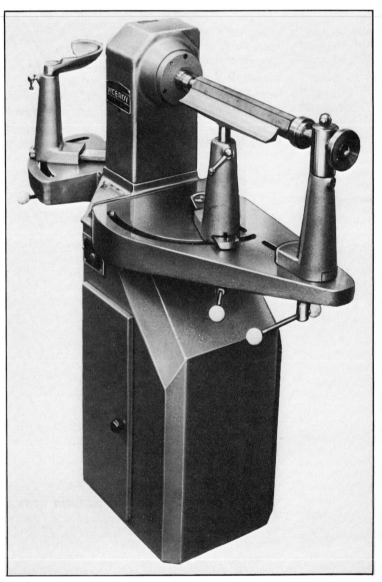

Figure 196   'Viceroy' short bed lathe with l.h. outrigger for bowl turning and r.h. capacity for bowl turning when not working between centres

cut right at the heel (the short corner). Then with a slight sideways movement and a rotation of the chisel, the heel can be made to form the rounded contour, enlarging it to size with several cuts. Both sides of the bead and the bulbous curve at E can be worked along together, using the chisel point to get right into the quirk (corner) against the square. The hollow contour at D can be worked with the round-nose gouge, finishing the long flat curve with a skew chisel. The bead can be cut in at B and the taper cut in with the chisel point. This corner could be made square if desired, but the little taper gives two sharp corners and a clean cut look to the contour. If the taper were turned first, the short grain at the corner would break out when turning the curve. The ball foot is turned in the same manner as the bead. The marking out of four identical legs is done by means of a stick on which distances are clearly marked for transfer to each leg in turn.

Face-plate work

Bowl turning The lathe is readily adapted for bowl turning by screwing face plates on either end of the spindle and with this branch of the craft becoming ever more popular, bowl-turning machines as seen in Fig. 196 are now marketed. Small bowls can be mounted on a screw flange chuck seen in Fig. 201, but it is safer for the beginner to use a face plate with four screws holding the work firmly. The outside is usually turned first and with the top side planed flat, the disc is screwed centrally to the face plate. Naturally, the top will be chosen so that any defects can be turned away or so that any specially attractive grain markings are retained. Before screwing the face plate on to the spindle, both threads should be cleaned and lightly oiled so that they do not jam together.

In bowl turning, low speeds should be employed, not only to avoid vibrating the lathe with unbalanced work before the disc is trued up, but also because for any given r.p.m., the peripheral speed increases in direct proportion with the diameter of the work. To keep the peripheral speed within reasonable limits therefore, we reduce the r.p.m. of the lathe for large diameter work. High speeds are not desirable in bowl turning as there tends to be more rubbing of the cutting edge than cutting and tools dull more rapidly.

The gouges used in bowl turning should not be large and it is important that they are always used with the bevel rubbing. In turning the outside of a bowl, the tee rest will need constant adjustment to the work to avoid too large a gap, but with insides, the curved tool rest is a great help in this respect. A bowl base should be turned slightly hollow so that it stands firmly and if a screw flange chuck is used, the centre of the work should be clearly located with pencil or chisel point to help in centring when the work is turned over. If a sectional drawing has been prepared, there should be no difficulty in checking the curve by eye as it is turned and it will be found easier to check the shape looking at the far side of the bowl as turning proceeds. If there is any doubt, then a cardboard template can be cut out and offered up to the work. A scraper tool will be of use in dealing with any short grain that tears out, or a finely sharpened cabinet scraper can be used with the work stationary. Fine glasspaper can be folded and held in the fingers when finishing or it can be folded over a small cork block which, if cut thin will readily spring to the contour.

It is always better if a bowl can be turned over and hollowed immediately, for the extensive opening up of the wood will eventually result in some movement and if all turning is completed before this happens, it will probably be of little consequence. It is a good thing for the wood to be sealed and this should certainly be done if there is to be any delay before completion. Sealing can be done with one or two generous brush coats of clear or white polish (or a proprietary sealer), put on as soon as work is completed. If the work

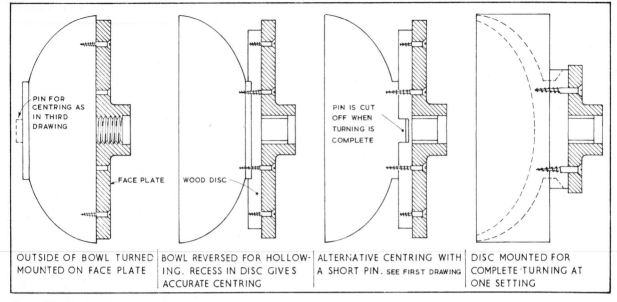

| PIN FOR CENTRING AS IN THIRD DRAWING | | PIN IS CUT OFF WHEN TURNING IS COMPLETE | |
| FACE PLATE | WOOD DISC | PIN IS CUT OFF WHEN TURNING IS COMPLETE | |

OUTSIDE OF BOWL TURNED MOUNTED ON FACE PLATE | BOWL REVERSED FOR HOLLOW-ING. RECESS IN DISC GIVES ACCURATE CENTRING | ALTERNATIVE CENTRING WITH A SHORT PIN. SEE FIRST DRAWING | DISC MOUNTED FOR COMPLETE TURNING AT ONE SETTING

Figure 197   Bowl turning

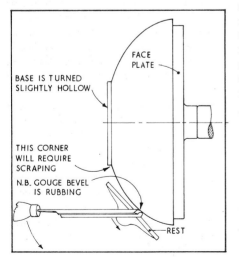

FACE PLATE

BASE IS TURNED SLIGHTLY HOLLOW

THIS CORNER WILL REQUIRE SCRAPING

N.B. GOUGE BEVEL IS RUBBING

REST

Figure 198   Bowl turning

must be stored for a while, it must be put in a cool, dry place and well away from any heat source. Hollowing should not be delayed for long as even a slight deformation can be quite a nuisance when re-centring and it may be necessary to re-turn the outside. When mounting the bowl for hollowing, note should be made of the screw length to avoid striking them and spoiling tool and work. Having worked out the maximum safe depth for hollowing, the depth can be checked at intervals, measuring from a stick laid across the rim.

When turning the insides, scraper tools are often used because it is not so easy to keep the gouge bevel rubbing on the inside curve. Made from flat files, the edges can be ground to any shape with the top surfaces smooth. Any tearing at short grain areas can often be rectified with a very keen scraper tool used lightly, or a shaped cabinet scraper can be used with the work stationary. Heavy glasspapering ought to be avoided on the principle that wood should be cut with tools and in any case, it is unpleasant to work amidst a cloud of fine dust. Scraper tools should be presented horizontally or even pointing downwards slightly, but not too steeply or the tool may catch and become caught between work and tool rest. If inclined upwards, they will readily dig in. Tool over-hang should be kept as small as possible by adjustment of the shaped tool rest when necessary and when glasspapering, the rest should be moved away to avoid accidents. If the glasspaper is held in the fingers, they should be trailed across the surface to avoid getting them burnt if the paper should be snatched away. Small, shaped cork blocks are useful in glasspapering, their corners being well rounded and the faces domed with a rasp or coarse glasspaper. On completion, the inside can be sealed as described and when hard, the surface can be cut down with fine paper in readiness for polishing.

It is not always necessary to make two separate operations for turning the inside and outside of a bowl. Where there is no great over-hang, work can often be mounted on a small face plate with a packing piece to bring it forward and then the whole job can be done at one setting (see Fig. 197).

Although bowl bases are often covered with felt or cork, it may occasionally be desired to avoid the appearance of screw holes in the base of a delicate job such as a shallow dish or a platter. After turning the outside with the work screwed to the face plate, it is glued by its base on to a disc which is screwed to the face plate. To ensure clean separation, a sheet of paper is sandwiched between the glued surfaces, the joint being put under pressure whilst it is drying out. For centring the work, a shallow recess can be turned in the disc to register the base as in Fig. 197, and if only a narrow rim is left around the recess, it can be split off and the work prised away by gently tapping a thin blade into the joint. Alternatively, centring can be effected with a small pin turned on the base, this method also being seen in Fig. 197. Obviously some care is needed with work mounted in this way and only light cuts should be taken if it is not to be pulled from its mounting.

Figure 199   Deep boring

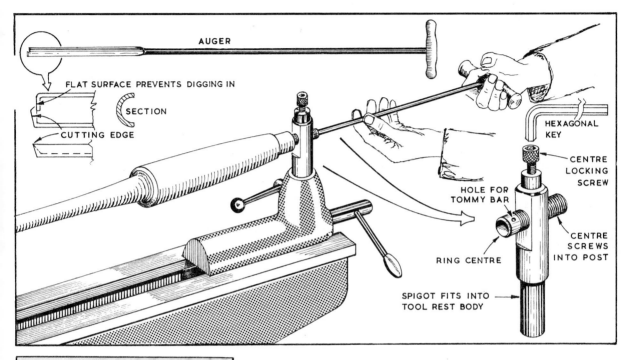

AUGER

FLAT SURFACE PREVENTS DIGGING IN

SECTION

CUTTING EDGE

HEXAGONAL KEY

CENTRE LOCKING SCREW

HOLE FOR TOMMY BAR

RING CENTRE

CENTRE SCREWS INTO POST

SPIGOT FITS INTO TOOL REST BODY

Figure 200   The 'Viceroy' quick release tailstock with hollow revolving centre for deep boring tail stock

Boring holes   One of the most useful of modern innovations is the facility for deep boring which is invaluable in making table and floor lamp standards. Using special augers, holes can be bored through long, slender work with no difficulty. The work is set up on a driving centre and the tailstock is dispensed with, a tubular centre being mounted in the tool rest body. The auger, passing comfortably through the hollow centre, is easily lined up with the work by eye. Where the auger is a snug fit in the hollow centre, this latter component must be correctly aligned before boring commences. The augers cut cleanly and quickly and once on course, do not wander readily. In boring short work, a depth mark should be chalked on the auger to avoid accidentally running the point against the fork centre. The lathe is run at only a moderate speed and the auger should be withdrawn at frequent intervals for clearing.

A useful tailstock and attachment for deep boring is seen in Fig. 200. A revolving back centre is used (it turns with the work) and the auger passes right through the tailstock barrel and the rotating centre.

Short holes can be bored with the work in a chuck and with an auger or twist drill in the tailstock chuck, and if these have taper shanks they can be fitted into the barrel direct. Boring in the ends of finished turning is not easy and this can sometimes be done first of all – in things such as candlesticks, using a brace and bit. If the lathe centre will not reach the bottom of the hole, a wood plug can be fitted and secured temporarily with one or two tiny dabs of glue. Removal of the plug later will present no great problem.

When boring holes, one tends to think only of augers and drills, but it is possible to bore holes using hand tools with the work on a face plate or in a chuck. An initial hole with a bit provides an entry for a scraper chisel which will need sharpening on side and end. If the hole is more than about an inch in depth, the tool will need firm handling to avoid snatching.

Chucks

Several kinds of chucks are used and among these are the self-centring chucks as used in metal trurning. These latter are useful in holding small jobs firmly, but there is an ever-present danger from the protruding jaws and many wood turners fight shy of using them.

The screw flange chuck is useful in holding small work for boring or turning and when the work is mounted end grain on, some care must be taken to ensure that the screw holds firmly. Its holding power can be increased considerably by passing a piece of dowel rod right through the work across the grain, giving the screw something to bite into. As the screw is driven, it will raise a small ridge around the hole and to prevent this from forming and causing the work to wobble, the hole should first be countersunk.

The bell chuck holds work firmly and can be used in turning things like egg cups, pepper pots and so on. A similar chuck can be made from a hardwood block mounted on the face plate, turning the work to a push fit in the hole and securing it with a wood screw driven in from the side.

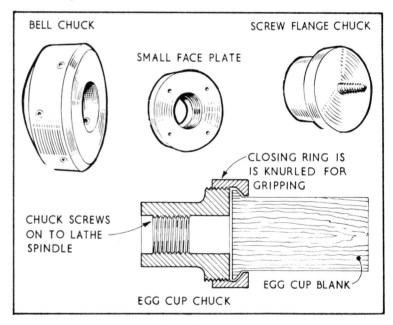

Figure 201   Chucks and face-plate (large face plate shown in Fig. 198)

The egg cup chuck shown in Fig. 201 is most efficient. It holds the work very firmly and the whole job can be done at one setting. The work requires some preparation for chucking, but the time is well spent.

The mandrel This simple device, mounted on centres, of any desired size and with a slight taper over its length is useful in mounting work which has been bored out and requires turning on the outside. Serviette rings, bored out in a chuck, can be slid along the mandrel until friction holds them tight enough for turning. In making salt and pepper pots, the blanks can be bored out and then pushed on to a mandrel (or more correctly, an 'arbor') which is held in a chuck and turned to fit the bore precisely. With his work mounted this way, the turner has clear access all round.

Polishing

Practically all woods need some kind of finishing treatment, not only to keep

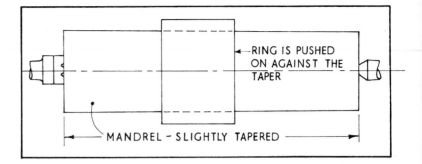

RING IS PUSHED
ON AGAINST THE
TAPER

MANDREL – SLIGHTLY TAPERED

Figure 202   Serviette ring mounted on a mandrel for turning

out dirt and moisture, but also to enhance their natural colours and grain markings. The use of French polish as a sealer has been mentioned and this will form a good base for further treatments. The grain will have become partly filled and further applications can be made, using a polishers' mop (a large soft brush) and smoothing the surface down with fine glasspaper when each coat is hard. The idea is not to build up a thick coating of polish, but simply to fill the grain; when this has been done no more polish should be applied. The only objection to this method is that although the actual working time is short, waiting for the polish to harden each time does tend to spin the job out. Beeswax is quite useful in filling, but if the work is to be finished with polish, then all excess wax must be removed from the surface.

A very nice finish is obtained by French polishing to a full shine, using a rubber and spinning the lathe by hand. When hard, this high polish is gently cut down using a pad of No. 000 steel wool charged with a little white polishing wax. Surplus wax is wiped away and later, the work is burnished with a soft cloth.

Wax polishing can be done without the sealing or bodying in with polish, but beeswax has a sticky feel about it, however sparingly it is applied. Carnauba wax is much harder and takes on a good, lasting shine when burnished with a cloth against the rotating work. Either kind of wax can be applied over a sealer.

Clear varnishes and lacquers can be used, but they give hard, shiny surfaces and are not generally favoured. Stains are not mentioned here as the trend today is for the wood to show its natural colours and markings. Linseed oil is sometimes used to bring out the natural beauty, some of the mahoganies responding well to this treatment. Linseed oil will produce a very mellow and lasting polish, but it takes a long time, a little oil being rubbed in with a cloth every other day or so. The oil oxidizes and hardens on exposure to the atmosphere.

10

The history of design

Many of the syllabuses for examinations in woodwork require the candidates to make a study of the period styles of furniture. This may be regarded as a good trend, for in fulfilling their obligations, the students will acquire a sound and useful background to their craft which might otherwise remain vague and neglected in their preoccupation with the 'smoothness' of the contemporary styles and modern methods of production.

They will find that just as modern styles are influenced by changing woods and living standards, by new materials and techniques – so in bygone years, designers and craftsmen were helped and influenced by the availability of 'new' timbers, improving techniques, better tools and revised living standards. Strong external influences which resulted from people's extended travel abroad also became apparent.

Apart from the historical interest of such studies much will be found that is undeniably very beautiful and craftsmen's estimations of such things soar when they come to a full appreciation of the artistry and skill of the people who set the standards of good taste of their day. Unaided by the fine machines of today, timber was laboriously sawn over the pit, whilst all preparation, shaping and joint constructions were performed by strong and skilful hands. Probably the greatest handicap under which these people worked was that imposed on them by the slow-cutting and inferior sharpening stones of their days. This must have caused much delay and hardship in maintaining keen edges on their tools and is something which is difficult to visualise in retrospect, pampered as we are today with good, standard quality steel cutters and the means to keep them in good working order.

In spite of these difficulties, much of the work of centuries ago was so well designed and so soundly constructed that it is still in a good state of preservation whilst the work of the master craftsman is still highly prized and eagerly sought after by collectors the world over.

English period styles (furniture)

1485–1603	Tudor
1603–1649	Jacobean
1649–1660	Cromwellian
1660–1688	Charles II and James II
1689–1702	William and Mary
1702–1714	Queen Anne
1714–1727	Early Georgian
1745–1779	Chippendale (*Thomas Chippendale, 1718–1779*)
1760–1792	Adam (*Robert Adam, 1728–1792*)
1760–1790	Hepplewhite (*George Hepplewhite, died 1786*)
1790–1810	Sheraton (*Thomas Sheraton, 1751–1806*)

The wood ages in furniture making

Before studying in detail the historical periods of furniture styles, which is the generally accepted method, it should be mentioned briefly that the whole history of styles can be divided into ages according to the woods which were in common use at different times. This is claimed by some to give a more satisfactory picture for there is no doubt that the wood itself, because of its variations of texture and strength and adaptability, has some influence on the degree of refinement, on the general proportions and on the finish of articles made from it. The question of availability of the different woods also influenced the changes of fashion and material.

(1) The age of oak

Oak was in common use for practically all forms of woodwork until towards the end of the 17th century, after which its popularity for furniture making waned. The characteristics of English oak are its toughness and strength, its great durability and the difficulty with which it is worked even when thoroughly seasoned. The grain is of a wide and sometimes awkward nature and this consideration had a marked effect on the carved work which at that time was rather simple and quite rudely finished. Because of the difficulty of hand working oak generally, most of the furniture of the age was characterised by a simple and robust dignity in construction, decoration and overall design.

(2) The age of walnut

With the Restoration of the throne in 1660 and the return of the court from exile there came a demand for new and better furniture styles fashioned in walnut, not only in the solid but in the form of veneered work.

Walnut is a timber of even grain and fine texture and is fairly hard, whilst it works well and takes a fine polish readily. These factors enabled the cabinet makers to execute very finely detailed carved work of graceful proportions and elegance.

The one weakness or defect of walnut is its liability to attack by the woodworm, but apart from this, it has everything to commend it.

(3) The age of mahogany

Although Sir Walter Raleigh discovered, and reported favourably on mahogany in the time of Elizabeth, it was not until after 1733 that the timber was introduced into this country in any quantity – from South America – with the abolition of the import tax. The cabinet makers soon found it to be a wood ideally suited to their work and used it extensively; since then it has never gone out of favour. It was found to have all the qualities of walnut since it can be carved very finely, it can be worked with great precision into the most delicate shapes, it takes a beautiful polish, and in addition it is not given to twisting or excessive shrinkage and is not prone to attacks by the woodworm.

Mahogany furniture at first followed very closely the styles used in walnut but later it was used in much lighter amd more elaborate forms, pierced, carved, turned and in the form of veneers.

Gothic

The history of furniture really begins at about the beginning of the 16th century with the coming of the Renaissance to Britain.

Prior to this, in the Gothic period, domestic furniture was of the simplest form, due to the unsettled conditions and to the general poverty of the country. At the best, a household's furnishings would consist of a bench and table and a chest, made from 'riven' or hewn oak and decorated mainly by painting in bright colours. Of these, the chest was probably the most important item for it served as a receptacle for clothes, valuables and weapons and was used as a seat long before chairs, which only the wealthy could afford, came into common use. Such chairs as were made were reserved for the head of the house or for ceremonial purposes.

Fitted with handles, the chest became a travelling trunk and was frequently pressed into service as a bed. The early methods of construction were crude, planks being held together with iron bands or nails of a sort, but even before the 16th century the mortise and tenon joint was used, secured with pins.

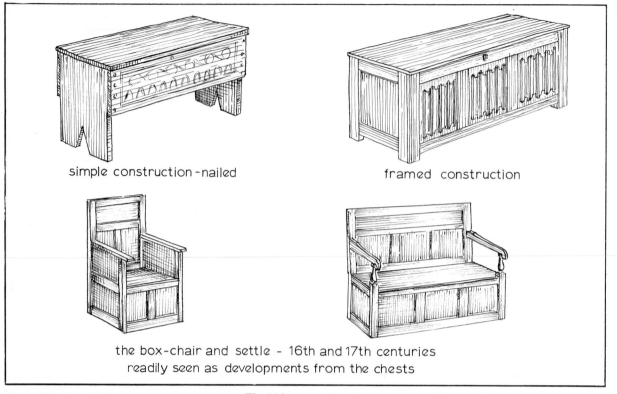

simple construction - nailed

framed construction

the box-chair and settle - 16th and 17th centuries
readily seen as developments from the chests

Figure 203   Early 16th century chests

The 16th century box chair and settle will be readily recognised as developments from the chest, to which were added back-rest and arms. At first quite plainly built, they were later panelled and decorated with the linenfold and other devices.

The chest or coffer of the Middle Ages was also an important item in the furnishing of the churches, many fine examples of which, in the Gothic style, can be found throughout the country. Indeed, most of the finest woodwork of the Gothic period is to be found in the churches and cathedrals of those times, in the form of carved bench ends, stalls, screens, roods, canopies and so on, for the Church has ever been a patron of the arts, and the craftsmen naturally turned to her for their employment. They were influenced by the Gothic style which came to Britain from Western Europe together with many craftsmen – mainly from Holland. Their work reflected this ecclesiastical inspiration until after the beginning of the 16th century when the effects of the Renaissance began to be seen.

The Renaissance
The Renaissance marked the re-awakening of learning and its influence on architecture was shown in the appreciation of the Classical forms, both Roman and Greek. The effects of this 'New Birth' spread from Italy, throughout Europe and, finally, to Britain in its isolation, causing a breakaway from the Gothic tradition which had so long influenced all forms of art and architecture.

From this time onwards, design in all the arts began to show the Classical influence. Although the dates of the Renaissance are given as from 1475 to 1525, and although there were unmistakable signs of the influences at work, it is very difficult to state with any precision the date at which Gothic could be said to have given way to the Tudor style.

Early Tudor, 1485–1558
The early Tudor period marked the transition from the Gothic style when

the Renaissance influence began to become an inspiration to our craftsmen. The furniture of the period included chests, coffers, stools and tables, all of which were of oak, decorated freely with chip carving and simple forms of inlay work. The carving took the form of low relief work or panels depicting portraits, medallions, the Tudor Rose, flowers, foliage, the human figure, birds, fruit and so on, all of which marked a change from the heavy Gothic style with its pointed arches and tracery of earlier times. It was during this period that the linenfold panel was introduced to England. It represents,

Figure 204   A selection of period chairs from 16th to 18th century (can be seen at the Victoria and Albert Museum)

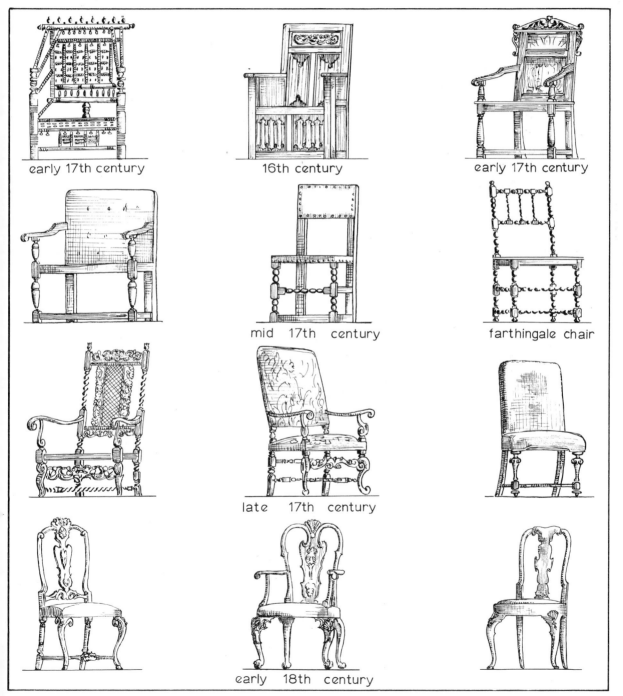

early 17th century   16th century   early 17th century

mid 17th century   farthingale chair

late 17th century

early 18th century

as its name implies, fabric folded over on itself and was carved in various and sometimes elaborate fashions.

Elizabethan, 1558–1603

As time passed, craftsmanship showed marked improvements and designs became more elaborate, special features being the draw-leaf table with large turned legs of bulbous shape and very vigorous carving freely used on practically every available surface.

The court cupboard – a piece of furniture of massive proportions – made its appearance together with the huge four-poster beds in the wealthier houses, still with strongly carved designs which included fluting and reeding. At this time inlays began to be used extensively. They included such woods as holly and bog oak because of colour contrasts – light and dark. The 'cupboard' has now come to mean an enclosed space for storing rather than a table or cup-board.

Jacobean, 1603–1649

As with all changes of period there is a certain amount of overlapping which is inevitable, but the Jacobean period which covered the reigns of James I and Charles I, soon showed a marked quietening of the richly decorated and heavily built furniture of the Elizabethan age. A note of severity was introduced, by the use of geometrical shapes, in panelled work and on drawer fronts in the form of diamond or lozenge shapes. The heavy bulbous turnings gave way to more slender shapes which were produced in much greater variety whilst split turnings were frequently used as planted-on decorations. Much of the embellishment was done by planting on simple frets, diamond-shaped tablets and carvings which gave the effect of high relief work. Punched and decorated leather was used for chairs and upholstery.

The reader will have noted that drawer fronts have been mentioned, for it was during this period that the drawer became a recognised part of furniture design.

Figure 205

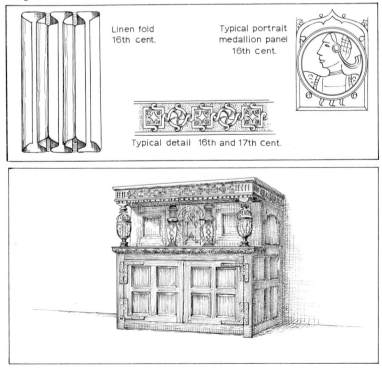

Figure 206 Carved oak court cupboard. Dated 1610 (can be seen at the Victoria and Albert Museum)

Cromwellian (Commonwealth) 1649–1660

This was the Puritan régime and was unmarked by any big changes in the styles except perhaps for further simplification of ornament, with planted mouldings.

In this period are found bureaux made in the manner of a desk, the continued use of leather upholstery on chairs and the free use of turning with twist turning just introduced from the Continent.

Restoration, 1660–1688 (*Charles II and James II*)

The Restoration marked the return of Charles II and his court from exile and with them came the call for new styles of furniture, for they had experienced the more luxurious continental furnishings which were much in advance of English standards. New ideas and techniques had to be absorbed and developed and during this period the continental influences, Dutch, Flemish, French, Italian and Spanish are to be seen.

Although oak was still the main wood used for commonplace articles and in rural districts, walnut was used increasingly both in the solid and in the form of veneers. It was the demand for veneered work which caused the craftsmen to abandon the sturdy oak construction with its pinned mortise and tenon joint and panels in favour of flush and smooth surfaces on which to lay veneers. Glued dovetailing helped largely in this direction.

Towards the end of the period, marquetry work in the Dutch fashion, depicting birds, foliage and flowers in many different woods and materials such as ivory and mother-of-pearl appeared. The burr also was used freqently in veneering.

The gate-leg table in the form in which we know it, made its appearance during this period; upholstery was used much more extensively, whilst richly

Figure 207   Examples of turning. The Flemish scroll

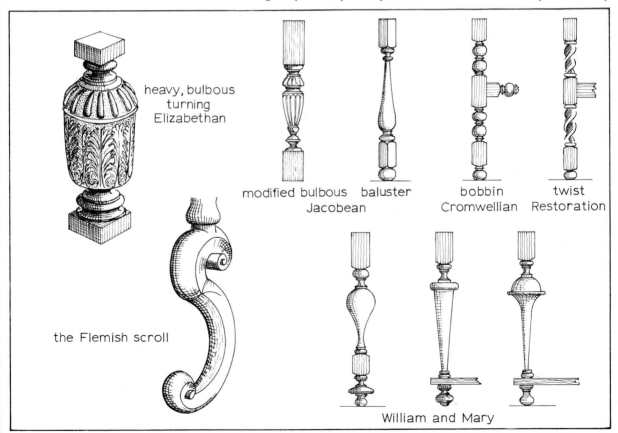

heavy, bulbous turning
Elizabethan

modified bulbous
Jacobean

baluster

bobbin
Cromwellian

twist
Restoration

the Flemish scroll

William and Mary

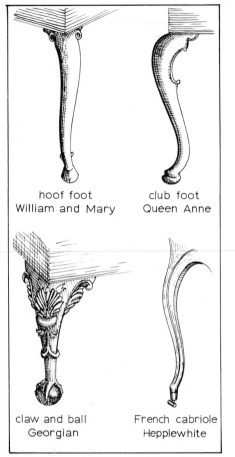

hoof foot
William and Mary

club foot
Queen Anne

claw and ball
Georgian

French cabriole
Hepplewhite

Figure 208   The cabriole leg

carved work was often silvered or gilded. The Dutch influence is seen in high-backed chairs, often with split cane panels and boldly carved. The Flemish scroll in various forms is found in work of late Restoration period.

William and Mary, 1689–1702

During this period there was a great influx of foreign craftsmen into this country and their influence on design is continually observed.

Features of the period include the flat stretcher rails and frames seen on chairs and tables. The frames, sometimes rectangular in form and sometimes crossing diagonally with a halved joint are usually found with a curved or 'serpentine' shaping to the edges. The halved joint in the diagonal frame was always secured with a dowel pin and ornamented with a neatly turned finial.

The Flemish scroll was used in shaping chair legs whilst a typical turned leg of the period had a large 'swell' near the top with a straight or trumpet shaped taper down to the stretcher rail. The 'swell' took various forms, sometimes like an inverted hemisphere, sometimes like an inverted narrow-necked vase and sometimes resembling a flattened ball.

The first cabriole legs appeared towards the end of the century; they were finely finished, resembling an animal's leg with a hoof and were strengthened with stretcher rails. The club foot also appeared at this time.

The high-backed and boldly-carved chair was still very much in evidence and the shaped 'splat' was seen for the first time, late in the period.

New items of furniture included many smaller 'pieces' such as card tables, bureaux and cabinets of all kinds especially those for the display of china associated with the 'new' habit of tea drinking.

All furniture of the period was elaborately decorated by silvering, gilding, staining and later by skilfully executed marquetry work.

It was at this time that Grinling Gibbons produced much of his masterly wood carving, of which plenty is still to be seen, including that in St. Paul's Cathedral for which edifice he designed and executed a large quantity of exquisite work in collaboration with Sir Christopher Wren.

Queen Anne, 1702–1714

This period, in the main, carried on the traditions of the William and Mary style with several marked developments in various directions. Whilst oak was still used for commonplace articles and for rural furnishings, walnut became the most popular timber for any work of quality.

In general the furniture was much more luxuriously designed and finished, especially as regards upholstering which was at times voluminous, hiding most of the woodwork. This craft had become firmly established as a subsidiary trade to that of cabinet making.

Much large furniture is attributed to this period, including tall-boys, chests of drawers raised on underframing, together with bookcases and cabinets which were ornamented with heavy pediments.

The Serpentine underframing typical of William and Mary disappeared whilst chair design showed marked changes in that they became much more graceful in their form. The cabriole leg was developed and became a well-known feature of the period on all kinds of furniture. It was made much fuller at the knee which was at first carved with the 'shell' pattern and later, much more elaborately. The claw and ball foot was most commonly carved on the cabriole leg, being known also as the 'lion's paw' foot. The smooth, fiddle shaped splat was another feature which distinguished the chair of the Queen Anne period, which saw also the introduction of the upholstered easy chair, the sofa and many types of stool.

Although marquetry work was still used, there was a marked tendency to employ plain, matched veneers, particularly on cabinets and drawer fronts, ornamented with cross bandings of veneer.

Although its exact date and place of origin are a little vague, the Windsor chair made its appearance in this period. It is a 'country' chair and has been manufactured in various forms ever since.

Georgian, 1714–1840

The early Georgian period at first showed no very marked changes, weighty pediments and the carved cabriole leg were still in evidence together with many elaborate decorative features such as richly moulded and carved doorways, fireplaces and the use of gilded wood and gesso work. Gesso work is the moulding of raised designs with a mixture of whiting and size on flat wood surfaces and is done with small brushes and moulding tools.

Spanish mahogany had already been imported in small quantities but was very costly and was used only for the very finest furniture.

It was with the abolition in 1733 of the import tax on 'exotic' woods that mahogany came into general use and from 1740 onwards there follows a succession of personalities through whose influence the period is often referred to as the 'Golden Age of Cabinet Making'.

The cabinet maker and the carver in particular immediately appreciated the value of mahogany for their work and with an increasing French influence for lighter and more dainty furniture, changes in style soon became evident.

Thomas Chippendale (1718–1779)

A Yorkshireman and son of a furniture maker, he was a most prolific designer of sometimes comparatively simple but graceful styles and of much distinctive work richly decorated by shaping, piercing, fretting and carving.

He established himself in London where he was soon recognised as a master craftsman and designer. Later, he published his well-known *Gentleman and Cabinet Maker's Directory* containing many fine designs which were freely copied by his contemporaries.

Figure 209   18th century chair backs

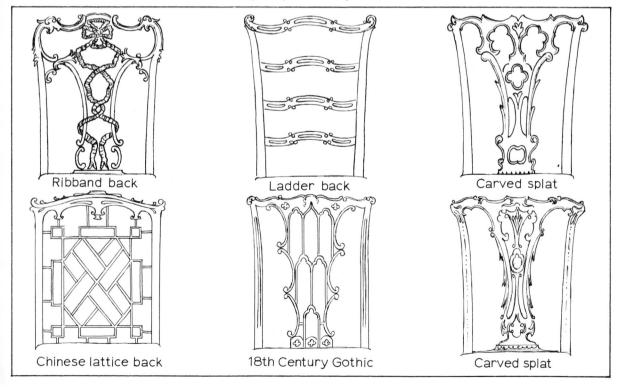

Ribband back   Ladder back   Carved splat

Chinese lattice back   18th Century Gothic   Carved splat

Figure 210   Embellishments

Prominent among the many features of his work are the finely proportioned cabriole leg enriched with knee carving, the claw and ball foot and the scroll foot, together with several very distinctive chair-back treatments. Notable among these chair backs are the 'ladder' back with three horizontal splats slightly curved and pierced, the ribbon or 'riband' back which is a rich pattern of interlacing ribbons, and lastly, a beautifully shaped, pierced and carved vertical splat. Chinese Chippendale is easily recognised, one example being shown in the trellis-backed chair with straight legs and stretcher rails. Chippendale modified the heavy pediments and cornices of the Queen Anne period, lightening them with fret cutting and he frequently introduced a dentil course.

Figure 211   Two armchairs in the Hepplewhite style (can be seen at the Victoria and Albert Museum)

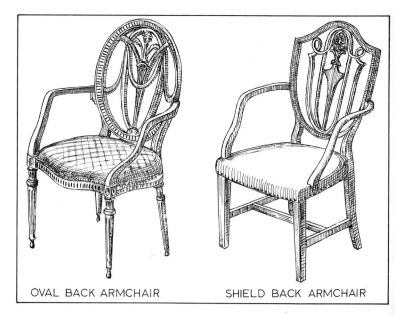

OVAL BACK ARMCHAIR   SHIELD BACK ARMCHAIR

Robert Adam (1760–1792)

Robert Adam was an exponent of the Classical style in both architecture and interior furnishings. He was the son of a Scottish architect and acquired his knowledge of the style with which he is always associated during his travels in Italy. Many buildings together with the interiors and the furniture which Adam frequently designed to ensure complete harmony are to be seen today, fireplaces and porticos being items for which he is perhaps most commonly known.

Details frequently used in the Adam style included rams' heads, 'swags', festoons and drapery, cupids and caryatids. Adam was a designer – not a craftsman.

Hepplewhite (1760–1790)

The work of George Hepplewhite is outstanding for its delicacy and charm which was achieved, not with the usual luxuriant flourish of the Georgian style, but with purely graceful form and contour. Two innovations for which he is known are the oval and the shield back chairs whilst his work is notable for the restrained use of carved embellishment which would have been quite superfluous to his finely balanced designs.

He abandoned the cabriole leg, for it would have been quite out of keeping with his style, and adopted various types of shaped, square-turned and tapered legs.

Sheraton (1790–1806))

The work of Thomas Sheraton bears some semblance to the style of Hepplewhite in its lightness and originality. A profusion of attractive chair designs justly earned him some distinction and, like Hepplewhite, he abandoned the cabriole leg. His chair backs were generally rectangular in shape and in many cases were fitted with shaped vertical splats between top rail and an extra rail just above the seat level. Chair arms were made to form a graceful and continuous sweep, springing from the back of the chair.

Sheraton used a variety of timbers, including satinwood, tulipwood, rosewood and mahogany, together with much delicate marquetry work, whilst carving and other ornamentations were reduced to a minimum for he abhorred the indiscriminate use of such embellishments.

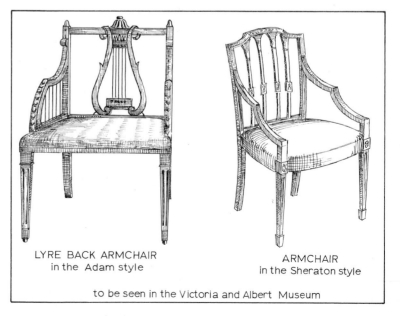

LYRE BACK ARMCHAIR
in the Adam style

ARMCHAIR
in the Sheraton style

to be seen in the Victoria and Albert Museum

Figure 212   Armchairs

In these and in other respects his work represented a very different school from that of Chippendale whom he regarded as being quite outmoded.

It is sad to record that, in spite of his great talent, Sheraton spent much of his life in a state of poverty and that at one time his work fell very much short of his usual high standard when he succumbed to the demands of popular appeal.

19th century styles

(1) Regency, 1800–1820

The end of the 'golden age' was marked by a deterioration in the styles of furniture, beginning with the Regency period which is generally regarded as covering the first twenty years of the century.

This period was represented by a medley of styles in which the designers modelled their work on that of Roman, Greek and Egyptian origin with a flavouring of Gothic and Chinese influence to complete the mixture. The chairs of this time are noted for the continued use of japanned finishes, for their brass inlays, legs and arms carved in the forms of animals' heads and legs and winged female figures, all of which had a very superficial appeal as novelties.

(2) Victorian, 1840–1900

This is the period noted for its ugliness and its general air of confusion. One cannot rightly refer to the Victorian 'style' for in the feverish search for fresh novelties and decorations the whole period up to the end of the century became a hotch-potch of jumbled up Gothic, Empire, Japanese and Chinese influences.

Heavily upholstered furniture, bamboo whatnots, highly decorated overmantels, occasional tables, circular pedestal tables, upright pianos, screens and hideous china ornaments are but a few of the articles which crammed the Victorian drawing room.

This debasement of the standards of taste was in large measure due to the advent of machinery – particularly in the woodworking trades – with the consequent mass production of solidly constructed, but ill-designed articles.

The days of the craftsman-designer seemed to have passed until in about 1860, William Morris began his movement to restore some semblance of sanity and individuality to what remained of the contemporary standards of design. He threw himself wholeheartedly into the unequal struggle against the commercialisation of the crafts, becoming a master craftsman, designing and making tapestries, weaving and printing and working in wood and metal. With his followers, and through his writings, he fought to regain some respect and to restore some pride in hand craftsmanship.

There is no doubt that his work and his inspiration re-awakened an interest in the best traditions of English design and, although he could have done little about it at the time, there is also little doubt that his efforts would have borne better fruit much sooner had he forsaken his idealism and made an ally of the machine instead of trying to fight against it. His struggles in his attempt at craft revival were perhaps a natural reaction to the changes which the beginning of the machine age represented, but they served merely to confuse the issue which we see so clearly, now that the alliance of art and industry is so nearly complete. The man who was missing from the overall picture of the industrial scene was the man we now call the 'industrial designer'.

Before moving on, mention should be made of Ernest Gimson (1864–1919), a craftsman-designer who was inspired by William Morris and who followed in the same tradition. He had his own workshops, employing metal and wood workers who produced work to his designs which showed a marked tidying up of the nondescript Victorian muddle. Sidney Barnsley was another disciple of Morris and was for a time a partner of Gimson.

Modern trends

Today much is being done to educate people in the appreciation of well designed and soundly constructed articles by means of good advertising, by means of well produced and authoritative periodicals and through exhibitions of those things which represent all that is best and in good taste.

Furniture of the 20th century is typified by a general overall cleanness of outline with strict attention to the function of each piece and an almost complete abstention from the use of small and fussy ornament. The thought behind the designing has resulted in furniture of generally smaller proportions so that it is no longer overbearing in its mass or colour and no longer restricts the sense of freedom of movement in the home.

The use of plate glass is an innovation worthy of mention – the appeal is not only aesthetic for its employment in the form of sliding doors effects a considerable increase in the depths of bookcases and showcases.

It would be difficult to associate any particular design to any one designer for, broadly speaking, their work is along similar lines and always unmistakably recognised as 'twentieth century'.

Questions

(1) Describe some of the chief differences in the furniture of the later Stuart period from that made during Cromwellian times. Give sketches to aid your answer.

(O and C)

(2) Oak, walnut and mahogany in turn became either the best available or the most fashionable timber. Write notes on the influence of timber on design, showing the most important differences between the three periods suggested by these three timbers.

(SU)

(3) Make neat sketches of three types of chair from different periods or styles. Name the period or style and give dates.

or

Give a brief account of English furniture of the period when oak was the principal wood used.

(4) Describe a good piece of modern furniture or craftwork. How does it differ in construction and decoration from its counterpart of a hundred years ago?

(JMB)

11

Design

Having mastered the intricacies of their craft in some measure, students will sooner or later feel urged on to create something new which they themselves designed, and will need to solve a problem which requires careful thought and the consideration of the basic principles of design.

Good craftsmen do not necessarily make good designers, for the ability to create tasteful and satisfying design is not always found combined with high craft ability in the same personality. This, however, should not deter them from making the attempt to produce their own designs, for it is so easy to adopt the 'I don't think I could' attitude, when in fact they may be one of the people with a flair for this sort of work. It must be borne in mind that each of those persons now accepted as experts had to make a beginning at some time, not knowing whether their efforts would meet with any success.

Perhaps in some cases craftsmen's inability to design is due to their talent for self-expression with pencil or brush remaining dormant through incomplete training or because they have been content to follow the examples and designs of others. Whether they are able to design or not, they can at least learn to appreciate and assess the aesthetic values of well designed articles around them. By becoming thus enlightened and by their influence on others, they will help to reject what is vulgar and shoddy.

Of one thing we can be quite certain, if craftsmen are going to design, they must first learn to draw free-hand, for designs do not begin with tee-square and drawing instruments, they begin with ideas nurtured on experience and on observation and they are best developed by translating the mental picture thus formed into free-hand sketches made with soft pencil. In other words, some sort of artistic representation of the article is required so that it may be seen in relation to its surroundings, or as it might appear to someone entering the room perhaps, or from some other point of vantage.

The basic principles of design

The basic principles of design fall into distinct groupings:
(1) Function or fitness for purpose.
(2) Form and proportion in satisfying harmony.
(3) Sound construction.
(4) Materials and embellishments.
Each element of design is discussed further with the exception of (3) which is dealt with elsewhere.

Function

This aspect of design must always be given first consideration, the designer questioning whether the article will do the job for which it is intended, whether it could be made to render more satisfactory service, whether it will be strong enough for the conditions under which it is to serve and whether it will be generally efficient. Such questions will cause the designer to think about main dimensions such as the height of a dining table or a work bench, or the size and height of a bureau fall or of a chair or stool. All of these must be made to accommodate a normal person comfortably either in the sitting position or standing up at work.

Constructional details must also be decided upon so that unnecessary labour is avoided and so that the minimum amount of material is employed to the best possible effect.

Form

Form or shape, although placed under a separate heading is really an integral part with function and will be considered by the designer at the same time. It is in relating form and function that care must be taken so that the one does not take precedence over the other, not forgetting, of course that with strictly utilitarian items such as work benches, tool cupboards and so on, function is given the prime consideration.

It is in achieving a sound relationship between form and function that the designer's knowledge of the constructional methods and other details is so necessary, together with some knowledge of the physical limitations of the materials themselves.

The designer is aided greatly by the various types of plywood, laminboard and veneers which are to hand, all of which make it possible to plan work much more freely than in the days when the use of solid wood imposed restrictions on the surface areas, making it necessary to break them up into smaller panels, each with its moulded dust traps. In industrial furniture making, the use of preformed plywood panels (shaped panels) gives the designer even greater scope for free planning.

A comparison of the furniture styles of today with those of only a few decades ago reveals some striking changes, the most noticeable of which is the now almost complete absence of mouldings together with the fancy and 'finicky' contouring of any edges which came within reach of the designer. It is easy to recall the highly ornamented overmantels and other furniture of the late Victorian days, to which people clung so passionately in spite of all the dust traps along the edges, on the little shelves, brackets and around the mirrors with which they were adorned.

The code for the contemporary designer could be summed up as the embodiment of efficiency and simplicity of general form with the restrained use of embellishment. These take the form of small 'soft' mouldings and thoughtfully designed handles, large surfaces being relieved by the inlaying of different veneers or by changing the direction of the grains, whilst every opportunity is taken to exhibit the natural beauty of the wood, unstained and with a dull polish.

Proportion

In giving due consideration to function, the designer is first led to give some thought to main dimensions, around these arranging other dimensions of suitable proportions, remembering particularly the general surroundings in which the article is to be used so that it may harmonise by being 'in style' and in good general relationship.

As an example of this let us take a writing table or desk in which a space measuring two feet high by two feet wide by two feet deep might well be considered as ample knee room. Less than this might cause some inconvenience to the user whilst more would be unnecessary. Around these essential dimensions the designer can arrange a dainty writing desk or small bureau for the dwelling room, or can build an imposing desk.

It is very important to consider proportion in relationship to its surroundings and it is equally important to secure an internal harmony among the component parts.

These problems must be solved in the preliminary stages with the aid of sketches which can be altered or discarded until a satisfactory impression is obtained from which sizes can be taken. The designer's eye and sensitivity for the arrangement of mass and form must make the final decisions. In this respect also some thought should be given to colour, for dark woods add considerably to the heaviness of large areas.

Materials and embellishment

Although plywood and laminboard are used very extensively today they have not completely ousted construction in solid wood – for furniture carcasing is frequently made in the solid, often employing neat lap dovetailing in full view as a feature of the design. Where moulded edges are called for, the use of laminboard does not always represent a saving of labour as planted and mitred mouldings will be required. The display of plywood edges was at one time strongly disapproved of, but today multi-plywood with almost invisible lamination joints is frequently used with the edges showing and when nicely finished, the effect is quite pleasing.

The use of mouldings and other embellishments which are stuck on as additions is severely restricted nowadays, most designers limiting themselves to the use of finely proportioned door handles and draw pulls made in different woods or in stainless or laquered metals.

Designing a coffee table

The sketches in Fig. 214 have been made from memory of the designing stages, with the actual table shown in Fig. 213. They have been devised to show how one might develop a train of thought, trying out ideas in a succession of 'thumb-nail' sketches in which proportions and details are modified until we arrive at a form which satisfies aesthetically, at the same time showing promise of fulfilling functional requirements. In practice, erasures and alterations would be made, using just two or three sketches for a small piece like this, but of course, this approach in Fig. 214 would break the continuity of the demonstration.

These drawings bring out two important points: (1) that free-hand sketches must be used freely, and (2) that without a facility for self-expression with pencil and paper, one's ideas must for ever remain locked away. The question on whether the finished work embodies good design is, of course, largely a matter of personal opinion and although this particular item is not claimed as startling or revolutionary, it does at least serve as an example for demonstration.

Figure 213   Coffee table

Figure 214 (opposite)   Designing a coffee table.

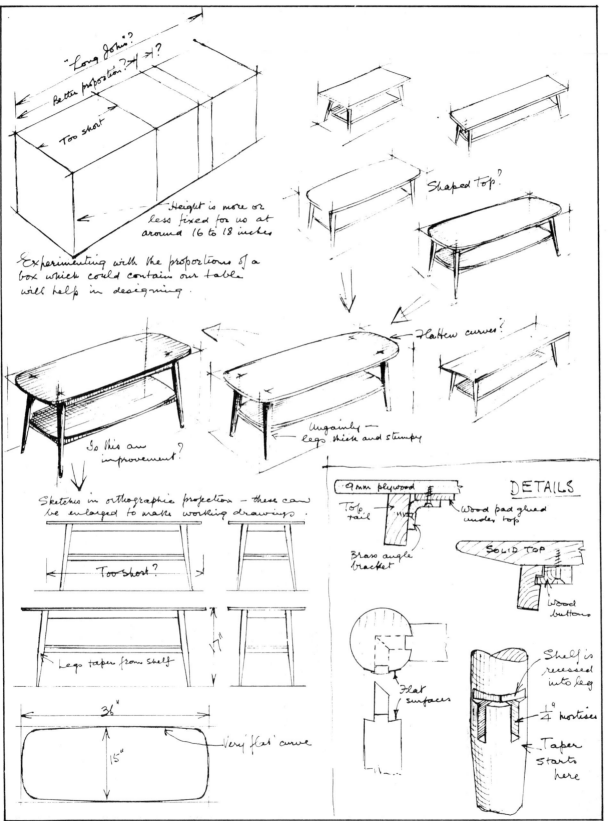

"Long John"?

Better proportion? ?

Too short

Height is more or less fixed for us at around 16 to 18 inches

Experimenting with the proportions of a box which could contain our table will help in designing.

Shaped top?

Flatten curves?

Is this an improvement?

Ungainly — legs thick and stumpy

Sketches in orthographic projection — these can be enlarged to make working drawings.

Too Short?

Legs taper from shelf

7"

36"

15"

Very 'flat' curve

DETAILS

9mm plywood

Top rail

Wood pad glued under top

Brass angle bracket

SOLID TOP

Wood buttons

Flat surfaces

Shelf is recessed into leg

$\frac{1}{4}$" mortises

Taper starts here

12

Test exercises

Orthographic drawings are in first angle projection.
All dimensions are in mm.

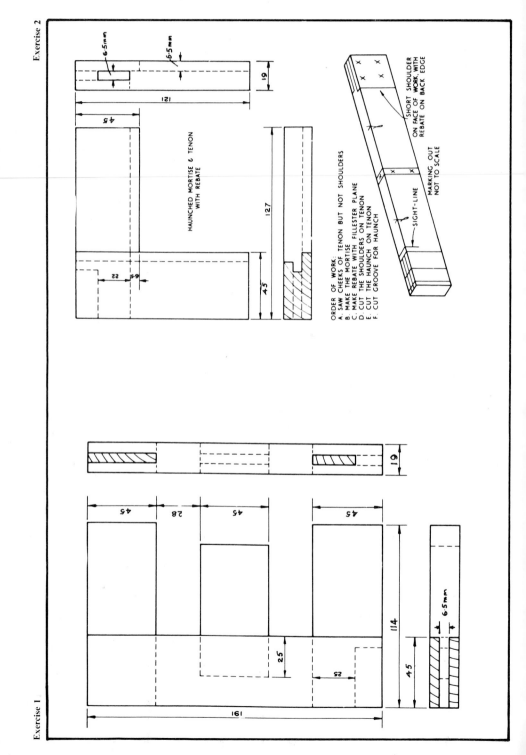

Exercise 2

HAUNCHED MORTISE & TENON
WITH REBATE

6·5mm
6·5mm
121
45
19
127
45
22
6·5

ORDER OF WORK:
A. SAW CHEEKS OF TENON BUT NOT SHOULDERS
B. MAKE THE MORTISE
C. MAKE REBATE WITH FILLESTER PLANE
D. CUT THE SHOULDERS ON TENON
E. CUT THE HAUNCH ON TENON
F. CUT GROOVE FOR HAUNCH

SHORT SHOULDER
ON FACE OF WORK, WITH
REBATE ON BACK EDGE

SIGHT-LINE

MARKING OUT
NOT TO SCALE

Exercise 1

161
45
28
45
45
114
25
25
45
19
6·5mm

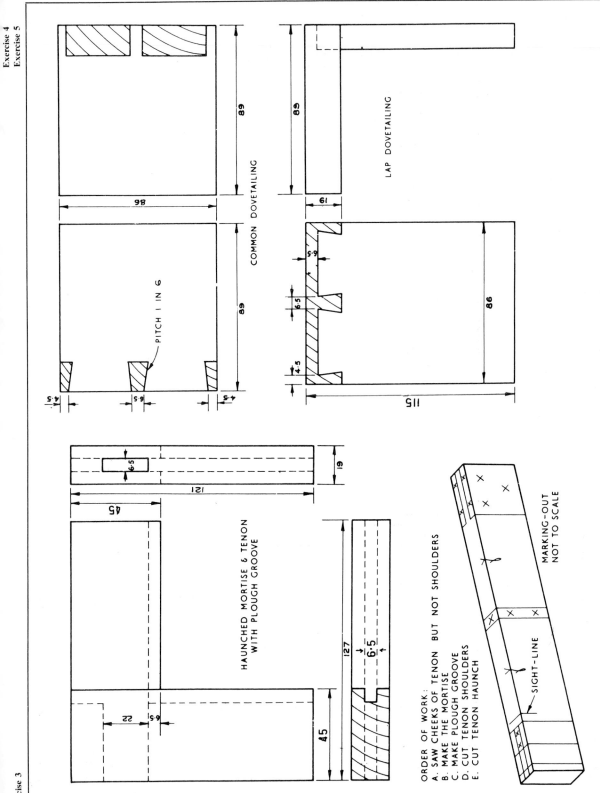

Exercise 4
Exercise 5

COMMON DOVETAILING

LAP DOVETAILING

PITCH 1 IN 6

HAUNCHED MORTISE & TENON
WITH PLOUGH GROOVE

ORDER OF WORK:
A. SAW CHEEKS OF TENON BUT NOT SHOULDERS
B. MAKE THE MORTISE
C. MAKE PLOUGH GROOVE
D. CUT TENON SHOULDERS
E. CUT TENON HAUNCH

MARKING-OUT
NOT TO SCALE

SIGHT-LINE

Exercise 3

Exercise 7

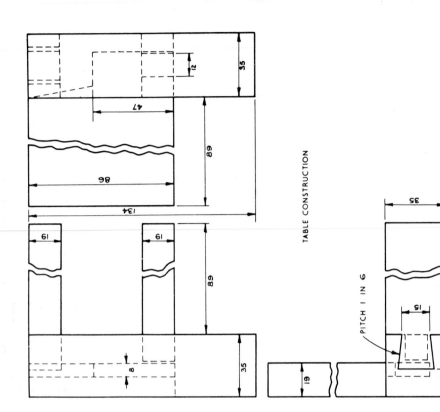

TABLE CONSTRUCTION

PITCH I IN 6

Exercise 6

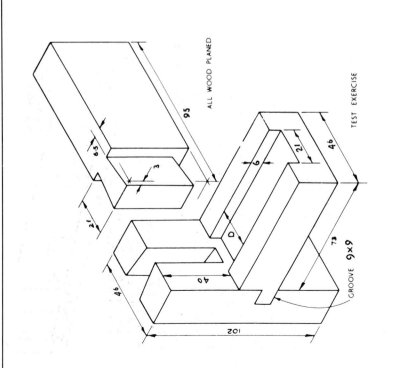

ALL WOOD PLANED

GROOVE 9×9

TEST EXERCISE

Instructions

This is not a model of any particular object, but is an example designed to test skill with saw and chisel.

The piece of wood should be 300 mm in length. Commence by squaring off one end, then cut the dovetail by sawing only. Cut off piece A. Next cut the socket to receive the dovetail, make the groove and cut off piece B.

The remaining piece is cut to length for piece C on one end of which the tongue is prepared. The groove is next marked out clearly with the gauge and with the wood held in the vice the sides of the groove D are sawn. The waste wood is pared away with a chisel, taking care to work with the grain to avoid going too deeply.

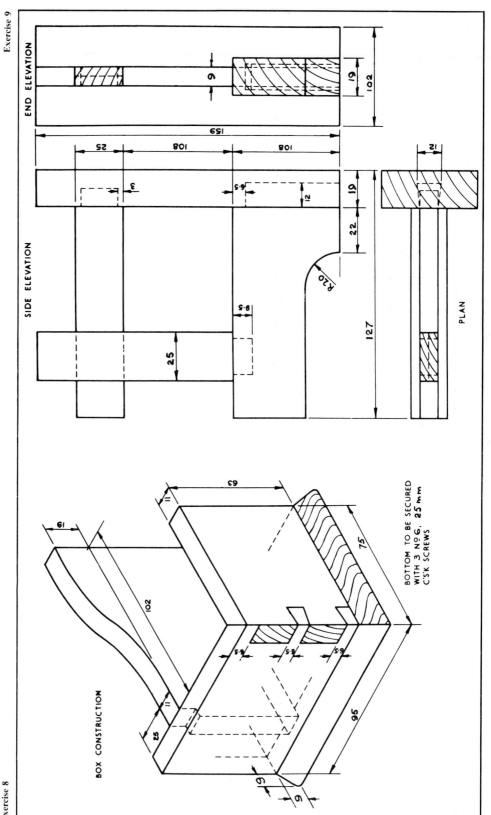

Exercise 9

END ELEVATION

SIDE ELEVATION

PLAN

Exercise 8

BOX CONSTRUCTION

BOTTOM TO BE SECURED
WITH 3 Nº 6, 25 mm
C'SK SCREWS

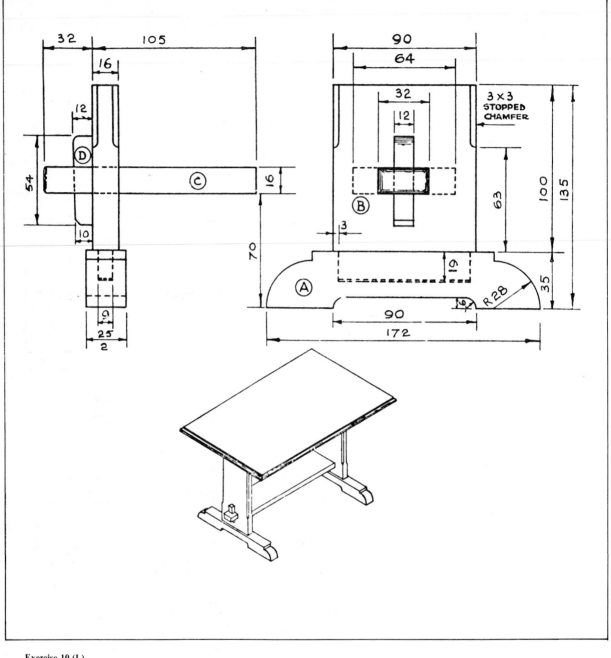

Exercise 10 (L)

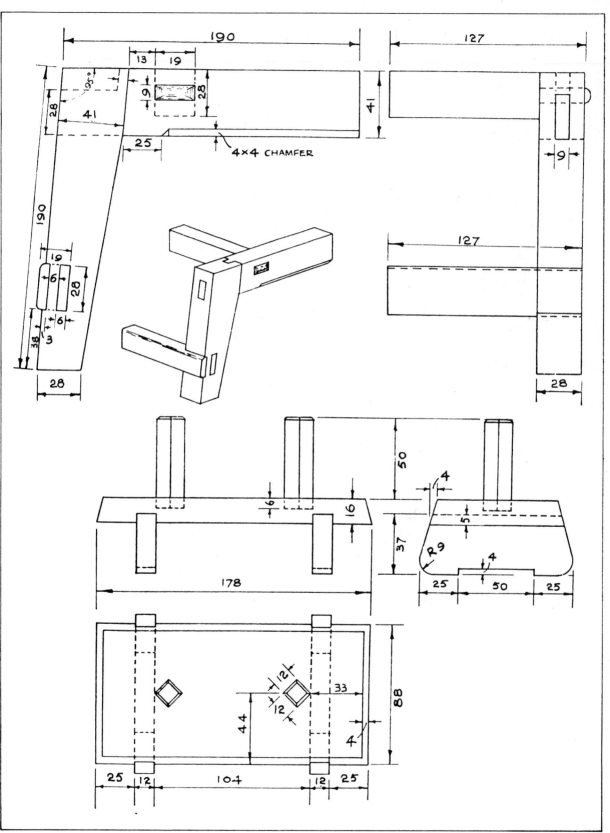

Bibliography

Historical design

DAVID JOEL, *The adventure of British furniture*, E. Benn
JOHN GLOAG, *English furniture*, A. & C. Black
FREDERICK S. ROBINSON, *English furniture*, Methuen
O. BRACKETT, *English furniture illustrated*, E. Benn
JOHN C. ROGERS, *English furniture*, Country Life
RALPH DUTTON, *The English interior*, Batsford
JOHN GLOAG, *The English tradition in design*, Penguin
CHARLES H. HAYWARD, *English period furniture*, Evans Bros.
THERLE HUGHES, *Old English furniture*, Lutterworth Press
RALPH EDWARDS F.S.A., *A history of the English chair*, Victoria and Albert
  Museum: H.M.S.O.

Modern design

NOEL CARRINGTON, *Colour and pattern in the home*, Batsford
S. H. GLENISTER, *Contemporary design in woodwork* vols. I and II, John Murray
BRUCE ALLSOPP, *Decoration and furniture: Principles of modern design* (2 vols.),
  Pitman
House and Gardens complete guide of interior decoration, Simon and Schuster,
  New York
H. WALTON CLIFFORD, *Plan your own home decoration*, Country Life

Timber and tools

F. H. TITMUSS, *A concise encyclopedia of world timber*, Technical Press
RICHARD JEFFERIES, *The wood from the trees*, Pilot Press
H. L. EDLIN, *Woodland crafts in Britain*, Batsford
H. L. EDLIN, *Forestry and woodland life*, Batsford
E. H. B. BOULTON and B. ALWYN JAY, *British timbers*, A. & C. Black
TIMBER RESEARCH AND DEVELOPMENT ASSOCIATION LTD., various publications
Concerning saws, Messrs. Spear & Jackson, Ltd.
Planecraft, The Record Tool Co., Ltd.

Wood turning

G. T. JAMES, *Wood turning design and practice*, John Murray
F. PAIN, *The practical wood turner*, Evans Bros.

Index